Ferns and Lycophytes of
MINNESOTA

Ferns and Lycophytes of
MINNESOTA

The Complete Guide to
Species Identification

Welby R. Smith

Minnesota Department of Natural Resources

Photography by Richard W. Haug

UNIVERSITY OF MINNESOTA PRESS

MINNEAPOLIS · LONDON

The University of Minnesota Press gratefully acknowledges financial assistance provided for this book by the Minnesota Department of Natural Resources.

Unless otherwise credited, all photographs were taken by Richard W. Haug, copyright 2023 by the Minnesota Department of Natural Resources.

Published by the University of Minnesota Press
111 Third Avenue South, Suite 290
Minneapolis, MN 55401-2520
http://www.upress.umn.edu

ISBN 978-1-5179-1466-0 (pb)

A Cataloging-in-Publication record for this book is available from the Library of Congress.

Printed in Canada on acid-free paper

The University of Minnesota is an equal-opportunity educator and employer.

32 31 30 29 28 27 26 25 24 23   10 9 8 7 6 5 4 3 2 1

CONTENTS

PREFACE

The predecessor to this book is a modest work written by Dr. Rolla M. Tryon Jr. and illustrated by Wilma Monserud, titled *The Ferns and Fern Allies of Minnesota,* published by the University of Minnesota Press in 1954. Tryon was one of the leading pteridologists of the twentieth century and was on the faculty of the Department of Botany of the University of Minnesota from 1945 to 1947. The work was modest in its presentation but exemplary in its scholarship, and it served a broad audience for twenty-six years.

It was followed by an updated work in 1980 with a similar format and scope but with the simpler title *Ferns of Minnesota,* also authored by Tryon, with behind-the-scenes help from Dr. Gerald Ownbey, then curator of the herbarium of the Department of Botany of the University of Minnesota.

Another twenty years passed, and an updated version was contemplated. Dr. Warren H. Wagner of the University of Michigan, another great pteridologist, was anticipated to be the lead author along with myself. Wagner was to be responsible for the taxonomy—the "science"—and I was to use my local knowledge and contribute the natural history, maps, and photographs. The project became dormant after Wagner's death in 2000.

The project remained dormant for perhaps a decade before it was taken up again by myself, with help from numerous specialists, culminating in the present volume. The scope of the book has remained the same, but the title has changed to reflect the rapidly advancing science upon which the book is based. The goal of the present book is to use the knowledge derived from recent advancements in molecular biology and statewide field surveys to create a useful field guide that is current, relevant, and accessible.

My work as state botanist with the Minnesota Department of Natural Resources for more than forty years has involved ongoing botanical surveys throughout Minnesota. And my position as a research associate of the Bell Museum provided continued access to the research facilities of the University of Minnesota.

ACKNOWLEDGMENTS

This book was created as a project of the Minnesota Biological Survey (MBS), which is a program within the Minnesota Department of Natural Resources. Partial funding was provided by the Minnesota Environmental and Natural Resources Trust Fund as recommended by the Legislative-Citizen Commission on Minnesota Resources (LCCMR). The author was a full-time employee of MBS during the preparation of the book. Richard W. Haug and Malcolm MacFarlane were part-time contractors funded by MBS for fieldwork related to this project. Haug used his exceptional photographic skills to provide most of the field photographs used in this book, and MacFarlane contributed his unparalleled knowledge of *Botrychium* and *Sceptridium* to the project. The author prepared the text, keys, maps, and most of the comparison photographs that accompany each genus, with valuable contributions from Haug.

The author would not have attempted or even contemplated this book without the help of numerous collaborators, colleagues, and advisors. Those who contributed directly to the contents of the book include Tom Klein, Jared Cruz, Michael Lee, Courtney Millaway, Donna Perleberg, Karen Myhre, Rolf Dahle, Scott Milburn, Otto Gockman, Lynden Gerdes, Derek Anderson, Brett Whaley, Bobby Henderson, Dick Oehlenschlager, Tim Whitfeld, and Nathan Dahlberg. Those not mentioned who contributed field photographs are credited alongside their individual contributions. All field photographs that are not credited are the work of Richard Haug.

The specimens on which this book is based have been examined and annotated by a series of internationally recognized taxon experts, whose groundbreaking research fills the pages of modern scientific journals. Attention must be drawn to one group of ferns in particular, the moonworts—the genus *Botrychium*. Many specialists have contributed to our knowledge of *Botrychium* of Minnesota, principally Warren H. Wagner and Donald Farrar, both of whom made repeated trips to Minnesota to train local botanists, lead field trips, and give workshops. The treatment in this book follows their work as closely as possible. Malcolm and Rosemary MacFarlane worked closely with Farrar and have applied their many years of fieldwork to the task of contributing an accurate, accessible, and useful treatment of *Botrychium* and *Sceptridium,* and they served as mentors to the author.

The author would like to thank the many skilled and dedicated professionals at the University of Minnesota Press, whose commitment to printed books and high scholarship is a constant source of inspiration. Gratitude is also due the faculty and staff at the Bell Museum of Natural History, which houses the herbarium of the University of Minnesota, the great storehouse of botanical knowledge; the museum granted the author the status of research associate, which allowed access to essential resources.

THE COUNTIES OF MINNESOTA

INTRODUCTION

This book is not meant to be a monograph, an encyclopedia, or an exhaustive treatise. It is meant to be a problem-solving tool, used to answer the question "Which plant is that?" For that reason, the individual species profiles are kept brief and to the point, and everything about each species can be found on two facing pages. The design of the book does not require a road map or a "how to use this book" section. Hopefully, interested readers will pick up the book and find its function intuitive. At any time, a person can circle back to the introduction and get a little help with some basics.

A SPECIMEN-BASED BOOK

In preparation for this book, the author and a team of contractors, volunteers, and colleagues conducted a systematic, state-wide ground search for ferns and lycophytes. Where ferns or lycophytes were found, specimens were vouchered and deposited in the herbarium of the Bell Museum of the University of Minnesota. They were added to an existing wealth of specimens that span the preceding 150 years and now number about 15,000. The specimens have been examined and verified by internationally recognized taxon experts and studied in the light of the most recent scientific findings. They have been scanned and are available for viewing on the Biodiversity Atlas website (https://bellatlas.umn.edu).

THE MAPS WITH ALL THE DOTS ON THEM

The maps in this book were created from the location data on the labels of herbarium specimens. Only those specimens for which the identification could be verified and are curated in the permanent collections of public herbaria, principally the University of Minnesota herbarium, have been used. The maps provide a reasonable summary of what is known about the distribution and relative abundance of ferns and lycophytes in Minnesota at the time this book was written. Yet there are limitations. In the case of a few highly sought-after species, the maps may give the false impression of abundance. In the case of a few cryptic, understudied species, they may give the false impression of rarity. The maps only tell us where the species have been found in the past. There are still many exciting discoveries to be made in the future. This book can serve as a guide to many outdoor adventures.

TECHNICAL TERMS

Many people have an understandable aversion to technical terms. With that in mind, an honest attempt was made to use nontechnical terms wherever possible, and yet the glossary of technical terms used in this book (p. 307) has grown to more than 100 entries. The glossary is based largely on the work of David Lellinger (2002) but modified, where needed, to serve the particular objectives of this book. Technical terms are used most often in the description of each species that appears first in each species account. This is because of their inherent precision. Elsewhere in the book, more commonly used words were substituted if clarity and precision could be maintained. Hopefully, the use of technical terms will aid rather than hinder users of the book in their search for information. For those who seek a deeper knowledge of biology and its peculiar terminology, the bibliography at the end of the book will be of interest.

ORGANIZATION OF THIS BOOK

Identification of ferns and lycophytes is essentially a visual process. It involves seeing and recognizing patterns of shape and structure and being able to distinguish them on a fine scale. This is impractical to do without a carefully constructed guide. But how best to organize such a guide? Many schemes were considered but none were without serious drawbacks. The final decision was to group plants by their biological relationships, that is, the natural relationships that developed over millions of years of evolution. Specifically, ferns in this book are grouped by taxonomic "orders," each of which has a latinized name with the suffix "ales."

There are 8 orders of ferns and lycophytes in Minnesota. They are presented in this book in phylogenetic sequence. The earliest order to appear on the tree of life is presented first, Lycopodiales. The order that appeared last in evolutionary history is presented last—the Polypodiales. A key (p. xxiii) will guide the user to the correct order. From there, another key will direct the user to the correct genus and from there to the correct species. The genera and species are arranged alphabetically since evolutionary relationships at that level are poorly known. With a little practice, most users will be able to jump ahead to the correct order and maybe even the correct genus. It might be noticed that the organization does not emphasize family, which is the grouping between order and genus. Certainly, every species of fern and lycophyte is assigned to a family, but families of ferns and lycophytes are often difficult to recognize as such, even by many professional botanists.

A BRIEF INTRODUCTION TO FERNS AND LYCOPHYTES

What Are Ferns?

A lengthy discussion about the nature of ferns is not really needed here, but a brief overview might help put Minnesota's ferns in a useful context. So, what is a fern? We cannot really talk about a fern "family" in the way we might talk about a grass family, or an orchid family, because there are as many as 48 families of ferns. The next step upward in the taxonomic hierarchy is the category of "order." It turns out there are 11 orders of ferns in the world. We need to go one level higher to encompass all the ferns—to the category of "class," specifically, the class Polypodiopsida.

Among animals, mammals constitute a class. Insects and reptiles each constitute a class. The class of ferns contains approximately 10,500 species, although new species are being discovered every year, almost every day. Even our ability to recognize new species among the bewildering diversity of ferns is rapidly evolving.

The numbers may seem daunting, but no need to panic. Learning the ferns of Minnesota is an easy place to start, and a convenient introduction to 5 of the 11 fern orders. There are 29 genera of ferns in Minnesota and 80 species. Most will be immediately recognized as ferns, but there will be a few interesting surprises.

What Are Lycophytes?

We have learned that ferns are a "class" of plants encompassing many families, genera, and species. Lycophytes (sometimes called lycopods) are a separate class of plants called the Lycopodiopsida. This class contains 3 orders, each with a single family, a total of 18 genera and by one estimate 1,338 species. Representatives of all 3 orders and families are present in Minnesota, comprising 8 genera and 20 species. Lycophytes are well represented in Minnesota, especially in northern forests and lakes (yes, lakes).

The lycophytes used to be considered "fern allies," but we now know they are only distantly related to the ferns. In fact, flowering plants are more closely "allied" with the ferns than are the lycophytes. So, the phrase *fern allies* can be completely banished from the biological lexicon.

The most easily seen feature that makes lycophytes different from ferns is the structure of the leaf. Leaves of lycophytes are called microphylls. They are usually quite small and have a single vein running down the middle. They do not resemble ordinary leaves at all.

What Unites Ferns and Lycophytes?

Both ferns and lycophytes are considered vascular plants, meaning they have a system of veins to move fluids through their bodies, much like people do. Mosses are nonvascular plants. They rely on simple diffusion to move fluids, which is why they remain small. Ferns and lycophytes are also considered cryptograms because they reproduce using spores, not flowers or seeds. The combination of those two features (vascular system and spore producing) are what unite ferns and lycophytes, and what separates them from all other plants. Ferns and lycophytes together comprise the pteridophytes.

The Life Cycle of Ferns and Lycophytes (Made Easy)

Most people who have taken a basic biology course have been exposed to the concept of "alternation of generations," which is a simple concept but sometimes difficult to grasp. To understand it, you really need to know just two terms: sporophyte (spore-producing plant) and gametophyte (gamete-producing plant). The gametophyte is a very small, flattened structure that lives independently in the ground or on the surface of the ground. Very few people ever see a gametophyte, or would recognize one if they did, but it is very much a fern or a lycophyte. It is the sexual generation of a fern or lycophyte in that it produces eggs and sperm that unite to produce a zygote, much like in animals.

The zygote grows into the sporophyte, which is the plant we recognize as a fern or lycophyte. The sporophyte is the nonsexual generation. It produces spores that are released to the wind. A spore is not the same as a zygote. It has only half the chromosomes needed for reproduction. If a spore lands on a suitable substrate, it will "germinate" to become a gametophyte, completing the cycle. In flowering plants, the reduction of the gametophyte is quite extreme; it consists of just a few cells that grow entirely inside the sporophyte. When you see a flowering plant or a pine tree, you are looking at the sporophyte. This book deals almost exclusively with the sporophyte generation of ferns and lycophytes, although the term *gametophyte* may turn up from time to time.

Why Hybrids?

It will be noticed that hybrids are mentioned in many places throughout the book. This is something not seen in most plant guides. But ferns and lycophytes are not like most plants. Many of them hybridize readily. There are two basic kinds of hybrids among the ferns and lycophytes. The first kind can be illustrated by the firmoss *Huperzia porophila* (p. 28). It arose long ago as a cross between *H. lucidula* and *H. appressa*. That cross produced a fertile, well-adapted plant that found a niche in the environment and flourished as a true species. This happens quite often. Scientists call this reticulate evolution. The intrepid field botanist calls it an inscrutable puzzle. We generally do not call such plants hybrids even though they originated through hybridization; they are considered "true" species.

The second type of hybrid is a sterile plant that arises spontaneously at one time and one place and survives on the landscape as an individual rather than a member of a population. This is generally what taxonomists and field botanists mean when they talk about hybrids. This type of hybrid is often given a name like a species, but that name will have a multiplication sign before the epithet. It would be convenient to ignore these hybrids, but in the case of some genera, hybrids are simply too common to ignore.

Natural History and Ecology of Ferns and Lycophytes in Minnesota

Minnesota ferns and lycophytes appear on the landscape in habitats that are not so different from those of other native plants. The habitat of a plant, meaning the place where it lives, can be broadly related to vegetation, which in turn relates to geography, climate, and glacial history—and, more recently, the ever-increasing effects humans are having on the landscape. Very few Minnesota ferns or lycophytes have adapted to human changes in the landscape. They generally survive in scraps of natural habitat that have remained more or less unaltered since before European American settlement.

Everything relating to the ecological setting of ferns and lycophytes in Minnesota comes down to location and history. Location puts Minnesota almost exactly in the middle of the North American continent, as far as possible from the moderating effects of ocean currents and the compounding effects of mountains. Location shapes the climate, particularly rainfall and seasonal variations in temperature.

History, in this context, refers to past events that have shaped the physical aspect of the landscape. In Minnesota, this is all about glaciers that scoured the surface multiple times, the most recent scouring ending about 10,000 years ago. The consequence of glaciers on the landscape can be summed up by the major substrate map (map 1).

The complex interaction of location and history produced the patterns of vegetation the first European American settlers saw when they arrived in the mid-nineteenth century. These basic patterns can still be seen today, although human activities have fragmented and greatly diminished what some people call the "original vegetation." The difficult task of reconstructing the vegetation of that period has been greatly aided by notes of the first land surveyors and is depicted in map 2.

Distilling all this down even further leaves us with a broad concept that divides Minnesota into four major vegetation zones called provinces (map 3), which can be thought of as biomes.

The Laurentian Mixed Forest Province

The Laurentian Mixed Forest Province covers a little more than 23 million acres (9.3 million hectares) of the northeastern part of the state. The province is characterized by broad areas of conifer forest, mixed hardwood and conifer forests, and conifer bogs and swamps. The landscape ranges from rugged lake-dotted terrain with thin glacial deposits over bedrock, to undulating plains with deep glacial drift, to large, flat, poorly drained peatlands. The wide diversity of habitats and the semihumid climate are favorable to a great diversity of fern species and even more so to lycophyte species.

The Eastern Broadleaf Forest Province

The Eastern Broadleaf Forest covers nearly 12 million acres (4.9 million hectares) of the central and southeastern parts of the state. This province serves as a transition, or ecotone, between semiarid prairie to the west and the semihumid mixed conifer-deciduous forests to the northeast. The northwestern and central portions of the province are covered by thick deposits of highly calcareous glacial drift of Wisconsin Age. The calcareous drift is not favored by ferns or lycophytes, as a rule, and few species except the most broadly adapted occur there. The southeastern part of the province was not covered by ice in the last glaciation. As a result, erosion of streams draining into the Mississippi valley exposed Paleozoic bedrock and pre-Wisconsin drift. For that reason, prevailing substrates are noncalcareous till and loess, and near-surface bedrock, which seem to favor high fern diversity but rather low lycophyte diversity.

Prairie Parkland

The Prairie Parkland Province covers just over 16 million acres (6.5 million hectares) in the western part of the state. This is the part of the state historically dominated by tallgrass prairie. Evapotranspiration is greater than precipitation across much of the province, resulting in semiarid conditions. The land surface

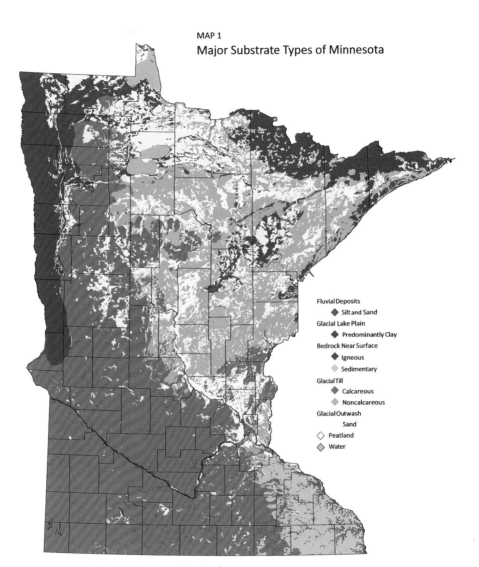

MAP 1

Major Substrate Types of Minnesota

Fluvial Deposits
◆ Silt and Sand
Glacial Lake Plain
◆ Predominantly Clay
Bedrock Near Surface
◆ Igneous
◇ Sedimentary
Glacial Till
◆ Calcareous
◇ Noncalcareous
Glacial Outwash
Sand
◇ Peatland
◇ Water

source: Agricultural Experiment Station, University of
Minnesota, Minnesota Soil Atlas Project, 1969–81.

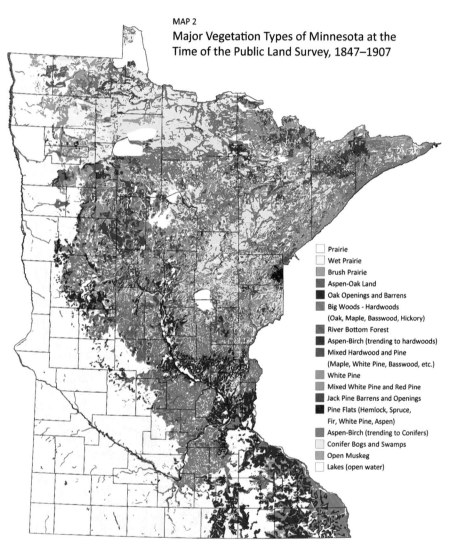

MAP 2

Major Vegetation Types of Minnesota at the
Time of the Public Land Survey, 1847–1907

Prairie
Wet Prairie
Brush Prairie
Aspen-Oak Land
Oak Openings and Barrens
Big Woods - Hardwoods
(Oak, Maple, Basswood, Hickory)
River Bottom Forest
Aspen-Birch (trending to hardwoods)
Mixed Hardwood and Pine
(Maple, White Pine, Basswood, etc.)
White Pine
Mixed White Pine and Red Pine
Jack Pine Barrens and Openings
Pine Flats (Hemlock, Spruce,
Fir, White Pine, Aspen)
Aspen-Birch (trending to Conifers)
Conifer Bogs and Swamps
Open Muskeg
Lakes (open water)

source: Marschner 1974.

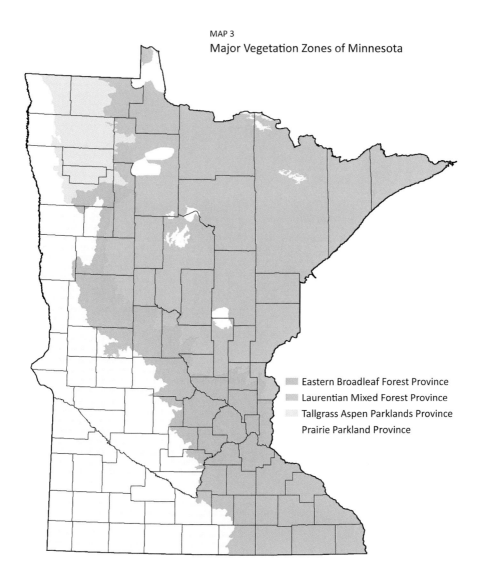

MAP 3

Major Vegetation Zones of Minnesota

Eastern Broadleaf Forest Province

Laurentian Mixed Forest Province

Tallgrass Aspen Parklands Province

Prairie Parkland Province

of the province was heavily influenced by the most recent glaciation, that of the Wisconsin Age. Ice sheets crossed the province several times during the period, depositing calcareous drift in the southern part of the province. Glacial Lake Agassiz deposited deep-water sediments over the northern part of the province. None of this is conducive to ferns or lycophytes. In fact, only 3 species in Minnesota (all ferns) specialize in prairie habitats.

Because of the thick mantle of drift covering most of the province, bedrock exposures are rare, being limited to the deeply downcut Minnesota River valley and a few places where quartzite bedrock protrudes through thinner drift in the southwestern corner of the province. Such bedrock exposures provide habitat for a few additional species.

Tallgrass Aspen Parklands

Tallgrass Aspen Parklands is very much a hybrid or transitional biome that combines aspects of both forest and prairie. It covers a small part of northwestern Minnesota, about 3 million acres (1.2 million hectares). The province forms a transition, or ecotone, between semiarid prairie landscapes to the west and semihumid forests to the east. The province is comparatively cold and dry, with evapotranspiration greater than precipitation. Low precipitation and desiccating winds from the Great Plains promote frequent spring fires, resulting in a landscape dominated by prairie and open, fire-dependent woodland communities. A small number of fern and lycophyte species occur in this province, but none exclusively.

Ferns for the Garden

Ferns make an excellent addition to a garden, especially a shade garden. Those ferns in the orders Polypodiales and Osmundales are most suitable. There is no single "best" fern for a garden. Lady fern and maidenhair fern are among the most popular. They will require no special care. A few ferns, like bracken and ostrich fern, are perhaps too aggressive for a small, neatly tended garden. Greatest success will be achieved if garden conditions closely mimic the corresponding natural habitat. For most fern species, that will include shade, moderate moisture, and weakly acidic soil. Although ferns in a garden can be a great source of pleasure, please do not take ferns from the wild, certainly not from public lands such as parks or nature preserves. All the ferns that are suitable for Minnesota gardens can be bought at local nurseries, especially those nurseries specializing in native plants.

KEY TO THE ORDERS OF FERNS AND LYCOPHYTES FOUND GROWING WILD IN MINNESOTA

Most of the 8 orders that occur in Minnesota are visually distinct. Admittedly, some species may seem out of place in any grouping, yet all have been accommodated. That is why some orders appear at multiple places in the key. If in doubt, jump ahead and check the photo page that accompanies each of the 8 orders to get an idea of the type of plant in hand.

1. Plants fully or partially aquatic.
      2. Leaves resembling slender hollow tubes like the quill of a feather
      . . . . Isoetales (quillworts), p. 49
      2. Leaves resembling four-leaf clovers (*Marsilea*), or duckweed floating on the surface of water (*Azolla*). . . . . Salviniales (water ferns), p. 161
1. Plants not aquatic although sometimes growing in wet soil or from shallow water.
      3. Stems with regularly spaced joints (nodes), each joint marked by a cylindrical sheath encircling the stem . . . . Equisetales (horsetails and scouring rushes), p. 63
      3. Stems not jointed, not sheathed.
            4. Leaves very small, often scalelike (microphylls), only 1–12 mm long (Lycophytes).
                  5. Leaves 1–3.5 mm long, margins with cilia or spiny projections
                  . . . . Selaginellales (spikemosses), p. 57
                  5. Leaves 1–12 mm long, margins sometimes toothed but not with cilia or spiny projections . . . . Lycopodiales (clubmosses, firmosses, and ground-cedars)
            4. Leaves much larger (megaphylls), usually recognizable as a fern leaf.
                  6. Sporangia borne on a separate stalk of the leaf; the two parts of the leaf connected at a common petiole; petiole round in cross-section, somewhat succulent
                  . . . . Ophioglossales (adder's-tongue ferns), p. 89
                  6. Sporangia borne on a separate leaf entirely, or on dedicated pinnae within an ordinary leaf, or in discrete sori on the undersides of ordinary green leaves; petioles sometimes round but more often grooved or channeled longitudinally, not succulent.
                        7. Sporangia born in discrete sori on the undersides of ordinary green leaves, and usually covered by indusia or leaf margins
                        . . . . Polypodiales ("true ferns," in part), p. 171
                        7. Sporangia borne on entirely fertile pinnae of ordinary green leaves, or on a highly modified separate leaf that lacks green color.

8. Sporangia borne on a highly modified separate leaf that lacks green color.
  9. Sterile leaves 1-pinnate-pinnatifid.
    10. Sterile leaf with a persistent tuft of hairs at the base of each pinnae (dorsal side); lateral veins of segments bifurcate, blade elliptic; fertile leaf cinnamon colored, ephemeral (Osmundastrum)
    . . . . Osmundales (royal ferns, in part), p. 147
    10. Sterile leaf lacking tuft of hairs at the base of each pinnae; lateral veins of segments unforked, blade oblanceolate; fertile leaf dark brown to blackish; persistent (Matteuccia) . . . . Polypodiales ("true ferns," in part), p. 171
  9. Sterile leaves 1- or rarely 2-pinnatifid
  . . . . Polypodiales ("true ferns," in part), p. 171
8. Sporangia borne on entirely fertile pinnae of an ordinary green leaf
  . . . . Osmundales (royal ferns, in part), p. 147

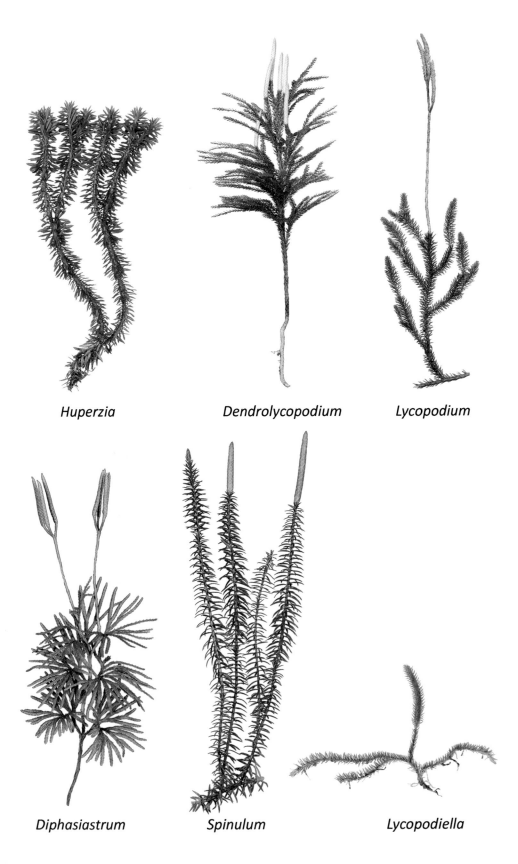

Huperzia

Dendrolycopodium

Lycopodium

Diphasiastrum

Spinulum

Lycopodiella

Chapter 1

The Lycophyte Order Lycopodiales (Clubmosses, Firmosses, and Ground-Cedars)

As currently classified by most botanists, the order Lycopodiales consists of a single family, Lycopodiaceae. Members of the order occur throughout the world with a total of 16 genera and perhaps 388 species. We have 6 genera and 15 species in Minnesota (by current count).

KEY TO GENERA OF LYCOPODIALES

1. Sporangia borne in the axils of ordinary leaves, not in cones; gemmae (small, green, flattened structures) often present in leaf axils near the top of mature stems; rhizomes absent . . . . *Huperzia*

1. Sporangia borne in distinct cones at the tips of the branches or stems; gemmae not produced; rhizomes present and often prominent, either on the surface of the ground or underground.

    2. Vertical stems 3–12 cm tall at maturity (including cones), unbranched; horizontal stems (rhizomes) growing on the surface of the ground, < 15 cm long . . . . *Lycopodiella*

    2. Vertical stems 12–40 cm tall at maturity (including cones), evidently branched; horizontal stems (rhizomes) deep underground (*Dendrolycopodium*), or if on the surface then > 15 cm long.

        3. Branches of the vertical stems flattened in cross-section, 1–4 mm wide (measured across the branch, leaf tip to leaf tip); individual leaves 0.5–2 mm long . . . . *Diphasiastrum*

        3. Branches of the vertical stems roundish in cross-section, 4–18 mm wide (measured across the branch, leaf tip to leaf tip); individual leaves 2–10 mm long.

            4. Cones on long, slender, nearly leafless stalks; leaves with a slender hairlike extension at the tip, 1–4 mm long . . . . *Lycopodium*

            4. Cones unstalked (sessile); leaves narrowly pointed or spine-tipped but without a hairlike extension at the tip.

                5. Vertical stems of the plant with horizontal branches (resembling a miniature tree); rhizomes buried deep underground; leaves 2–5 mm long . . . . *Dendrolycopodium*

                5. Vertical stems lacking horizontal branches (looking more moss-like than tree-like); rhizomes at or near the surface (may be covered with mosses or leaf litter); leaves 4–10 cm long . . . . *Spinulum*

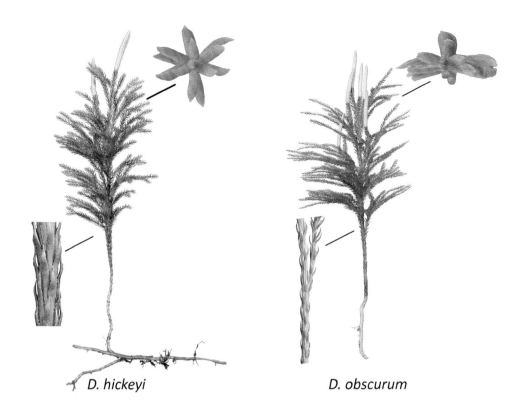

D. hickeyi   *D. obscurum*

D. dendroideum

DENDROLYCOPODIUM
(TREE CLUBMOSSES)

There are currently believed to be 5 species of *Dendrolycopodium* in the world. There are 3 species in North America, all of which are found in Minnesota. The *dendro-* part of the name is Greek for tree, which is especially apt for this group of lycophytes.

The rhizome of *Dendrolycopodium* is a horizontal stem growing deep underground. Each year the rhizome typically grows 15–20 cm and produces one lateral branch and one vertical shoot. The vertical shoot emerges aboveground its second year, and for the next two years it will add height and lateral branches. The third year aboveground, it normally produces one or more cones at the tips of the upper branches. It dies the fourth year along with the segment of rhizome to which it was attached. This is called determinate growth—it survives for a predetermined period of time. Meanwhile, the growing tip of the rhizome continues to grow indefinitely. This is called indeterminate growth. It is unclear if species of *Dendrolycopodium* hybridize, or how to identify them if they do. None have been given names. To date, no convincing hybrids have been found in Minnesota.

KEY TO *DENDROLYCOPODIUM*

1. Leaves on the lower portion of the main stem diverging from the stem at an angle of 45–90 degrees (most meaningful below the branches but above the leaf litter); side branches with 2 rows of leaves on the top, 1 row on each side, and 2 rows on the bottom . . . . *D. dendroideum*

1. Leaves on the lower portion of the main stem closely appressed to the stem or divergent at an angle ≤ 30 degrees (most meaningful below the branches but above the leaf litter); side branches with 1 row of leaves on top, 2 rows on each side, and 1 row on the bottom.

   2. The bottom row of leaves of the branches distinctly shorter than the lateral rows of leaves (½ to ¾ as long), and often appressed, causing the branches to appear somewhat flattened on the underside when viewed end on . . . . *D. obscurum*

   2. The bottom row of leaves of the branches about the same length as all the other leaves, and not noticeably appressed, causing the branches to appear ± round when viewed end on (a circle formed by the leaf tips) . . . . *D. hickeyi*

Dendrolycopodium dendroideum (Michx.) A. Haines
Prickly Tree Clubmoss

[*Lycopodium dendroideum* Michx.; *L. obscurum* var. *dendroideum* (Michx.) D. C. Eaton]

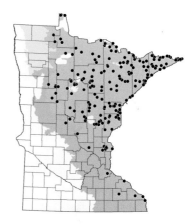

PLANTS evergreen. **RHIZOMES** subterranean. **AERIAL STEMS** 15–40 cm in height at maturity (measured from rhizome). **LEAVES ON CENTRAL STEMS** spreading at an angle of 45–90 degrees from axis, firm, prickly to the touch, lanceolate, 3–5 mm long, 0.5–0.8 mm wide; margins entire; apex pointed or spine-tipped. **LEAVES ON BRANCHES** like those on central stems but somewhat shorter; arranged in 6 ranks (rows), 2 ranks pointing obliquely upward, 2 ranks pointing obliquely downward, and 1 rank pointing straight outward from each side; the arrangement causing the branch to appear ± round when viewed end on. **CONES** sessile, 1–4.5 cm long, 1–10 in number. **PHENOLOGY:** Cones typically begin development in spring of the third year. They mature slowly during the summer and shed spores in late autumn and early winter of the same year.

IDENTIFICATION: *Dendrolycopodium dendroideum* is very much like *D. hickeyi* and *D. obscurum*, but the leaves on the central stem point straight outward or slightly upward. This gives the stem a prickly look and feel. The corresponding leaves of *D. hickeyi* and *D. obscurum* point more nearly upward, with the tips held closer to the stem, causing the stem to look and feel smooth. This feature is most pronounced on the portion of the main stem below the first branch but above the leaf litter. If that portion of the stem is short, with few leaves to judge, look around for one with a longer stem.

NATURAL HISTORY: *Dendrolycopodium dendroideum* ranges across the cooler parts of North America and Asia. In Minnesota, it is relatively common in a wide variety of northern forest types, less common going southward. It is most common in conifer forests but is also found under hardwoods, primarily oak, aspen, and birch. Soil conditions vary but tend to be somewhat acidic and coarse-textured, often with a large component of woody or leafy humus. It is sometimes found in swamp forests where the substrate resembles damp peat but not saturated or water-logged peat. It can be found growing side by side with *D. hickeyi* in the north, but statewide *D. dendroideum* is more common.

Stem leaves point outward.

Resembling a miniature tree, Kanabec County—October 14.

Stems are evergreen, stand out in autumn, Isanti County—October 18.

Dendrolycopodium hickeyi (W. H. Wagner, Beitel, & Moran) A. Haines
Hickey's Tree Clubmoss

[*Lycopodium hickeyi* W. H. Wagner, Beitel, & Moran; *L. obscurum* var. *isophyllum* Hickey]

PLANTS evergreen. **RHIZOMES** subterranean. **AERIAL STEMS** 15–40 cm in height at maturity (measured from rhizome). **LEAVES ON CENTRAL STEM** ascending at an angle ≤ 30 degrees from axis; those below the branches appressed; lanceolate, 3.5–5 mm long, 0.4–0.7 mm wide; margins entire; apex pointed or spine-tipped. **LEAVES ON BRANCHES** like those on central stem but somewhat shorter; arranged in six ranks (rows), with 1 upper rank, 1 lower rank, and 4 lateral ranks (two on each side of the branch); the arrangement giving the branch a circular

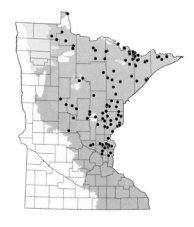

appearance when viewed end on. **CONES** sessile, 1–4.5 cm long, 1–10+ in number. **PHENOLOGY:** Cones typically begin development in spring of the third year. They mature slowly during the summer and shed spores in late autumn and early winter of the same year.

IDENTIFICATION: There is very little difference between *D. hickeyi* and the two other species of *Dendrolycopodium*. To get a reliable identification, it is essential to check the details. The easiest detail to see is the orientation of the leaves on the main stem. Those of *D. dendroideum* point distinctly outward. Those of *D. hickeyi* and *D. obscurum* point more nearly upward. To separate *D. hickeyi* and *D. obscurum,* look at one of the branches end on. The arrangement of the leaves will cause the branches of *D. hickeyi* to appear round (imagine a circle formed by the leaf tips) and *D. obscurum* to appear flat-bottomed. For a final check, focus on the bottom row of leaves on any branch. Those of *D. obscurum* are distinctly shorter than the other leaves; those of *D. hickeyi* are not.

NATURAL HISTORY: *Dendrolycopodium hickeyi* occurs primarily in the northeastern United States and adjacent parts of Canada. In Minnesota, it occurs in essentially the same forest habitats as *D. dendroideum* and *D. obscurum.* If fact, all three species may be found growing together where their ranges overlap. These are primarily subboreal, northern-type forests, either deciduous or coniferous. They may be old-growth forests or forests in middle or late stages of regeneration following logging. Soils vary but are often coarse-textured, noncalcareous, dryish or somewhat moist.

Stem leaves point upward.

Sherburne County—September 20.

Conspicuous after snow melts in spring, Anoka County—March 25.

Dendrolycopodium obscurum (L.) Haines
Flat-Branched Tree Clubmoss

[Lycopodium obscurum var. obscurum L.]

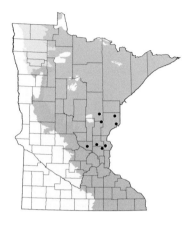

PLANTS evergreen. **RHIZOMES** subterranean. **AERIAL STEMS** 15–40 cm in height at maturity (measured from the rhizome). **LEAVES ON CENTRAL STEMS** ascending at an angle ≤ 30 degrees from the axis; those below the branches appressed, lanceolate; 3.5–5 mm long, 0.6–0.7 mm wide; margins entire; apex pointed or spine-tipped. **LEAVES ON BRANCHES** like those on central stem but somewhat shorter; arranged in 6 ranks (rows) with 1 upper rank, 1 lower rank, and 4 lateral ranks (two on each side of the branch); those of the lower rank somewhat appressed and ½–¾ the size of those in the other ranks, causing the branch to appear somewhat flat when viewed end on. **CONES** sessile, 1.2–6 cm long, 1–10+ in number. **PHENOLOGY:** Cones typically begin development in spring of the third year. They mature slowly during the summer and shed spores in late autumn and early winter of the same year.

IDENTIFICATION: None of the *Dendrolycopodium* can be told apart at any great distance, but each can be identified with just one or two subtle details. First, check the leaves on the lower part of the main stem to see if they point outward from the stem or if they point upward. Upward will lead to *D. hickeyi* and *D. obscurum*. If that is the case, then check to see if the side branches look round when viewed end on or if they look flat on the bottom. Round indicates *D. hickeyi*; flat indicates *D. obscurum*. If still uncertain, check to see if the bottom row of leaves is distinctly smaller than the other leaves (*D. obscurum*) or about the same size (*D. hickeyi*).

NATURAL HISTORY: *Dendrolycopodium obscurum* occurs in the northeastern United States and adjacent parts of Canada, extending westward only as far as eastern Minnesota. It was overlooked in Minnesota until 2020, and its distribution and habitat preferences are still imperfectly known. So far, habitats appear similar to those of other *Dendrolycopodium*: primarily dry-mesic forests of oak, pine, and aspen. Soils are humus-rich sand, somewhat dry at the surface but only slightly higher in elevation than adjacent ground-water-maintained wetlands. All three species of *Dendrolycopodium* may grow intermingled where their ranges overlap.

Leaves on underside are small.

Cones, still green on September 6, will ripen before winter.

Stem leaves point upward.

On the floor of an oak forest, Anoka County—November 2.

D. digitatum

D. tristachyum

D. complanatum

DIPHASIASTRUM (GROUND-CEDARS)

There are about 20 species of *Diphasiastrum* in the world, primarily in north temperate and subarctic regions. There are 5 species in North America and 3 in Minnesota.

The growing tip of the rhizome will lengthen 10–30 cm each year depending on habitat conditions. Each annual segment of the rhizome will produce 5–15 aerial stems, a similar number of stout roots, and occasionally a side branch. Each year thereafter, the aerial stems will grow, adding height and branches until the age of five or six, when cones are produced. The following year, the cohort of stems that produced the cones will senesce and die along with the segment of rhizome to which they were attached. But the growing tip of the rhizome keeps extending, producing a continual series of aerial stems, as will any successful side branch of the rhizome. Each leaf on the underside of a branch has a narrow, pointed "free portion" that is shaped like a canine tooth, and a portion fused to the branch. It is the free portion that is measured.

KEY TO *DIPHASIASTRUM*

1. Ultimate branches 1–1.5(2) mm wide, excluding any flaring leaf tips; leaves on the undersides of the ultimate branches 1–1.5 mm long, similar in length to the leaves on the sides of the branches; rhizomes well belowground, frequently buried deeper than 5 cm . . . . *D. tristachyum*

1. Ultimate branches 1.5–2.5 mm wide, excluding any flaring leaf tips; leaves on the undersides of the ultimate branches 0.5–1 mm long, measurably shorter than the side leaves; rhizomes at or near the surface.

    2. Mature branches without annual constrictions, the branches oriented in horizontal planes; cones 2–3.5 cm long, often with a slender sterile tip . . . . *D. digitatum*

    2. Mature lateral branches each with 1 or 2 annual constrictions, the branches oriented somewhat irregularly in relation to the horizontal; cones 1–2.5 cm long, always lacking a sterile tip . . . . *D. complanatum*

DIPHASIASTRUM HYBRIDS

All *Diphasiastrum* species in Minnesota hybridize freely, producing fertile offspring. That means they can form backcrosses with the parent species, even trihybrids with a nonparent species. This makes positive identification of hybrids extremely difficult. Despite the possibilities, most of the *Diphasiastrum* encountered in Minnesota appear to be one of the 3 nonhybrid species.

Diphasiastrum complanatum (L.) Holub
Northern Ground-Cedar

[*Lycopodium complanatum* L.]

PLANTS evergreen. **RHIZOMES** to 1+ m
long, infrequently branched, superficial or
shallowly buried in humus. **AERIAL STEMS**
typically rising to an aboveground height
of 15–20 cm (excluding cones) at maturity;
with 3–6 primary branches. **BRANCHES**
usually 6–9 cm long at maturity, repeatedly
forked, ± flat in cross-section, 1.5–2.5 mm
wide (excluding any protruding leaf tips),
with 1 or 2 annual constrictions each.
LEAVES joined to the branch for at least half
their length; the free portion narrowed
evenly to a pointed tip; leaves on the
underside of the branch 0.5–1 mm long,

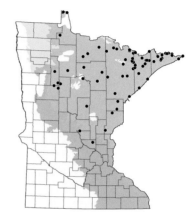

½–¾ the length of those on the sides of the branches. **CONES** 1–2.5 cm long,
borne on a common stalk 2–6 cm long; each stalk typically bearing 1–5 cones.
PHENOLOGY: Cones start to develop in the spring, mature during summer, and
release spores in late summer and early fall. Old cones and their stalks turn
brown but stay on the branch through the winter.

IDENTIFICATION: The overall appearance of *D. complanatum* compared to
D. digitatum is one of a somewhat larger plant with a tangle of long, disheveled,
or disorganized branches. Each branch will have 1 or 2 annual constrictions,
which appear as an abrupt narrowing of the branch. They mark the end of one
year's growth and the beginning of the next. They should be visible on every
branch that is more than one year old. The branches of *D. digitatum* only grow for
one year, so they are shorter and have no annual constrictions. Both species differ
from *D. tristachyum* in that the leaves on the undersides of the branches are
smaller than those on the sides of the branches.

NATURAL HISTORY: *Diphasiastrum complanatum* ranges across northern parts of
North America and much of Eurasia. It is not uncommon in the northern third of
Minnesota. It occurs in a variety of habitats loosely associated with upland forests,
especially where conditions are somewhat dry and at least partially shaded by trees
or shrubs. Soils are usually shallow, with a coarse texture, and sandy or rocky. It
seems to do fine in rather barren settings such as bedrock-influenced habitats
where mosses or lichens dominate.

Branches showing annual constrictions.

Cones nearing maturity, Lake County—
August 21.

With stiff clubmoss and large-leaved aster,
Lake County.

Spores have been shed—September 18.

Diphasiastrum digitatum (Dill. ex A. Braun) Holub
Fan Ground-Cedar

[*Lycopodium complanatum* var. *flabelliforme* Fern.; *L. flabelliforme* (Fern.)
  Blanch.; *L. digitatum* Dill. ex A. Braun]

PLANTS evergreen. **RHIZOMES** to 1+ m
long, seldom branched, superficial or
shallowly buried in humus. **AERIAL STEMS**
typically rising to a height of 10–15 cm
(excluding cones) at maturity, occasionally
to 20 cm, with 1–4 primary branches.
BRANCHES usually 4–6 cm long at maturity,
repeatedly forked, becoming ± flat in cross-
section, 1.5–2.5 mm wide (excluding any
protruding leaf tips), lacking annual
constrictions. **LEAVES** joined to the branch
for at least half their length, the free
portion narrowed evenly to a pointed tip;
leaves on the undersides of the branches

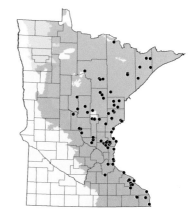

0.5–1 mm long, about half the length of those on the sides of the branches.
CONES 2–3.5 cm long, often with a short sterile tip, borne on stalks 3–9 cm long;
each stalk typically bearing 4 cones. **PHENOLOGY:** Cones start to develop in the
spring, mature during summer, release spores in fall and winter, and remain until
the following spring or summer.

IDENTIFICATION: Only with much practice can the 3 Minnesota species of
Diphasiastrum be reliably told apart without a close look at the branches.
Compared to the other species, the branches of *D. digitatum* are typically shorter,
fewer in number, and radiate fanlike in 2 or 3 horizontal or slightly drooping
layers. For confirmation, look for annual constrictions, which are easily seen
on the branches of both *D. complanatum* and *D. tristachyum* but absent from
D. digitatum. Furthermore, the cones of *D. digitatum* often have a slender sterile
tip that is not seen in the other species. Unfortunately, cones are not always
present.

NATURAL HISTORY: *Diphasiastrum digitatum* is endemic to forests in temperate
regions of eastern North America. It is found in eastern portions of Minnesota,
most commonly in sandy, noncalcareous forest soils. Forest types include
mid- to late-successional upland stands of hardwoods or conifers. Although
fundamentally a forest species, *D. digitatum* is sometimes found where a forest
borders a sunny opening, yet it does not compete well with sun-adapted plants.
In ideal conditions, it becomes established quickly and spreads rapidly, sometimes
forming dense colonies several meters across.

Note the fan-shaped branches—
October 7.

An extensive colony in spring—May 15.

Rhizomes grow over the surface of the ground.

Spores are released in fall
and winter.

Diphasiastrum tristachyum (Pursh) Holub
Blue Ground-Cedar

[*Lycopodium tristachyum* Pursh]

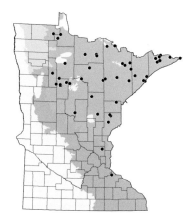

PLANTS evergreen. **RHIZOMES** to 1+ m long, infrequently branched, belowground to a depth of 1–12 cm. **AERIAL STEMS** typically rising to an aboveground height of 12–18 cm (excluding cones) at maturity, main axis (if discernible) with 3–7 primary branches. **BRANCHES** repeatedly forked, with 1 or 2 annual constrictions each; the ultimate branches 1–1.5(2) mm wide (excluding any protruding leaf tips). **LEAVES** joined to the branches for at least half their length, the free portion narrowed evenly to a pointed tip; leaves on the undersides of the branches 1–1.5 mm long, about equal in length to those on the sides of the branches. **CONES** 1–2.5 cm long, borne on stalks 5–10 cm long; each stalk typically bearing 2–4 cones.

PHENOLOGY: Cones begin to develop in early summer, reach maturity during the summer, and release their spores in late summer and fall of the same year.

IDENTIFICATION: The branches of *D. tristachyum* are comparatively narrow and sometimes appear more cordlike than distinctly flat. Another feature of *D. tristachyum*, the eponymous blue-green color, seems to develop in response to sunny conditions and might not be noticed in shade-grown plants. Similarly, the characteristic deep rhizome might not be deep where the soil is thin or rocky. The one feature to count on is the row of narrow, pointed leaves on the underside of each slender branch. They are essentially the same size as the leaves that line the margins of the branches. In fact, leaves on all four sides of the branch are about the same size.

NATURAL HISTORY: *Diphasiastrum tristachyum* ranges through north temperate and boreal regions of eastern and central North America and Eurasia. It can be found regularly, but not commonly, in the northeastern half of Minnesota. It is most often associated with pine forests, especially jack pine, or the types of places one might expect to find jack pine. Expect it to be growing in dryish, sandy, forest soil, or sometimes in loose gravely residue on large boulders or bedrock outcrops. Habitats are most often in partial shade but sometimes in direct sunlight in small clearings. It is often associated with bracken, lichens, or blueberries.

Plants often have a blueish cast—
September 18.

In a dry, rocky habitat, Lake County—July 19.

Branches are slender, show annual constrictions.

Spores recently shed—
September 18.

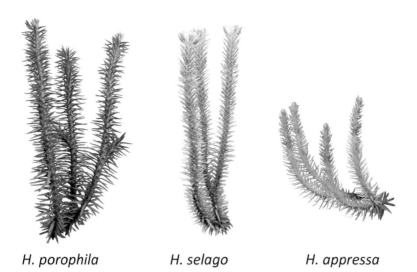

H. porophila   *H. selago*   *H. appressa*

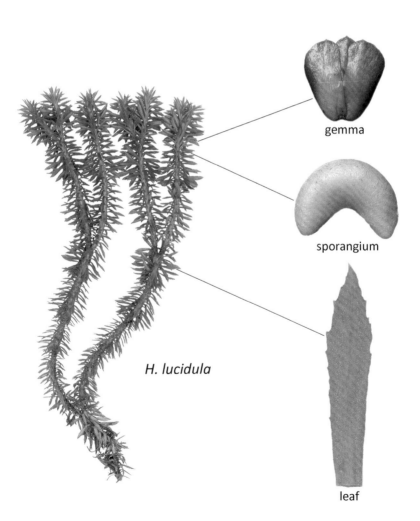

gemma

sporangium

H. lucidula

leaf

HUPERZIA (FIRMOSSES)

The genus *Huperzia* consists of about 25 species, with the greatest diversity in temperate and subtropical regions of the Northern Hemisphere. There are 7 species in the United States and 4 in Minnesota.

Minnesota *Huperzia* are built around a simple body plan, yet they have at least two unique features that set them apart from similar lycophytes. First, they reproduce vegetatively by gemmae. These are fully preformed plantlets that are produced each year once the plant reaches maturity. Although the gemmae are shed each year, the short branches on which they are produced persist and are easy to see among the leaves. Second, the sporangia are produced along the leafy stems, not in distinct cones.

In addition, two pieces of specialized knowledge are needed to navigate the key. First: trophophylls versus sporophylls. Sporophylls are the leaves that have sporangia at their base. They are found in the upper parts of mature branches. They are somewhat smaller than the trophophylls, which are the leaves without sporangia that are found in the lower parts of the branches.

The second key feature is the stomates. These are round, donut-shaped cells on the surface of the leaves that function in gas exchange between the leaf and the environment. Under magnification, they stand out from the normal rectilinear cells of the leaf epidermis. They do require magnification to see, but not any special preparation.

Hybrid *Huperzia* are common wherever two species occur together. They are sterile but can proliferate via gemmae. Knowing if a specimen is a hybrid involves looking at the spores under magnification (at least 50×). In the case of hybrids, 25–50 percent of the spores will have a variable and imperfect shape; they will not be spherical. Making this determination requires experience and access to a microscope; it is not practical otherwise.

Two keys are provided: one key to the 4 species of *Huperzia* that can be found in Minnesota, and another key to the 4 sterile hybrids that occur in Minnesota. Disclaimer: If you have determined that your specimen has abortive spores and is therefore a likely hybrid, then the key to hybrids may help determine the parents. Otherwise, do not use the key to hybrids. Do not assume that just because you had poor success with the key to species that you will have better luck with the key to hybrids—the result will likely be the opposite.

KEY TO THE NONHYBRID SPECIES OF *HUPERZIA*

1. Leaves widest above the middle, tapering toward the base; most leaves with 1–8 irregular but distinct teeth on each margin; stomates present only on lower surface of leaves; gemmae (pressed flat and dried) 4–5 mm long and 3–5 mm wide . . . . *H. lucidula*

1. Leaves widest at the base or somewhere between the base and the middle, or the proximal half of the leaf with sides nearly parallel; leaf margins entire or with a few barely distinguishable teeth; stomates present on upper and lower surfaces of leaves; gemmae (pressed flat and dried) 3–4.5 mm long and 2–4 mm wide.

    2. Gemmae (or the persistent branches that bear them) scattered throughout the middle and upper portions of the branches; trophophylls 4–6 mm long; sporophylls 2–3.5 mm long (measure the longest); sporangia-bearing portions of branches 5–8 mm wide (including leaf tips); entire plant 5–12 cm in height, pale yellowish green . . . . *H. appressa*

    2. Gemmae produced only at the apex of each season's growth (expect them to be spaced at ± regular intervals of 1–3 cm corresponding to the end of each year's growth); trophophylls 6–9 mm long; sporophylls 3–5 mm long (measure the longest); sporangia-bearing portions of branches 7–15 mm wide (including leaf tips); entire plant 8–28 cm in height, uniformly green.

        3. Upper surface of leaves with 1–50 stomates, trophophylls 7–9 mm long (measure the longest) . . . . *H. porophila*

        3. Upper surface of leaves with > 60 stomates; trophophylls 6–8 mm long (measure the longest) . . . . *H. selago*

KEY TO THE HYBRID *HUPERZIA*

1. Sporophylls (sporangia-bearing leaves on the upper portion of the branches) 3–4 mm long and visibly shorter than the trophophylls (sterile leaves near the base of the branches); gemmae (pressed and dried) 3.5–4 mm long.

    2. Stomates numbering 70–120 on upper surface of leaves; sporangia-bearing portion of branches 6–12 mm wide . . . . *H. ×josephbeitelii*

    2. Stomates numbering 1—60 on upper surface of leaves; sporangia-bearing portion of branches 10–15 mm wide . . . . *H. ×protoporophila*

1. Sporophylls (sporangia-bearing leaves on the upper portion of the branches) 5–7 mm long and not visibly shorter than the trophophylls (sterile leaves near the base of the branches); gemmae (pressed and dried) 4–4.5 mm long.

    3. Upper surface of leaves with 5–60 stomates . . . . *H. ×buttersii*

    3. Upper surface of leaves with 1–10 stomates . . . . *H. ×bartleyi*

HUPERZIA ×BARTLEYI (*H. LUCIDULA* × *H. POROPHILA*)

This entity looks most like *H. porophila* and has been found in cliff habitats near *H. porophila*. The leaves tend to be long like those of *H. lucidula* but show only rudimentary teeth along the margins or no teeth at all. Numerous stomates are found on the lower surface but only a few on the upper surface. Among the hybrids, it most closely resembles *H. ×buttersii*.

HUPERZIA ×JOSEPHBEITELII (H. SELAGO × H. APPRESSA)

Although clearly intermediate between the parents, this hybrid more closely resembles *H. appressa* in that the gemmae are distributed throughout the apical portion of mature plants rather than in a single ring. It more closely resembles *H. selago* in being robust, and with larger gemmae.

HUPERZIA ×BUTTERSII (H. SELAGO × H. LUCIDULA)

Visually, this hybrid looks most like a slender *H. lucidula*. Among the hybrids, it is most similar to *H. ×protoporophila* and *H. ×bartleyi* but with barely noticeable winter bud constrictions and with fewer than 60 stomates on the upper surface of leaves. Gemmae are borne in a single ring at the top of each growth segment. It is most likely to occur in level forest terrain rather than specialized cliff habitats.

HUPERZIA ×PROTOPOROPHILA (H. APPRESSA × H. LUCIDULA)

The mixing of parental features causes this hybrid to closely resemble *H. porophila*. Expect the number of stomates on the upper surface of each leaf to not exceed 60, and the margins of the leaves to be entire or with vague teeth toward the apex. The gemmae will be together in 1 or 2 (rarely 3) whorls at the apex of each annual growth segment. Typically found growing with *H. appressa* in exposed cliff-related habitats.

Huperzia appressa (Desv.) A. & D. Löve
Mountain Firmoss

[*Huperzia appalachiana* Beitel & Mickel]

PLANTS evergreen. **BRANCHES** 5–12 cm in length, with little if any portion decumbent; distal (sporangia-bearing) portion 5–8 mm wide (including leaf tips), proximal (non-sporangia-bearing) portion 7–13 mm wide; lacking visible annual constrictions. **LEAVES:** Trophophylls (sterile leaves) spreading to ascending; the proximal half with sides nearly parallel; entire, mostly 4–6 mm long. Sporophylls (fertile leaves) mostly 2–3.5 mm long, appressed, narrowly triangular, entire. **STOMATES** on both surfaces of leaves, numbering 70–120 on upper surface.

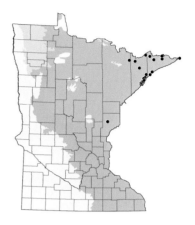

SPORANGIA in axils of nonspecialized leaves (sporophylls). **GEMMAE** 3–4 mm long, 2–3.5 mm wide (pressed and dried), produced throughout mature portions of the branches. **PHENOLOGY:** Reproductive maturity is reached in 2–4 years, then sporangia and gemmae are normally produced each year throughout the growing season. The sporangia shed spores about 1.5 years after formation; the gemmae are dispersed after about 1 year.

IDENTIFICATION: *Huperzia appressa* is the smallest of Minnesota firmosses. Each branch is about the size of an ordinary pencil. It has a distinctive pale yellowish-green color and slender upright stems. In its genetically pure form, it is rather distinctive. It is most likely to be mistaken for *H. selago* but is somewhat smaller in all respects. The best single character is the gemmae, which in *H. appressa* appear to be scattered randomly throughout upper portions of mature stems. In *H. selago,* the gemmae are confined to a single ring at the top of each year's growth.

NATURAL HISTORY: *Huperzia appressa* is found in arctic and cold temperate regions of eastern North America and Eurasia. In Minnesota, it is found on shaded ledges, shelves, and chutes associated with north-facing cliffs and talus of igneous rock. It is quite rare in Minnesota, or at least suitable habitat is rare in Minnesota, comprising some small part of 1 percent in the northeast corner of the state. Unlike most other *Huperzia,* the individual stems of *H. appressa* are reported to be determinate in growth pattern. Apparently, the whole plant dies after 12–15 years, after having produced spores and gemmae for 6–10 years. Other species of firmoss live about the same length of time but don't seem to die on cue as this one does.

Growing with lichens *Cladonia uncialis* and *C. squamosa*.

Slender, yellowish branches live 12–15 years.

Bouldery talus at the base of a cliff, Lake County—prime habitat for *H. appressa*.

Huperzia lucidula (Michx.) Trevisan
Shining Firmoss

[*Lycopodium lucidulum* Michx.]

PLANTS evergreen. **BRANCHES** 12–45 cm in length, the lower 5–15 cm often decumbent; 15–25 mm wide (including leaf tips), with noticeable annual constrictions. **LEAVES:** Trophophylls (sterile leaves) oblanceolate, clearly widest above the middle, spreading to reflexed, 7–12 mm long, with 1–8 teeth on each margin toward distal end. Sporophylls (fertile leaves) 5–8 mm long, otherwise similar to trophophylls. **STOMATES** only on lower surface of leaves. **SPORANGIA** in axils of nonspecialized leaves (sporophylls).

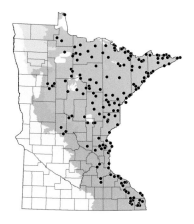

GEMMAE 4–5 mm long, 3–5 mm wide (pressed and dried), produced in 1 whorl at the summit of each season's growth (seen just below the annual constriction). **PHENOLOGY:** Reproductive maturity is reached in about 6 years. Sporangia are produced each year thereafter in early summer and released in the autumn of the following year. Gemmae are produced in late summer and released 1 year later.

IDENTIFICATION: *Huperzia lucidula* is the largest *Huperzia* in Minnesota, although only a bit more than ankle high. It can be separated from other *Huperzia* by a quick look at the leaves. They taper from above the middle to a slender base, and the margins have jagged teeth toward the tip. *Spinulum annotinum* (p. 44) is a surprising look-alike, but the aerial stems of all *Spinulum* grow from a long rhizome and have sporangia in cones at the top of the stems. All *Huperzia* lack rhizomes and have sporangia mixed in with the leaves.

NATURAL HISTORY: *Huperzia lucidula* is endemic to cool temperate and subboreal regions of eastern North America. It is relatively common in Minnesota, although never abundant. It is found in a variety of moist, shaded, forested habitats, primarily in uplands under broad-leaved or needle-leaved trees. It also occurs in swamp forests, where it might be found on slightly elevated microsites such as around the base of a tree or on a mossy hummock. It sometimes forms dense patches a meter or more across. Such patches apparently come about through the release of gemmae since there is no true rhizome to propagate the plant. What might appear to be a rhizome is simply the lower portions of the stems that sag with age until a greater and greater portion is lying on the ground.

The pale structures that hug the stem are sporangia.

A large colony in Washington County—September 7.

The round, yellow cells are stomates.

Gemmae above; sporangia below.

Huperzia porophila (F. E. Lloyd & Underw.) Holub
Rock Firmoss

[*Lycopodium porophilum* F. E. Lloyd & Underw.]

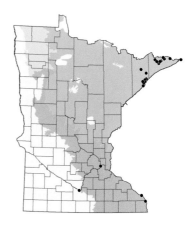

PLANTS evergreen. **BRANCHES** 10–22 cm in length, a small portion decumbent; distal (sporangia-bearing) portion 10–15 mm wide (including leaf tips); proximal (non-sporangia-bearing) portion 14–18 mm wide; annual constrictions indistinct. **LEAVES:** Trophophylls (sterile leaves) ascending, spreading or slightly reflexed; proximal half with sides nearly parallel, 7–9 mm long; margins entire or with a few indistinct serrations toward apex. Sporophylls (fertile leaves) 4–5 mm long, narrowly triangular, entire. **STOMATES** on both surfaces of leaves, 1–50 on upper surface. **SPORANGIA** in axils of nonspecialized leaves (sporophylls). **GEMMAE** 3.5–4.5 mm long, 2–3.5 mm wide (pressed and dried), produced in 1–3 pseudowhorls at summit of each annual growth segment. **PHENOLOGY:** Reproductive maturity is reached in 4–5 years, then sporangia and gemmae are normally produced each year, in distinct zones. Sporangia release spores in autumn of the second year. Gemmae disperse in late summer of the second year.

IDENTIFICATION: At times, *H. porophila* will resemble a small *H. lucidula,* which can be ruled out by characteristics of the leaves (dichotomy 1 of the key). Distinguishing it from *H. selago* is more difficult. When seen side by side, the branches of *H. porophila* will generally look slightly thicker and darker green than those of *H. selago,* but there is considerable overlap. Identification may come down to a careful measurement of the trophophylls (pick the largest) and the ability to count the stomates on the upper surface of a leaf. If doubt lingers, it might be time to consult a specialist.

NATURAL HISTORY: *Huperzia porophila* is endemic to cool temperate regions in eastern and central North America. It is quite rare in Minnesota, found on moist, shaded, moss-covered ledges on north-facing cliffs and bouldery talus. It occurs on sandstone in the southeast and various igneous rocks in the northeast. It is believed to be an allopolyploid that began its existence long ago as a chance fertile hybrid between *H. appressa* and *H. lucidula*. It subsequently found a unique ecological niche and now lives entirely independent of its parent species. Curiously, *H. appressa* and *H. lucidula* will still form occasional hybrids, and although the hybrids look very much like *Huperzia porophila,* they are sterile and are given the name *H.* ×*protoporophilla.*

Gemmae in separate rings.

A single plant with 10 or more branches.

Trophophore.

In shallow soil on a ledge of a north-facing cliff, Lake County.

Huperzia selago (L.) Bernh. ex Schrank & Mart.
Northern Firmoss

[*Lycopodium selago* L.]

PLANTS evergreen. **BRANCHES** 8–28 cm in length, a small portion decumbent; 7–15 mm wide (including leaf tips), with indistinct annual constrictions or none. **LEAVES:** Trophophylls (sterile leaves) spreading to ascending, proximal half with sides nearly parallel, 6–8 mm long, margins entire or with a few small irregular serrations. Sporophylls (fertile leaves) ascending to appressed, 3–6 mm long, narrowly triangular, entire. **STOMATES** on both surfaces of leaves, numbering > 60 on upper surface. **SPORANGIA** in axils of nonspecialized leaves (sporophylls).

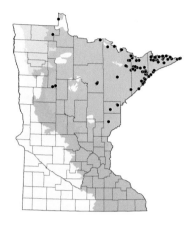

GEMMAE 4–5 mm long, 2.8–4 mm wide (pressed and dried), produced in 1 whorl at the apex of each season's growth. **PHENOLOGY:** Reproductive maturity is reached at 2–4 years, then sporangia and gemmae are produced each year in distinct zones on all the branches. Sporangia are produced during the first part of the growing season and release spores in autumn of the following year. Gemmae are produced at the end of the growing season and are dispersed about 1 year later.

IDENTIFICATION: In most situations, *H. selago* will look very much like *H. porophila*. Separating the two can be daunting, and not reliably done in the field. The smaller trophophylls of *H. selago* (dichotomy 3) is a useful distinction, but it is a fine distinction and there is overlap. It is usually necessary to count stomates. There is considerable variation in this feature, so check more than one leaf. Also, be aware that *H. selago* is relatively common and occurs in a variety of habitats; *H. porophila* is rare and found only in cliff habitats.

NATURAL HISTORY: *Huperzia selago* ranges broadly across temperate, boreal, and arctic regions of North America and Eurasia. Among the *Huperzia*, it can be considered relatively common in parts of northeastern Minnesota, less so in the north-central counties. The preferred habitat in Minnesota seems to be in rugged, rocky terrain, often among lichens and mosses. It does particularly well in crevices, ledges, and chutes on cool, shaded, north-facing cliffs, or on exposed, bouldery talus at the base of cliffs. It can also be found in level terrain in upland forests, and even in swamp forests on slightly elevated microsites where its roots are above the saturated peat.

A single ring of gemmae.

A thriving plant with 10 branches.

On a boulder in Lake County, with rock polypody and the lichens *Cladonia rangiferina* and *C. amaurocraea*.

L. inundata

LYCOPODIELLA (BOG CLUBMOSSES)

There are perhaps 15 species of *Lycopodiella* in the world, with the greatest diversity in the New World tropics. There are at least 8 species in North America and 1 in Minnesota. Our one species, *L. inundata* (northern bog clubmoss), is perhaps the widest ranging of any species in the genus, ranging across North America, most of Europe, and parts of Asia.

Outwardly, *L. inundata* resembles nothing more or less than a miniature or simplified version of *Lycopodium*, as the name implies. And yet, *Lycopodium* and *Lycopodiella* are separated by more than 200 million years of evolution. The technical differences separating the two genera are corroborated by DNA evidence but of little use in field identification. We generally recognize *Lycopodiella* in the field by its small size and delicate structure. It exists more on the scale of a moss than a lycophyte.

Lycopodiella inundata (L.) Holub
Northern Bog Clubmoss

[*Lycopodium inundatum* L.]

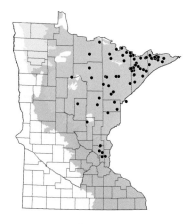

PLANTS deciduous, dying back to a winter bud at the end of each growing season. **RHIZOMES** (stolons) growing on the surface of the ground, often with a peculiar arch, and rooting along their length; to 15 cm long, branching once or twice or remaining unbranched. **AERIAL STEMS** 1 or occasionally 2 in number, 4–12 cm long (including cones), unbranched, each bearing a single cone. **LEAVES** 3–6.5 mm long, 0.5–0.7 mm wide, narrowly triangular to linear-lanceolate; margins entire; apex acute to acuminate. **CONES** 1–5 cm long, 5–10 mm wide (leaf tip to leaf tip), distinctly wider than the stem that supports it, sessile, solitary or rarely 2.

PHENOLOGY: Cones turn yellow and release their spores in late autumn and early winter. Stems and branches die over winter.

IDENTIFICATION: The small size, simplified structure, and soft branches will distinguish *Lycopodiella* from *Lycopodium*. Although it is a lycophyte, *L. inundata* may initially appear more like a true moss than a lycophyte. Unlike mosses, there will be a spore-bearing cone at the top of each vertical shoot. The cone looks much like the stem itself, only slightly thicker. Most of the plant hugs the ground; only the cone-bearing branch stands upright, but rarely as much as ankle high.

NATURAL HISTORY: *Lycopodiella inundata* occurs in cool temperate regions across North America and Eurasia. It is sometimes hard to find in Minnesota, but it is not uncommon in good habitat. Good habitats are generally small and imbedded in, or marginal to, larger habitats. Examples include seasonally inundated habitats, such as lakeshores and margins of beaver ponds, where it may grow on the surface of bare sand, peat, or organic silt. It is also found in relatively stable habitats such as fens or floating vegetation mats. Most habitats are natural in origin, although some are abandoned man-made habitats such as sediment basins or sand mines where ponded water fluctuates with the seasons or with ground-water levels. The one necessary requirement is wet ground. It is considered a perennial, but only a bud on the rooted tip of each branch survives the winter to begin growth the following spring. It multiplies vegetatively when two branches are produced, each leaving a bud to overwinter.

Cone not yet ripe on August 15.

Cones stand erect; rhizomes hug the ground—
August 15.

Aerial stems turn yellow and
fade in autumn—September 26.

Typical shore fen habitat, Lake County—September 9.

MICHAEL D. LEE

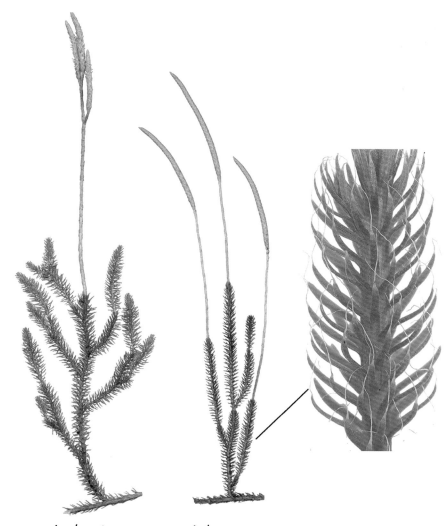

L. clavatum   *L. lagopus*

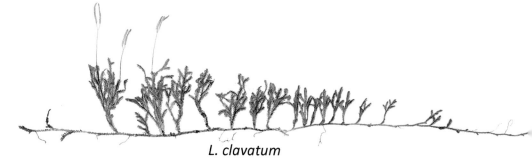

L. clavatum

LYCOPODIUM (CLUBMOSSES)

There are believed to be about 15 species in the genus *Lycopodium,* with just 2 species in North America, both of which are found in Minnesota. There are two simple features that easily distinguish plants in this genus: the cones are on slender, nearly leafless stalks, and the individual leaves have long, hairlike extensions at the tips.

The species of *Lycopodium* that occur in Minnesota have horizontal stems (rhizomes or stolons) that grow over the surface of the ground, averaging per-haps 50 cm per year. Each year, the newest segment of the stolon will produce a number of vertical branches (aerial stems) that grow for 4 or 5 years, then produce cones that bear the sporangia. The following year, the cone-bearing branches die, along with the segment of stolon that bore them. However, the tip of the stolon continues to grow, producing a succession of new vertical branches.

KEY TO *LYCOPODIUM*

1. Cones usually 2–4 per stalk, each cone borne on a short but separate branch at the top of the stalk; leaves spreading to ascending, 4–6 mm long (excluding hairlike extension); branches of aerial stems 8–15 mm wide (measured leaf tip to leaf tip, excluding hairlike extension) . . . . *L. clavatum*

1 Cones usually 1 per stalk; if a second cone is present, then both are sessile at the top of the stalk; leaves ascending to appressed, 3–4.5 mm long (excluding hairlike extension); branches of aerial stems 5–8(9) mm wide (measured leaf tip to leaf tip, excluding hairlike extension) . . . . *L. lagopus*

Lycopodium clavatum L.
Common Clubmoss

PLANTS evergreen. **RHIZOMES** (stolons) superficial, to 3+ m long. **AERIAL STEMS** 6–18 cm in height at maturity (excluding cones and cone stalks), 8–15 mm wide (leaf tip to leaf tip), producing 5–15+ (usually 6–12) unequal branches (count each branch tip). **BRANCHES** spreading to ascending; the primary branches typically forming an angle with the axis ≥ 45 degrees. **LEAVES** linear-lanceolate, spreading to ascending, 4–6 mm long, 0.4–0.6 mm wide; margins entire; apex with a slender hairlike extension 1–4 mm long.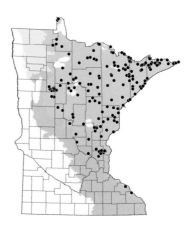
CONES 3–5 cm long, numbering 1–4 (usually 2 or 3); each borne on a separate 1–5 mm branch of the common stalk; common stalk 5–13 cm long. **PHENOLOGY:** Stalks that bear the cones typically begin to develop as growth commences in the spring of the fourth year. Spores are released in autumn of that year, then the aerial stem senesces and dies before the end of the next growing season.

IDENTIFICATION: Compared to *L. lagopus,* the leaves of *L. clavatum* are somewhat longer and they tend to project straight outward, giving the branches a "bristly" appearance. Also, the branches of the aerial stems are more numerous and tend to spread more widely. In any large colony of *L. clavatum,* the majority of mature stems will have at least 2 cones, and each cone will be on a short but separate branch at the top of the stalk. There may be a few stalks with only one cone, but they will be in the minority.

NATURAL HISTORY: *Lycopodium clavatum* is found in temperate and boreal habitats in much of the world. In Minnesota, it is comparatively common in a variety of upland forest types, apparently favoring fire-dependent forests on light or sandy soil. It is also found in swamp forests, where it will avoid the wettest areas. The stolons are quite agile, easily crisscrossing mossy or lichen-encrusted boulders or decomposing logs. It seems to thrive even where mineral nutrients or water seem to be in short supply. Perhaps because the plant sits lightly on the surface of the ground, and roots are few and shallow, the habitat below the top few centimeters does not really matter.

Each cone is on its own stalk.

Mass sporulating is not uncommon, Lake County—September 18.

A cloud of spores—September 7.

Rhizomes easily traverse fallen logs, Lake County—August 21.

Lycopodium lagopus (Laest. ex Hartman) Zinserl. ex Kuzen.
One-Cone Clubmoss

PLANTS evergreen. **RHIZOMES** (stolons) superficial, to 2+ m long. **AERIAL STEMS** 3–12 cm in height at maturity (excluding cones and cone stalks), 5–8(9) mm wide (leaf tip to leaf tip), producing 2–10+ (typically 2–7) unequal branches (count every branch tip). **BRANCHES** ascending to erect; the primary branches typically forming an angle with the axis < 45 degrees from vertical. **LEAVES** linear to linear-lanceolate, ascending to appressed, 3–4.5 mm long, 0.4–0.6 mm wide; margins entire; apex with a slender hairlike extension 1–4 mm long.

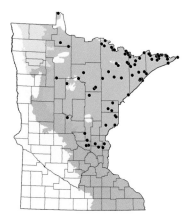

CONES 1–6 cm long, numbering 1 or occasionally 2; if 2 cones present, then both sessile at the top of the stalk; common stalk 3–10 cm long.

PHENOLOGY: Stalks of the cones typically begin to develop as growth commences in the spring of the third year. Spores are released in October and November of that year, then the aerial stem senesces and dies before the end of the next growing season.

IDENTIFICATION: Only small details separate *L. lagopus* from *L. clavatum*. In the case of *L. lagopus,* the leaves are consistently smaller and held closer to the branches, and the branches themselves are fewer in number and more upright. Significantly, *L. lagopus* usually has only 1 cone at the top of each stalk. Sometimes a stalk will have 2 cones, in which case the 2 cones will be sessile. It will look like they are joined at the base rather than attached separately to the stalk. Do not rely on a sample of just one or two cone-bearing stems. Inspect several stems from the same stolon.

NATURAL HISTORY: *Lycopodium lagopus* occurs in cold regions of North America and Eurasia. It occurs throughout the forested region of northern Minnesota but can be considered common only in the northeastern counties. It is typically found in fire-dependent forests of pine, sometimes oak, aspen, birch, spruce, fir, or other trees. It is often found creeping over talus, bedrock, or thin dry stony soil, sharing habitat and resources with lichens and mosses. Habitats are not much different from those of *L. clavatum,* and the two can sometimes be found growing together, but *L. lagopus* is less likely to be found in swampy places.

Leaves tipped with long hairs.

Most stalks have one cone, Lake County—August 8.

If cones paired, then sessile.

Rhizomes crisscross to form dense colonies.

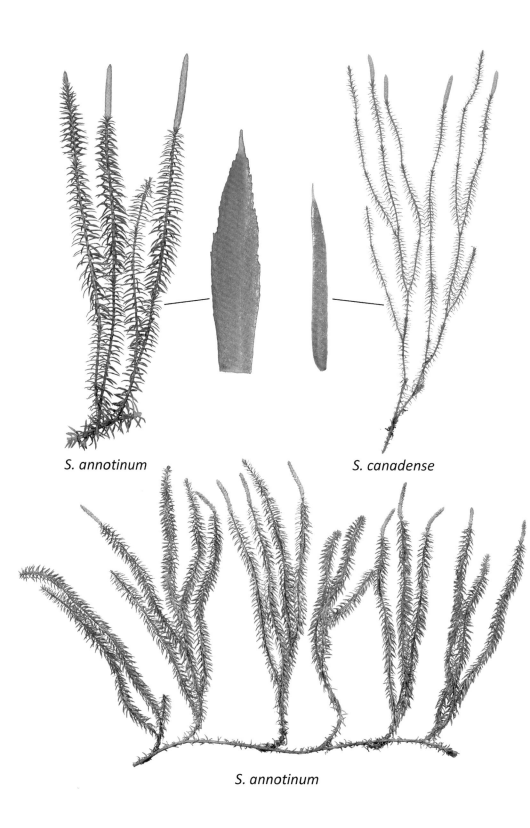

S. annotinum

S. canadense

S. annotinum

SPINULUM (BRISTLY CLUBMOSSES)

The genus *Spinulum* is believed to consist of 4 species occurring in various parts of the Northern Hemisphere. There are 3 species in North America and 2 in Minnesota. The genus has been segregated (taxonomically speaking) relatively recently from the genus *Lycopodium*. The most obvious differences between the 2 genera are the cones, which in *Spinulum* are sessile at the tips of leafy stems. In *Lycopodium,* they are at the ends of long, nearly naked stalks. Also, each leaf of *Spinulum* has a firm, spinelike tip (hence the genus name); each leaf of *Lycopodium* has a slender, hairlike extension.

The stolons of *Spinulum* grow horizontally over the surface of the ground, often hidden by mosses or covered with leaf mold. This is how they spread and forage for nutrients. Each rhizome will add 30–50 cm of growth each year and produce a number of vertical stems that grow for 5 or 6 years before producing cones and dying. The tip of the rhizome will continue to grow, producing a new cohort of vertical stems each year. If the tip is damaged, it will trigger the growth of side branches to perpetuate the process.

KEY TO *SPINULUM*

1. Leaves 4–6 mm long, 0.6–0.9 mm wide; the margins entire; leaves generally broadest at or near the base (most consistently seen on leaves immediately above an annual constriction); stems 7–12 mm wide (measured leaf tip to leaf tip); cones 1.5–2.5 cm long at maturity . . . . *S. canadense*
1. Leaves 6–10 mm long, 0.8–1.4 mm wide; the margins distinctly serrated; leaves generally broadest at or above the middle; stems 13–18 mm wide (measured leaf tip to leaf tip); cones 2–4 cm long at maturity . . . . *S. annotinum*

Spinulum annotinum (L.) A. Haines
Stiff Bristly Clubmoss

[*Lycopodium annotinum* var. *annotinum* L.]

PLANTS evergreen. **RHIZOMES** (stolons) superficial, to 3+ m long; branching suppressed by apical dominance. **AERIAL STEMS** 15–28 cm long at maturity (including the cones), 13–18 mm wide (leaf tip to leaf tip); with 1–4 branches arising from near the base. **LEAVES** narrowly oblanceolate to narrowly elliptic, held horizontally or slightly ascending, 6–10 mm long, 0.8–1.4 mm wide; distal margins serrate; apex with a firm spine about 0.5 mm long; stomata absent from upper surface although present on both surfaces of leaves at annual constrictions. **CONES**

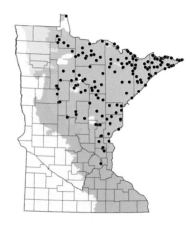

sessile, 2–4 cm long at maturity, solitary (one per branch). **PHENOLOGY:** Cones begin to develop when growth commences in the spring of the fourth or fifth year. They develop during the summer and shed spores in autumn of the same year; stems senesce the following year.

IDENTIFICATION: With practice, *S. annotinum* and *S. canadense* can be told apart from a distance, but even with a good search image it is always advisable to check the details. Start with the leaf margins; those of *S. annotinum* typically have irregular, jagged teeth toward the tip. If that feature is not clear, it may be necessary to do some fine-scale measuring (dichotomy 1). Without cones, *S. annotinum* bears an uncanny resemblance to *Huperzia lucidula* (p. 26), which often occurs in the same habitat. It is usually possible to see yellowish sporangia among the leaves of *Huperzia* but never on a *Spinulum*.

NATURAL HISTORY: *Spinulum annotinum* is widespread and common in mountainous and colder parts of North America and Eurasia. In Minnesota, it is a typical component of lycophyte communities in northern forests. It is somewhat of a forest generalist, occurring in a variety of upland coniferous and deciduous forests and occasionally swamp forests. It is usually found in stable older forests but sometimes in "working" forests if the native ground flora has not been severely compromised. Even though the best habitats may appear lush and green, there will be relatively few mineral nutrients available to the shallow roots of *S. annotinum*. And the plant is constantly foraging for better habitat as it creeps along at 30–50 cm per year.

Foraging plants are not deterred by fallen logs—May 5.

Cones sit directly atop stems—no stalks.

Perched on a mossy boulder, Cook County—
October 20.

Spinulum canadense (Ness.) A. Haines
Northern Bristly Clubmoss

[*Lycopodium annotinum* var. *pungens* (L.)
La Pylaie ex Desv.]

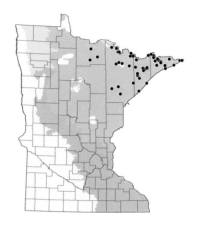

PLANTS evergreen. **RHIZOMES** (stolons)
superficial on the substrate (usually peat)
but often buried in living moss, to 2+ m
long, branching suppressed by apical
dominance. **AERIAL STEMS** 15–35 cm long
at maturity (including cones), 0.7–1.2 cm
wide (leaf tip to leaf tip); with 3–10
branches, most originating in the lower
half of the stem. **LEAVES** lanceolate to
narrowly triangular, spreading to
ascending, 4–6 mm long, 0.6–0.9 mm
wide; margins entire; apex with a firm
spine about 0.5 mm long; stomata on both
surfaces. **CONES** sessile, 1.5–2.5 cm long at maturity, solitary (one per branch).

PHENOLOGY: Cones begin to develop when growth commences in the spring of
the fourth or fifth year. They develop during the summer and shed spores in
autumn of the same year; fertile stems and the attached portion of the rhizome
senesce the following year.

IDENTIFICATION: The aerial stems of *S. canadense* typically look thinner and paler
than those of *S. annotinum*. Also, the leaf margins are smooth, with no hint of
serrations, and tend to be widest near the base. Leaves of *S. annotinum* typically
have jagged, irregular serrations toward the tip and are widest near the middle.
Size differences seem to be consistent (dichotomy 1) but require a practiced eye or
careful measurements.

NATURAL HISTORY: *Spinulum canadense* is found across much of arctic, boreal,
and cool temperate regions of North America. It is a decidedly northern species,
occurring primarily in Canada and Alaska. It can be found with some regularity in
the northeastern counties of Minnesota, and occasionally in the north-central
counties. It is somewhat less common in Minnesota than *S. annotinum*. It is also
limited to a smaller portion of the state and a narrower range of habitats. Habitats
occur primarily in conifer swamps under a canopy of black spruce, and
sometimes in adjacent treeless fens. It seems to always grow on wet peat among
mosses, primarily *Sphagnum* moss. These tend to be acidic, nutrient-poor
habitats. Sparse colonies seem to be the rule, or sometimes just solitary plants
roaming, unanchored, across the forest floor.

Stems produce a cone in their fourth or fifth year.

In a black spruce bog, Lake County—September 17.

Leaves are slender, with smooth margins.

Spores are shed in autumn—September 17.

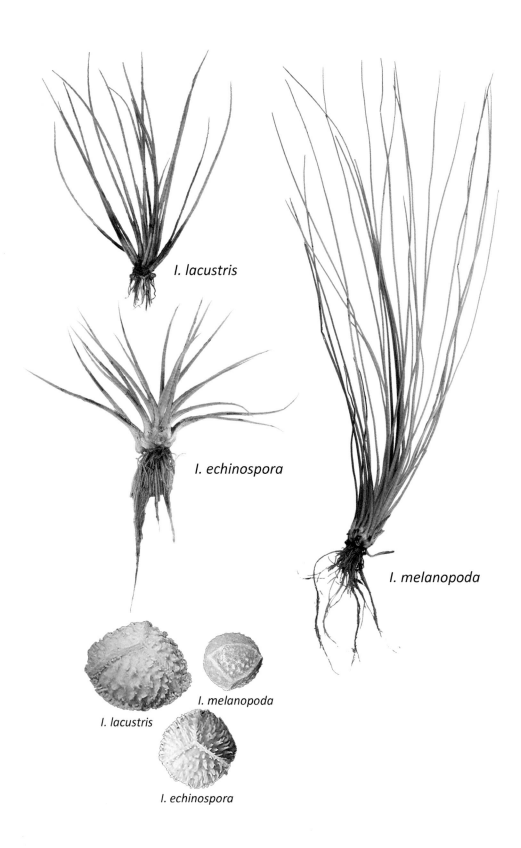

I. lacustris

I. echinospora

I. melanopoda

I. lacustris

I. melanopoda

I. echinospora

Chapter 2

The Lycophyte Order Isoetales (Quillworts)

The order Isoetales contains a single ancient family (Isoetaceae), which contains a single genus (*Isoetes*), with about 250 species. They are found nearly worldwide, with about 25 species in North America and 3 in Minnesota.

All species of *Isoetes* have tufts of slender leaves that resemble the quill of a feather. Each leaf will have a solitary sporangium. It is a sac embedded in a cavity at the base of each leaf (inward side) and covered by a thin flap of tissue called a velum. It can be found by gently pulling a leaf away from the plant.

A single quillwort will produce two types of spores: microspores (male) and megaspores (female), each borne in separate sporangia. It is the megaspores that are used to identify the species. They are chalky white and can be seen with the unaided eye, but a strong hand lens is needed to clearly see the surface features. Each megaspore has four bold ridges: an equatorial ridge encircling the spore and three equally spaced radial ridges that originate on the equatorial ridge and converge at one of the poles. The surface between these ridges will have a distinctive texture that is referenced in the key.

In Minnesota, lake-inhabiting *Isoetes* often grow with similar rosette-forming aquatic plants, particularly *Eriocaulon aquaticum* (pipewort), *Subularia aquatica* (water awlwort), *Lobelia dortmanna* (water lobelia), *Juncus pelocarpus* (brown-fruited rush), and *Littorella uniflora* (American shoreweed). To recognize *Isoetes*, check for pointed leaves that are round in cross-section, have visible cross-partitions (septa), and have a dilated base that contains the sporangia.

KEY TO *ISOETES*

1. Plant growing in pockets of wet soil on rock outcrops in prairies of southwestern Minnesota; leaves mostly about 20 cm long; leaves typically black toward base; megaspores 0.28–0.4 mm in diameter . . . . *I. melanopoda*

1. Plant growing rooted in the bottom of soft-water lakes and streams in the forested region of Minnesota; leaves mostly about 10 cm long; leaves pale toward base; megaspores 0.4–0.75 mm in diameter.

    2. Megaspores covered with narrow, jagged ridges forming a loosely connected network; megaspores 0.55–0.75 mm in diameter. . . . . *I. lacustris*

    2. Megaspores covered with stout spines and discrete projections that have separate bases, not fused into ridges or a network; megaspores 0.40–0.55 mm in diameter
    . . . . *I. echinospora*

Isoetes echinospora Durieu
Spiny-Spored Quillwort

[*I. braunii* Durieu; *I. muricata* Durieu]

PLANTS aquatic, perennial. **LEAVES** monomorphic, bright green to reddish green, pale toward base, tufted, erect to spreading or somewhat recurved, 5–25 (usually ca. 10) cm long at maturity, stiff yet pliant, gradually tapering toward tip, abruptly dilated at base. **SPORANGIA** solitary, embedded in a cavity at the base of a leaf (inward side) and covered by a velum. **MEGASPORES** white, 0.40–0.55 mm in diameter, the surface covered with stout spines (echinate). **MICROSPORES** gray to light brown, 0.02–0.03 mm, smooth to spinulose. **PHENOLOGY:** Spores mature about mid-July and remain in the sporangia until the leaves senescence. The leaves are reported to be deciduous, but their seasonality has not been confirmed in Minnesota.

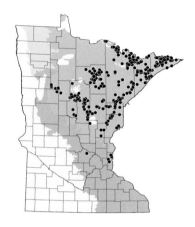

IDENTIFICATION: True to its name, the megaspores of *I. echinospora* look spiny with 10× magnification. At 20× the spines can be told from the jagged ridges of *I. lacustris.* The difference is consistent, although there is reported to be a hybrid with intermediate characteristics. Nothing else reliably distinguishes the two species. Young plants that have not yet reached reproductive maturity usually remain unidentified.

NATURAL HISTORY: *Isoetes echinospora* is a northern species with a circumboreal distribution. In Minnesota, it is common in the littoral zone of soft-water lakes, large and small, as well as permanent ponds and gently flowing streams. It is found in clear water up to about 2 m in depth. Favorable habitats coincide with regions of the state influenced by near-surface bedrock and noncalcareous glacial deposits. The water chemistry will be slightly acidic and nutrient-poor, meaning the water will be free of the large-scale "algae blooms" that plague nutrient-enriched lakes in midsummer. However, certain epiphytic algae often grow on the leaves of *I. echinospora,* making them difficult to detect through the water. *Isoetes echinospora* is a long-lived, slow-growing plant with a dense mass of rather coarse, dark roots that penetrate deeply into rocky, stony, gravely, or sandy substrates—anywhere it can root firmly. Sometimes it will root successfully in soft organic sediments if wave action is not too severe. It does not survive if stranded above the water line, and the spores will not germinate if they become dry.

Spine-covered
megaspores.

Typical underwater habitat, Aitkin County—September 22.

Megaspores in open sporangium.

Leaves taper to the tip, round in cross-section.

Isoetes lacustris L.
Lake Quillwort

[*I. macrospora* Durieu]

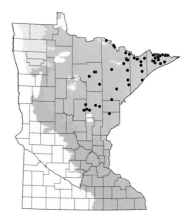

PLANTS aquatic, perennial. **LEAVES** monomorphic, dark green to reddish green, pale brown toward base, tufted, erect to spreading or somewhat recurved, 5–20 (usually 5–10) cm long at maturity, stiff yet pliant, gradually tapering toward tip, abruptly dilated at base. **SPORANGIA** solitary, embedded in a cavity at the base of a leaf (inward side) and covered by a velum. **MEGASPORES** white, 0.55–0.75 mm in diameter; the surface covered with narrow, jagged ridges (cristate). **MICROSPORES** gray, 0.033–0.045 mm, papillose. **PHENOLOGY:** Spores reach maturity about mid-July and remain in the sporangia until the leaves senesce. Leaves are sometimes reported to be evergreen, but there are no winter observations from Minnesota to confirm this.

IDENTIFICATION: Seeing the jagged ridges on the megaspore of *I. lactustris,* as opposed to the pointed spines on *I. echinospora,* can usually be accomplished without much difficulty, if not rushed and if not averse to using a strong hand lens. Essentially every leaf of every mature plant will have sporangia at its base, although the spores may not be fully developed until mid-July. Roughly half of the sporangia will have just megaspores and half will have just microspores. The microspores are so small they will be barely visible. They can be ignored.

NATURAL HISTORY: *Isoetes lacustris* is found in northern portions of eastern and central North America and northern parts of Eurasia. In Minnesota, it is found in cool, clear, slightly acidic soft-water lakes and low-gradient streams in the northeastern quarter of the state, most often in firm, rocky, sandy, or gravely bottoms, sometimes in soft, silty sediments. Suitable habitats are not obviously different from those of *I. echinospora.* In fact, where *I. lacustris* is found, it is likely that *I. echinospora* will also be found. But the reverse is seldom true. Random sampling indicates *I. lacustris* is less common, by a factor of probably 20 to 1. There is some evidence that *I. lacustris* can occur in deeper water than *I. echinospora* and persist in smaller populations, but that has not yet been demonstrated in Minnesota. Both species of *Isoetes* are mycorrhizal, meaning they get at least some of their nutrients from specialized fungi that inhabit the bottom sediments of lakes, which might reduce their dependence on sunlight.

Jagged ridges on
megaspores.

Firmly rooted among rocks—September 22.

Typical habitat near the shore of Blue Lake, Aitkin County.

Isoetes melanopoda subsp. *melanopoda* Gay & Durieu
Blackfoot Quillwort

PLANTS amphibious, perennial, although seasonally ephemeral. **LEAVES** monomorphic, deciduous, bright green, pale to lustrous black toward base, tufted, erect to spreading, to 40 (usually 15–25) cm long at maturity, stiff yet pliant, gradually tapering toward tip, abruptly dilated at base. **SPORANGIA** solitary, embedded in a cavity at the base of a leaf (inward side) and covered by a velum. **MEGASPORES** white, 0.28–0.44 mm in diameter, the surface covered with an irregular pattern of faint, low ridges. **MICROSPORES** gray, 0.02–0.03 mm, spinulose. **PHENOLOGY:** Spores mature in July and August, although timing may be weather dependent, and are released when leaves senesce at the end of the season.

IDENTIFICATION: The megaspores of *I. melanopoda* are significantly smaller than those of *I. lacustris* and *I. echinospora*. Also, the "surface ornamentation" is less pronounced and will not show up at 20× or even 30× magnification. The leaves are often black at the base (the "foot"), as its name implies, and the leaves are usually about twice as long those of the other two species. There are few other morphological differences to distinguish *I. melanopoda,* but distribution (southwestern vs. northeastern) and habitat (prairie rock pools vs. soft-water lakes) should make tentative identification of individuals found in Minnesota relatively easy.

NATURAL HISTORY: *Isoetes melanopoda* is endemic to parts of the central and southern United States. It is very rare in Minnesota and has been found only in pockets of shallow, silty soil on level outcrops of crystalline bedrock in the southwestern prairie counties. The soil will be only a few centimeters deep. It will become saturated or inundated after rainfalls, then dry out quickly. This sequence of wet/dry might happen several times during the growing season and is somehow essential to the success of *I. melanopoda*. No one knows how, but *I. melanopoda* responds quickly to such events. But even when drought fails to wet the soil, and excessive rain floods everything, *I. melanopoda* survives, even thrives. Although seemingly ephemeral, there is strong evidence that *I. melanopoda* populations are very durable and long-lived. We know of one population of *I. melanopoda* in Minnesota that has sustained itself for at least 76 years and counting.

FRED HARRIS

FRED HARRIS

Typical rock pool habitat.

In thin layer of mud, Rock County—June 24.

The eponymous "black foot."

Exposed sporangium.

Megaspores.

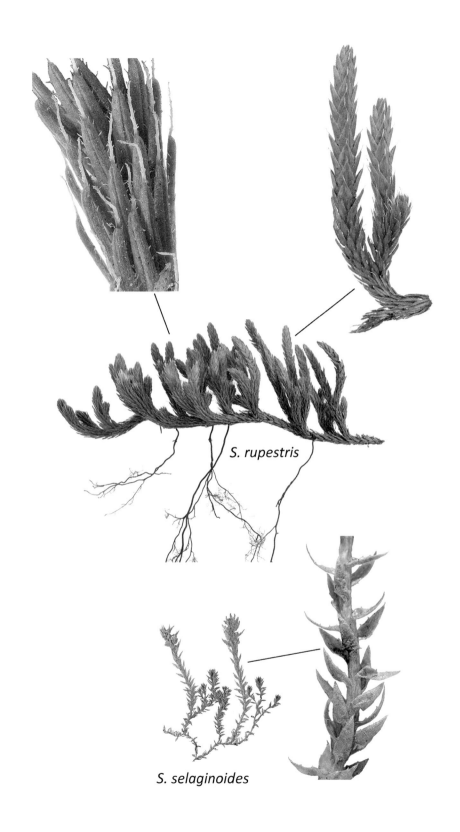

S. rupestris

S. selaginoides

Chapter 3

The Lycophyte Order Selaginellales (Spikemosses)

Worldwide, the order Selaginellales consists of just 1 family (Selaginellaceae), with 1 genus (*Selaginella*) and 700–800 species, which makes it the largest lycophyte family and genus. *Selaginella* is the most ancient and enigmatic group of plants the world has to offer. The oldest fossils that are clearly *Selaginella* date from nearly 350 million years ago, or 100 million years before the appearance of dinosaurs.

Species of *Selaginella* are distributed worldwide, with the highest diversity in the tropics and subtropics. There are 38 species in the United States, mostly in the southern and western states. There are 2 species presently known to occur in Minnesota. A third species, a prairie plant named *S. densa,* comes close to the northwestern border of Minnesota. Yet another species, a wetland plant named *S. eclipse,* approaches Minnesota from the southeast.

The common name, spikemoss, is an unfortunate misnomer. Although a *Selaginella* may look like a moss with spikes, they are true lycophytes. Mosses lack vascular tissue. They rely on simple diffusion to move water to all parts of the plant, and they do not have spikes. *Selaginella* have vascular tissue that actively moves fluids throughout the plant, and they have spikes that bear sporangia. In Minnesota, look for vertical branches poking up a few centimeters. Each will have a cone at the tip. The cone will look like the branch but is usually a bit wider and will have clam-shaped sporangia at the base of the leaves. As a final check, look for the spiny projections along the margins of the leaves.

KEY TO *SELAGINELLA*

1. Cones distinctly square (4-angled) in cross-section; leaves rigid and firm, each overlapping the bases of at least 3 other leaves, and held closely to the stems and branches, each with a white bristle at the tip; found on hot, dry bedrock exposures or barren sand
. . . . *S. rupestris*
1. Cones round in cross-section; leaves thin and fragile, each overlapping the bases of 1 or 2 other leaves, wide spreading, exposing the branch beneath, lacking a bristle at the tip; found in cool, moist habitats along the north shore of Lake Superior . . . . . . *S. selaginoides*

Selaginella rupestris (L.) Spring
Rock Spikemoss

PLANTS terrestrial, perennial. **STEMS** to about 15 cm long, decumbent, branching, mat-forming. **BRANCHES** 2–5 cm long; cone-bearing branches ascending, determinate. **ROOTS** slender, branching. **LEAVES** of stems and branches (trophophylls) monomorphic, in alternate pseudowhorls of 6, tightly appressed and overlapping, green to blue-green or gray-green, linear-lanceolate, 2 3 mm long, 0.2–0.4 mm wide; margins with slender spines; apex tipped with a white barbed bristle 0.5–1 mm long. **CONES** solitary at the tips of vertical branches, 4-angled, 0.5–3.5 cm long; leaves within the cones (sporophylls) triangular to ovate or broadly lanceolate, otherwise similar to trophophylls. **PHENOLOGY:** Stems and branches are evergreen, living 3–5 years. Cones are initiated the second year and continue to grow for about 3 years, releasing spores continually.

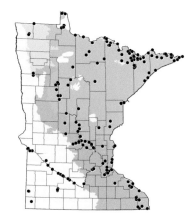

IDENTIFICATION: A close inspection will reveal *S. rupestris* to be covered in tiny, stiff, overlapping leaves, each with slender spines along the margins and a white bristle at the tip. Yet the plant is very small and rarely conspicuous. It can easily blend into the mosses and lichens with which it often occurs, or it can be hidden beneath overtopping vegetation, usually grasses or sedges.

NATURAL HISTORY: *Selaginella rupestris* occurs in temperate and boreal habitats over much of eastern and central North America. In Minnesota, it is found throughout the state, but it is spotty due to the scarcity of suitable habitat. It is found consistently on dry exposures of bedrock in full sunlight. Also found on dry exposed sand, but usually on indigenous sand that has been formed into dunes by the wind, or sand barrens on outwash plains. It is not found on ruderal sand, and not in places where it is likely to be trampled. Only rarely is it found on excavated sand such as road embankments or abandoned sand mines, and even then only after considerable time has passed and the habitat has been stabilized by lichens or mosses. In fact, it is often found half-buried in lichen mats, where it is easily overlooked. It is clonal, spreading outward from the founder, forming a circular clone if unimpeded. The individual branches of the clone are relatively short-lived, surviving only 3–5 years before turning brown and dying. But the branches proliferate, extending the life of the clone indefinitely.

A complete branch—August 30.

A nearly intact clone, Sherburne County—
September 26.

Cone with mature sporangia (yellow).

Cone (left); sterile branch (right).

Selaginella selaginoides (L.) P. Beauv. ex Mart. & Schrank
Northern Spikemoss

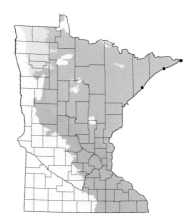

PLANTS terrestrial, perennial, evergreen. **STEMS** to 10 cm long (usually < 5 cm), decumbent, indeterminate, dichotomously branching and mat-forming. **LATERAL BRANCHES** upright, determinate, unbranched, 2–8 cm tall. **ROOTS** arising at the base of lateral branches. **LEAVES** of stems and branches (trophophylls) monomorphic, helically arranged, ascending, green, lanceolate, 1–3.5 mm long, 0.5–1.2 mm wide; margins with slender spines; apex pointed; base forming saclike structure with the stem. **CONES** solitary at the tips of upright branches, cylindrical, 1–2.5 cm long; leaves within the cones (sporophylls) somewhat larger than the leaves of the stem and branches, otherwise similar. **PHENOLOGY:** The upright, cone-bearing branches begin development in the spring and release spores as they senesce in the autumn. The decumbent stems survive one winter.

IDENTIFICATION: By any standard, *S. selaginoides* qualifies as mosslike. In fact, it will be very difficult to pick it out from the surrounding mosses. The cones might catch the eye, if looking closely. They are about the size of a paper clip. The rest of the plant is even smaller. Normally, every plant will produce at least one cone each year. If uncertain about the identification, check the leaves. They have distinct spines along their margins, although the leaves are so small that a hand lens is needed to see them clearly.

NATURAL HISTORY: Although quite rare in Minnesota, *S. selaginoides* is a circumboreal species common in a wide variety of habitats farther north, including cliffs, seeps, and bogs. In Minnesota, it requires cool, moist, boreal-like conditions, which it finds at a few special places along the north shore of Lake Superior. Look for it in the narrow zone of exposed bedrock just far enough from the lake to escape waves in the summer and ice in the winter. In this zone, there are sometimes distinct communities of plants that develop around shallow rainwater pools. The cornerstone of such communities is a small number of sedge species that, over time, develop raised hummocks of roots, rhizomes, and fine windborne silt. The living hummocks are colonized by mosses and eventually a few species of specialized vascular plants, including, on rare occasions, *S. selaginoides*.

The cones stand erect but not very tall.

Sporangia are buried deep in cones.

Barely distinguishable from the surrounding mosses.

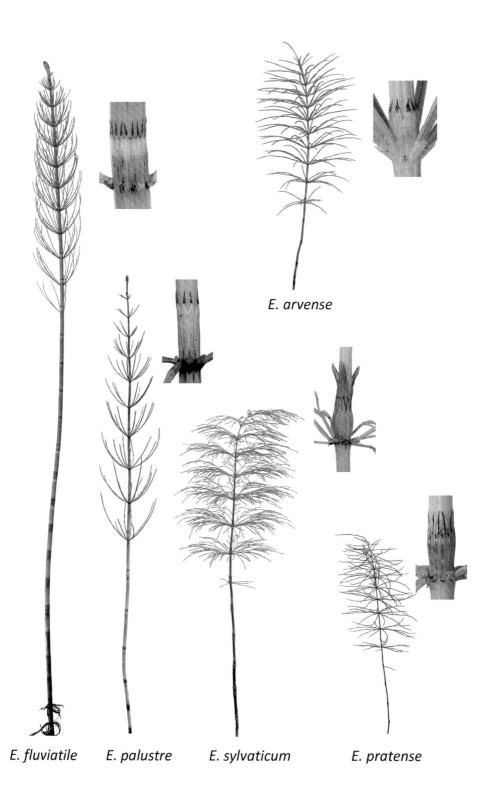

E. arvense

E. fluviatile   *E. palustre*   *E. sylvaticum*   *E. pratense*

Chapter 4

The Fern Order Equisetales (Horsetails and Scouring Rushes)

The order Equisetales consists of a single living family (Equisetaceae) with a single living genus (*Equisetum*) with 18 living species, concentrated in nontropical regions of the Northern Hemisphere. There are 10 species in the United States and 9 in Minnesota.

Species of *Equisetum*, as such, are easy to recognize. The stems are hollow, to one extent or another, and have conspicuous, regularly spaced joints (nodes). At each joint is a collar-like sheath (highly modified leaves) and sometimes a whorl of slender branches. In spite of their curious appearance, *Equisetum* are true ferns, as revealed by molecular phylogenetic studies.

Our species belong to 2 separate subgenera: horsetails (subg. *Equisetum*), generally recognized by stems that produce side branches and die back in winter; and scouring rushes (subg. *Hippochaete*), with stems that lack side branches and generally survive over winter.

All *Equisetum* are perennial and spread underground through an extensive system of rhizomes. They can also reproduce sexually in the same way as other ferns, which sometimes results in hybrids. In fact, each of the 9 species of *Equisetum* that occurs in Minnesota is known to hybridize with at least one other species of *Equisetum*, although only within their respective subgenus. Hybrid *Equisetum* may produce cones, but the spores are generally sterile. Although sterile hybrids can persist and spread through nonsexual reproduction, only ×*ferrissii* (the hybrid between *E. praealtum* and *E. laevigatum*) is common and has been included in the key.

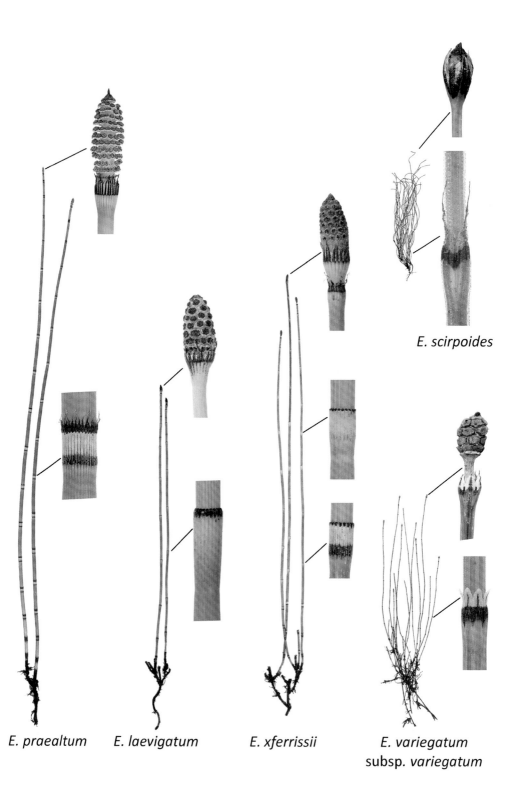

E. praealtum   E. laevigatum   E. xferrissii   E. variegatum
subsp. variegatum

E. scirpoides

1. Stems and sheaths pale pinkish brown, with black or dark-brown teeth on the sheaths (no green or orange color present); stems fleshy, stems unbranched, bearing a cone at the summit, ephemeral, seen only in April or May.

    2. Sheaths at mid-stem 8–15 mm long (excluding teeth), 5–10 mm wide at their widest; teeth of sheaths predominately black or blackish with thin brown margins
    . . . . *E. arvense* (in part)

    2. Sheaths at mid-stem 6–10 mm long (excluding teeth), 4–6 mm wide at their widest; teeth of sheaths with a narrow brown stripe down the center and whitish flanks and margins . . . . *E. pratense* (in part)

1. Stems or sheaths at least partially green (teeth may be orangish); stems not fleshy, stems branched or unbranched; cones present or not; stems seen past May and throughout the growing season.

    3. Stems with regular whorls of slender side branches (horsetails, subgenus *Equisetum*).

        4. Branches compound (primary branches producing secondary branches at some or all of the nodes); teeth of sheath on main stem 3–15 mm long, orangish, adhering along margins to form 3–5 discrete groups; ridges of stem with needlelike spicules or spicules absent. . . . . *E. sylvaticum*

        4. Branches simple (primary branches unbranched); teeth of sheaths on main stems 0.5–6 mm long, predominately brown or blackish, appearing distinct and separate, 7–25 in number; ridges of stem with blunt spicules or spicules absent.

            5. Sheaths at mid-stem 4–8 mm long (excluding teeth); teeth 7–25 in number; stem 2–9 mm wide.

                6. Teeth of sheaths at mid-stem 1.5–3 mm long, 15–25 in number; stems with thin walls and a large hollow center, easily compressed to a nearly flat cross-section . . . . *E. fluviatile* (in part)

                6. Teeth of sheaths at mid-stem 3–6 mm long, 7–12 in number; stem walls not particularly thin, center not entirely hollow, not so easily compressed to a flat cross-section . . . .*E. palustre*

            5. Sheaths at mid-stem 1.5–4 mm long (excluding teeth); teeth 4–15 in number; stem 1–3 mm wide.

                7. First internodes of the branches in the lowest whorl of branches shorter than the adjacent sheath and teeth of the main stem; teeth of the sheaths of the side branches merely acute; ridges of the main stem (especially on the upper internodes) with rows of evenly spaced, peg-shaped, silica spicules, feeling rough to the touch. . . . .*E. pratense* (in part)

                7. First internodes of the branches in the lowest whorl of branches equaling or surpassing the adjacent sheath and teeth of the main stem; teeth of the sheaths of the side branches attenuate; ridges of main stem appearing rough or bumpy under magnification but feeling more or less smooth to the touch
                . . . .*E. arvense* (in part)

    3. Stems unbranched, or atypically with a few scattered rudimentary branches on damaged stems (scouring rushes, subgenus *Hippochaete*).

        8. Stems typically < 30 cm long, 0.5–2 mm wide, feeling firm or solid when compressed.

9. Stems curled, twisted, or contorted, about 0.5 mm wide; sheaths 1–1.5 mm long (excluding teeth), each with 3–4 teeth . . . . *E. scirpoides*

9. Stems ± straight and erect, 1–2 mm wide; sheaths 1.5–3 mm long (excluding teeth), each with 4–6 teeth . . . . *E. variegatum* subsp. *variegatum*

8. Stems typically > 30 cm long, 1–13 mm wide, feeling thin-walled and somewhat hollow when compressed.

10. Stems weak, easily compressed to a nearly flat cross-section; sheaths with firm pointed teeth that persist all season; found in aquatic and wetland habitats . . . . *E. fluviatile* (in part)

10. Stems comparatively firm, not as easily compressed to a flat cross-section; sheaths with membranous hair-tipped teeth that may be shed early in the season; found in uplands and margins of wetlands.

11. Stems living two years (lower ⅔ of the stem from the previous year still alive and standing the second year); sheaths of second-year stems and first-year stems after about August 1 tan or gray with a black band around the rim and another just above the base; cone apiculate . . . . . *E. praealtum*

11. Stems living only one year; sheaths on the upper half of stems after about August 1 green with a black band only around the rim; cone apiculate or not.

12. Sheaths 3–7 mm wide at their widest; lower sheaths green with a narrow black band only around the rim; cone with a blunt tip; spores green, spherical . . . . *E. laevigatum*

12. Sheaths 5–9 mm wide at their widest; lower sheaths tan or gray with a black band around the rim and also near the base; cone with an apiculate tip; spores white, misshapen . . . . *E. xferrissii*

EQUISETUM HYBRIDS

Rare or infrequent *Equisetum* hybrids that are known to occur in Minnesota were excluded from the key and are not described or illustrated. Expect hybrids to appear intermediate in morphology between the parents but with sterile spores. Correct identification of hybrids is very difficult, and there is no practical way to confirm parentage of a suspected hybrid. The following are the hybrids that have been confirmed to occur in Minnesota. There are likely more hybrids that have been overlooked.

E. ×*jesupii* (A. A. Eaton) Christenh. & Husby = (*E. praealtum* × *E. variegatum*). Habitats of the parent species overlap in moist, open habitats, which is where the hybrid is found. Stems of the hybrid are in the range of 30–50 cm long, 4–5 mm wide, and they feel firm when compressed. It is usually easy to spot the hybrid if both parents are there for size comparison. Intermediate sheath characteristics are best for confirmation.

E. ×*litorale* Kuhlew. = (*E. arvense* × *E. fluviatile*). This hybrid is monomorphic like *E. fluviatile* rather than dimorphic like *E. arvense*. So, all stems are green, and all stems can potentially bear cones. This is the only hybrid in Minnesota that shows a narrow habitat preference and a distinct geographic range. Populations of *E. ×litorale* are perhaps self-sustaining in alluvial forests on the floodplains of the St. Croix and Mississippi Rivers.

E. ×mildeanum Rothm. = (*E. sylvaticum* × *E. pratense*). The parents are quite common and frequently share habitat in moist forests. Hybrids are surprisingly uncommon in Minnesota, but they do occur. The influence of *E. sylvaticum* is seen in the intermediate size and color of the sheaths on the stems and in the weakly compound branches.

E. ×nelsonii (A. A. Eaton) J. H. Schffn. = (*E. laevigatum* × *E. variegatum*). The parents of this hybrid rarely co-occur in Minnesota, providing few opportunities for hybridization. Hybrids, when they do occur, do not seem to persist in the habitat of either parent. Nor have they found an ecological niche of their own.

Equisetum arvense L.
Field Horsetail

AERIAL STEMS dimorphic.
NON-CONE-BEARING STEMS green,
branched, 10–60 cm long, 1.2–3 mm wide;
ridges with granular silica deposits yet feel
smooth; sheaths (excluding teeth), 2–4 mm
long and 2–3 mm wide; teeth persistent,
4–14 in number, predominantly dark
brown or black with narrow whitish
margins, 1–2.5 mm long. **BRANCHES**
simple; sheaths with 3–4 attenuate teeth;
first internodes of the branches in the
lowest whorl of branches equaling or
surpassing the adjacent sheath and teeth of
the main stem. **CONE-BEARING STEMS** pale

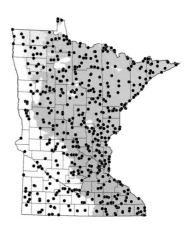

pinkish brown, unbranched, ephemeral, 10–40 cm long, 1.5–6 mm wide, smooth;
sheaths (excluding teeth) pale, 8–15 mm long, 5–10 mm wide; teeth 6–10 in
number, 4–10 mm long, predominately black or blackish with narrow brown
margins. **CONES** blunt or rounded at apex. **PHENOLOGY:** Fertile stems appear in
late April (south) or early May (north), reach their maximum height quickly,
release their spores, then vanish without a trace. Sterile stems emerge from the
same rhizome about a week after the fertile stems and persist until the advent of
winter.

IDENTIFICATION: From any distance, it is hard to tell *E. arvense* from the less
common *E. pratense*. That is true for both sterile and fertile stems. For the sterile
green stems, most botanists rely on the long first internode of the lowest branches
or the narrowly pointed teeth of the branch sheaths (dichotomy 7, p. 65). The
fertile, cone-bearing stems are an oddity. They appear very early in the spring, last
only a couple of weeks, then disappear without a trace. They more closely
resemble a mushroom than a fern. The more familiar green stems come shortly
after and last all season.

NATURAL HISTORY: *Equisetum arvense* occurs throughout North America and
much of the Northern Hemisphere, including temperate, boreal, and arctic
regions. In Minnesota, it is primarily a species of damp forests but is very
common in nearly all terrestrial habitat types, including agricultural habitats. It is
only absent from urban areas and active industrial sites. It will grow in deep shade
or direct sunlight, and in almost any substrate, but preferentially mesic or wet
soils near the middle of the pH scale. It also occurs in surface-dry soil if the deep-
growing rhizomes can reach moisture.

Fertile stem—May 10.   Mature sterile stem, Anoka County—July 29.

Cross-section of
sterile stem.

Lowest whorl of branches; note long first internode.

Equisetum ×ferrissii Clute
Ferriss' Scouring Rush

AERIAL STEMS monomorphic, unbranched, stiff and erect, minutely roughened with rows of knobby silica deposits on the ridges, dying back in the winter (in the climate of Minnesota), 30–80 cm long, 2–9 mm wide. **SHEATHS** 7–11 mm long (excluding teeth), 5–9 mm wide (l/w=1.2–1.7); upper sheaths green with a narrow black band or black markings at the summit; lower sheaths pale green or more often gray, with a black band at the summit and near the base; teeth blackish, 14–22 in number, 2–4 mm long; with slender whitish hairlike tips, mostly shed 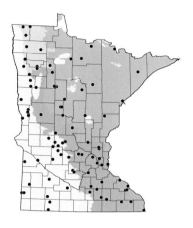 by midsummer, some surviving until autumn. **CONES** apiculate. **PHENOLOGY:** Most stems emerge in spring, sometimes with a second flush in midsummer. Cones seem to mature in July and August, but the spores are apparently infertile.

IDENTIFICATION: *Equisetum ×ferrissii* is the hybrid between *E. praealtum* and *E. laevigatum*. At maturity, the sheaths on the upper portion of the stem resemble those of *E. laevigatum* and those on the lower portion resemble *E. praealtum* (the proportion of each is variable). This is a reliable distinction once all the sheaths have matured after about August 1. Always check the cones. If the top is blunt, suspect *E. laevigatum*. A short point would indicate *E. praealtum* or *E. ×ferrissii*. Also, look around for living stems still standing from the previous season. Such stems might look ragged, and the upper portions might be missing, but they will still be green. Their presence strongly indicates *E. praealtum*.

NATURAL HISTORY: *Equisetum ×ferrissii* is usually sterile, which means the spores are infertile; hence no sexual reproduction. It spreads primarily by fragmentation of the stems and rhizomes, which it does extremely well. It is now widespread in temperate regions of North America and is quite common in Minnesota. It is generally found in grassy, sunny, moist or dry habitats, usually not far from roads, which gives support to the theory that fragments are inadvertently moved along transportation corridors. Although it often grows intermingled with one or both parents, it can be found far from both parents. Minnesota populations of *E. ×ferrissii* seem entirely self-sustaining and apparently do not rely on repeated hybridizations. It accomplishes this with a seemingly immortal rhizome system.

In a dry sand savanna, Sherburne County—July 10.

Lower sheaths are dark-
banded.

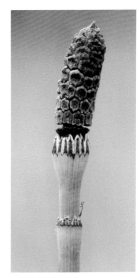

Upper sheaths are green.

Cones have a short
point.

Equisetum fluviatile L.
Water Horsetail

AERIAL STEMS somewhat dimorphic, being either branched or unbranched; green, smooth, thin-walled and easily compressed, dying back by winter, to 150 cm long, 2–9 mm wide; sheaths at mid-stem 4–8 mm long (excluding teeth); green, or reddish when young; teeth black, persistent, 1.5–3 mm long, 15–25 in number. **BRANCHES** (when present) occurring in regular or irregular whorls at nodes in the middle third of sterile stems or in the upper third of fertile stems, simple; sheaths with 4–6 narrowly pointed teeth. **CONES** blunt, occurring at the

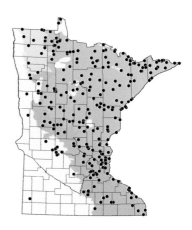

summit of the stem and occasionally at the tips of the branches. **PHENOLOGY:** The first stems typically emerge in early May (south) or late May (north). Cones typically mature and shed spores around the end of June.

IDENTIFICATION: *Equisetum fluviatile* is a tall, slender, graceful plant; usually with side branches, sometimes without. It is one of 4 similar species that are told apart by features of the nodal sheaths (starting at dichotomy 5, p. 65). This will require counting and measuring the teeth that line the top of each sheath. Another useful feature that becomes reliable with practice is the easily compressed stems of *E. fluviatile*. They collapse to a nearly flat cross-section with very little pressure.

NATURAL HISTORY: *Equisetum fluviatile* is widespread and common in temperate, boreal, and arctic regions of North America and Eurasia. In Minnesota, it is common in wetlands over much of the state, particularly in fens, sedge meadows, marshes, conifer swamps, hardwood swamps, ditch bottoms, and lake margins. It is notably absent from acidic bogs, and it does not venture far into the prairie region. Habitats may be perpetually wet, or wet for only a portion of the year. It competes especially well in habitats with seasonally fluctuating water levels. Plants are usually in full sunlight or moderate shade. Soils are often deep, soft sediments like peat or saturated silt, but sometimes soils are sandy or rocky. It is perhaps most conspicuous in the shallow margins of northern lakes, where it can grow emergent from water 50–100 cm deep. Their fragile stems are somehow unaffected by the tallest waves.

Mature cone—June 17.

Closely packed stems in shrub swamp—June 24.

Branches
beginning—
May 28.

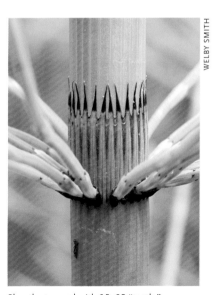

Sheaths topped with 15–25 "teeth."

Cross-section of stem.

Equisetum laevigatum A. Br.
Smooth Scouring Rush

[*E. kansanum* J. H. Schaffn.]

AERIAL STEMS monomorphic, unbranched, stiff and erect; smooth to the touch, lacking discernable silica deposits; dying back in winter, 30–80 cm long, 2–6 mm wide. **SHEATHS** somewhat flared at apex and tapered to base, 7–13 mm long (excluding teeth, if any present), 3–7 mm wide (l/w=1.4–2), green with a narrow black band at the summit; teeth 2–3 mm long, 10–30 in number, brown with twisted hairlike tips, deciduous early in the season. **BRANCHES** lacking or sometimes rudimentary branches developing following injury to the stem. **CONES** blunt-

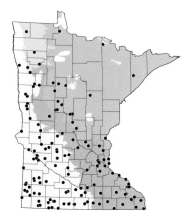

tipped or rounded. **PHENOLOGY:** Stems begin to emerge in early May; the earliest shed spores by July. Stems may linger through October, but generally no signs remain the following spring.

IDENTIFICATION: In its genetically pure state, *E. laevigatum* has slender, smooth, unbranched stems with green sheaths at the nodes. The sheaths are long and narrow with a thin black rim around the top. All the sheaths are the same, even the lowest one, and they do not change shape or color as the season progresses. If even the lowest sheath on the stem has a black band around the base, then it should be considered *E. ×ferrissii* or *E. praealtum*. The same would be indicated if the cone has a small point at the top. At the latitude of Minnesota, the stems of *E. laevigatum* and *E. ×ferrissii* die back each winter. Those of *E. praealtum* survive the first winter and can be seen the following summer among first-year stems, although looking ragged at the top.

NATURAL HISTORY: *Equisetum laevigatum* is endemic to prairie and grassland habitats in western and central North America. Although it is rarely abundant, it is found in prairies and savannas throughout western and southern Minnesota, even in small habitat fragments and remnants. Some habitats may not appear pristine, having endured ecological isolation or abusive land use. There are recent records from roadside habitats deep inside forested counties indicating *E. laevigatum* has a certain amount of mobility, although it is by no means aggressive. Native soils vary but are often sandy glacial deposits, usually calcareous in composition. Being a prairie plant, drought is easily tolerated, but not shade or prolonged inundation.

Cones have a rounded tip.

Stems are loosely clumped or single—May 29.

All sheaths are green.

Stem ridges lack spicules.

Stem walls are thin but rigid.

Equisetum palustre L.
Marsh Horsetail

AERIAL STEMS monomorphic, branched, dying back in winter, to 90 cm long, 2–5 mm wide, ridges smooth, feeling firm when compressed; sheaths (excluding teeth) 5–7 mm long (measured at mid-stem); teeth dark with green or colorless margins, or entirely dark distally, persistent, 3–6 mm long (at mid-stem), 7–12 in number. **BRANCHES** simple, ascending; sheaths with 5–8 teeth, each with a long-attenuate tip or hairlike extension; first internode of each branch shorter than the adjacent sheath on the stem. **CONES** blunt at apex, occurring at

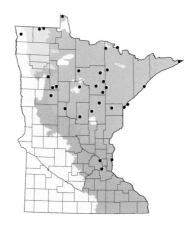

the summit of the stem and occasionally at the tips of branches. **PHENOLOGY:** Stems begin to emerge around the middle of May (in an average year). The cones begin to develop around the middle of June, release spores sometime in July, and wither soon after. The stems stay green until winter.

IDENTIFICATION: Under ideal conditions, *E. palustre* can become a large, robust plant with dark-green stems and relatively coarse upswept branches. The branches usually continue to the top of the fertile stems but not quite to the top of sterile stems. In that way, it will resemble *E. fluviatile*. But unlike *E. fluviatile*, the stems of *E. palustre* feel firm when compressed, and the teeth of the stem sheaths are longer and fewer in number (dichotomy 6, p. 65). To tell *E. palustre* from the ubiquitous *E. arvense*, count the number of teeth on the sheaths of the branches (not the main stem). *Equisetum palustre* has at least 5 and as many as 8; *E. arvense* will have only 3 or 4.

NATURAL HISTORY: *Equisetum palustre* is widespread in northern parts of North America and Eurasia. Although it ranges across much of northern and central Minnesota, it is decidedly uncommon. It is usually found growing in saturated peat or wet mineral soil, in deep or moderate shade. It seems to favor shallow groundwater pools or rivulets, or wetlands that are in some way influenced by groundwater. This would include certain types of conifer or hardwood swamps but exclude acidic bogs. This is a subset of habitats where the much more common *E. fluviatile* and *E. arvense* are often found, and indeed, all three species have been found together.

Sheaths topped with 7–12 "teeth."

In a cedar swamp, Clearwater County—July 7.

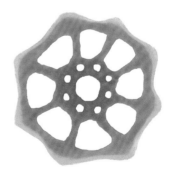

Cross-section of stem.

Cones release spores in July.

Equisetum praealtum Raf.
Common Scouring Rush

[*Equisetum hyemale* subsp. *affine*
(Engelm.) Calder & Taylor]

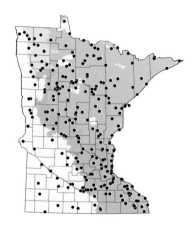

AERIAL STEMS monomorphic, unbranched, stiff and erect, roughened with rows of silica deposits on the ridges, 50–150 cm long, 3–13 mm wide, largely hollow but feeling stiff; lower portions remaining green over winter and the following summer. **SHEATHS** 5–12 mm long (excluding teeth), 4–10 mm wide; gray at maturity, with a black band at the summit and another above the base; teeth blackish, 2–4 mm long, 15–35 in number, with slender hairlike tips shed the first month. **BRANCHES** lacking, or sometimes rudimentary branches developing at nodes below an injury. **CONES** apiculate.

PHENOLOGY: The first flush of stems begins in late April or early May and continues into summer. Cones of the earliest stems mature and release spores in June. The second year, side branches may develop at upper nodes and produce small cones.

IDENTIFICATION: Identification of *E. praealtum* usually focuses on the sheaths. By August of the first year, there will be a black band around the rim and another just above the base. Before that, the sheaths on the upper part of the stem will lack the black band near the base and can be easily mistaken for *E. ×ferrissii*. It is useful to check for surviving second-year stems. They will look somewhat worn and weathered (especially the tops) after having survived the winter. Their presence is a strong indicator of *E. praealtum*.

NATURAL HISTORY: *Equisetum praealtum* ranges across nearly all of subboreal North America in a variety of habitats. In Minnesota, it is fundamentally a forest species, preferring moist or seasonally wet soil along streams and shores of lakes and ponds. It is supremely adapted to floodplains, where it seems immune to sedimentation and scouring. Within historic times, it appears to have spread along roadways to virtually all parts of the state, to habitats such as grassy roadsides and abandoned farm fields. Rhizomatous growth can result in dense clones an acre or more in size, with density as great as 500 stems per square meter. It occurs in a variety of soils, which may at times be dry at the surface but likely remaining moist at the depth where the rhizomes live.

New stems among the old—June 8.

Stems can be densely packed, Anoka County—
July 30.

Cones have a pointed
tip—Aug 31.

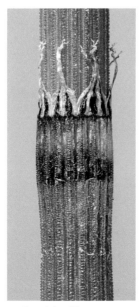

Teeth with hairlike tips.

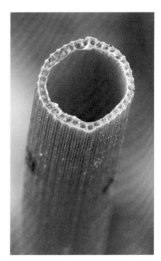

Stem cross-section.

Equisetum pratense Ehrh.
Meadow Horsetail

AERIAL STEMS dimorphic. **NON-CONE-BEARING STEMS** green, branched, 15–45 cm long, 1–2.5 mm wide, dying back by winter; ridges with rows of peg-shaped silica deposits; sheaths (excluding teeth), 1.5–3 mm long; teeth persistent, 9–15 in number, with a dark central stripe and broad whitish flanks, 0.5–2 mm long. **BRANCHES** simple; sheaths with 3 triangular teeth; first internodes of the branches in the lowest whorl of branches shorter than the adjacent sheath and teeth of the main stem. **CONE-BEARING STEMS** pale pinkish brown, unbranched, 10–30 cm long, 1.5–2.5 mm wide, smooth; ephemeral, or rarely becoming green and developing rudimentary branches; sheaths (excluding teeth) 6–10 mm long, 4–6 mm wide; teeth 6–9 in number, 3–9 mm long, persistent, with a narrow dark-brown stripe down the center and pale-brown or whitish flanks. **CONES** blunt or rounded at apex. **PHENOLOGY:** Cone-bearing stems (rarely seen) emerge about a week before sterile stems, typically in late April (south) or early May (north), and within 2–3 weeks reach full height and shed spores. A few may then turn green and develop whorls of rudimentary branches at the nodes; most quickly senesce.

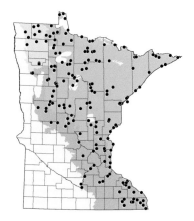

IDENTIFICATION: *Equisetum pratense* looks very much like *E. arvense*. It is generally a smaller, more delicate plant, but the two cannot be reliably told apart without a close inspection. This applies to the sterile green stems as well as the rarely seen fertile stems. The most often used character for sterile stems, and the one that rarely fails, is the relationship between the first internode on the branches on the lowest whorl of branches and the sheath of the adjacent stem; they are shorter (dichotomy 7, p. 65).

NATURAL HISTORY: *Equisetum pratense* is found in northern parts of North America and Eurasia. In Minnesota, it is a woodland species (the common name notwithstanding), usually in mesic woods or sometimes swampy woods, in deep to moderate shade under a variety of common tree species. Soils are usually loamy or peaty, circumneutral or weakly acidic. It is occasional to locally common in good habitat but often overlooked because of its superficial resemblance to the more ordinary and more common *E. arvense*.

Lowest whorl of branches; note short first internodes.

Sterile stem in late summer.

Fertile stem—May 4.

In transition.

Fertile stem—June 4.

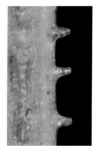

Peg-shaped spicules.

Stem cross-section.

Equisetum scirpoides Michx.
Dwarf Scouring Rush

AERIAL STEMS monomorphic; curled, twisted or contorted; unbranched, feeling solid if compressed, remaining green over winter; to 20 cm long if straightened but rarely more than 10 cm in actual height; about 0.5 mm wide; ridges minutely roughened with jagged rows of silica. **SHEATHS** (excluding teeth) 1–1.5 mm long, 0.6–1 mm wide; green proximally, black distally; teeth 1–2 mm long, 3–4 in number, persistent; with long, fragile, pale-brown, hairlike tips. **CONES** acutely pointed. **PHENOLOGY:** Stems remain green through winter and are replaced

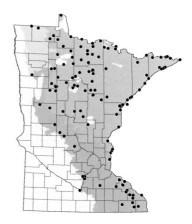

continually during the growing season. Cones develop in the latter half of the growing season and release their spores early the following spring.

IDENTIFICATION: *Equisetum scirpoides* is the smallest of the *Equisetum,* usually about ankle high. It grows in dense tufts of curled and twisted dark-green stems, which stay green through winter. At first, it might look like a disused animal nest, or some other leftover artifact of the forest, but all the usual hallmarks of an *Equisetum* are there. The stems are often numerous and tangled together so it may look like the stems have side branches (relevant when using the key). Untangle the mass and you find the stems have no side branches. The stems are very thin and wiry, and they have no central hollow, so they feel solid. Cones are small and inconspicuous.

NATURAL HISTORY: *Equisetum scirpoides* occurs in arctic, boreal, and cool temperate regions of North America and Eurasia. It is widely scattered throughout the forested region of Minnesota, although nowhere in the state is it common. Habitats in northern Minnesota include a variety of upland forest types associated with mature broad-leaved or needle-leaved trees, always cool and shady. It is also found in wet, swampy forests on raised mossy hummocks or around bases of trees where it is just above standing water. Soils are generally well-aerated peat or loam, although sometimes it is found on patches of bare mineral soil. Habitats in southeastern Minnesota are exclusively mesic forests, usually on north-facing slopes in stream-dissected terrain, always shaded, always moist and cool. Forests where it occurs are typically ecologically stable if not technically old-growth. It sustains itself with delicate short-lived rhizomes that grow just below the surface.

Streamside habitat, Washington County—
September 7.

Stands about ankle high.

Stems twist and contort—
September 7.

Stems are less than
1 mm wide.

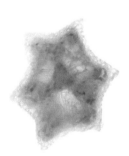

Cross-section of stem.

Equisetum sylvaticum L.
Woodland Horsetail

AERIAL STEMS partially dimorphic, dying back in winter. **NON-CONE-BEARING STEMS** green, branched, 30–75 cm long, 1.5–3.5 mm wide; with rows of slender, needlelike spicules on ridges (best seen just below nodes); sheaths (excluding teeth) 3–5 mm long, 3–5 mm wide; teeth persistent, orangish, adhering to form 3–5 groups, 3–8 mm long. **BRANCHES** compound; sheaths of branches with 3–4 attenuate teeth. **CONE-BEARING STEMS** at first pale green or yellowish green and unbranched, becoming green and branched before spore release, 15–40 cm long, 2–4.5 mm wide; needlelike spicules present or often absent; sheaths (excluding teeth) 5–15 mm long, 5–7 mm wide; teeth persistent, orangish, adhering to form 3–5 groups, 5–15 mm long. **CONES** blunt or rounded at apex. **PHENOLOGY:** Fertile stems develop cones as they emerge from the ground in late April or early May and shed spores about 4 weeks later. Sterile stems emerge about a week later than the fertile stems. All stems persist until the advent of winter.

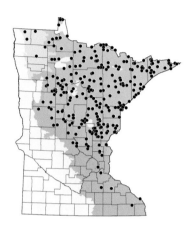

IDENTIFICATION: The compound branches of *E. sylvaticum* are conspicuous beginning in June and give the whole plant a distinctive lacy look. This makes it probably the easiest *Equisetum* to identify, although for a brief time in the spring the fertile stems look something like those of *E. arvense* and *E. pratense,* which might incorrectly lead to dichotomy 2. But the young plants quickly gain green color and sprout side branches, leading to dichotomy 3. At all times, the stem sheaths have large, flaccid, orangish teeth that define the species and confirm identification. The teeth grow together in 3–5 coherent groups, not singly like the other species.

NATURAL HISTORY: *Equisetum sylvaticum* occurs in arctic, boreal, and cool temperate regions of North America and Eurasia. It is common in forested regions of Minnesota, especially in the northern two-thirds of the state. Habitats are found in moist or wet forests as well as permanent shrub communities that often border open wetlands. It is generally found in full to moderate shade, or sometimes in direct sunlight at the edge of a forest opening. Soils are often peaty or woody in texture, or noncalcareous glacial till.

Branches are uniquely compound—June 4.

Persisting into fall, Kanabec County—
October 14.

Needlelike spicules.

Newly aboveground—May 20. Sheath and teeth.

Equisetum variegatum subsp. *variegatum* Schleich. ex F. Weber & D. Mohr
Variegated Scouring Rush

AERIAL STEMS monomorphic, unbranched, rigid, firm, ± straight, to 40 cm long (typically 15–20 cm), 1–2 mm wide, remaining green over winter, minutely roughened with rows of rounded silica deposits on the ridges. **SHEATHS** 1.5–3 mm long (excluding teeth), 1.5–2 mm wide, green proximally, black distally; teeth 1–2.5 mm long, 4–6 in number, persistent, primarily clear hyaline with a dark stripe down the middle, apex rounded after the hairlike extension is shed. **CONES** with a 1 mm long pointed tip (apiculate).

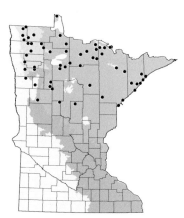

PHENOLOGY: Stems are replaced throughout the growing season after surviving portions of two summers and at least one winter. Cones are commonly seen all year, but spores appear to be shed in early spring.

IDENTIFICATION: There is nothing cryptic about this species, although it is not identifiable by any single character. Compared to most other scouring rushes, the stems of *E. variegatum* subsp. *variegatum* will appear short and slender. They will feel firm when compressed and will remain unbranched under essentially all circumstances, and they remain green over winter. They are typically clustered, forming dense, single-species mats. It seems to hybridize easily when in close contact with *E. praealtum*.

NATURAL HISTORY: *Equisetum variegatum* subsp. *variegatum* occurs in arctic, boreal, and cool temperate regions of North America and Eurasia, including Minnesota. The less common subsp. *alaskanum* is confined to the Pacific Northwest. Although wide-ranging, subsp. *variegatum* is rather scarce in Minnesota and limited to the northern third of the state. It is found most often in habitats associated with shallow wetlands, such as marshes, fens, meadows, and swales, as well as wet transitional habitats along lake margins or riverbanks. Soils are typically clay, shallow peat, or glacial till, and may be saturated or have a few centimeters of standing water. It does not seem to compete well with taller plants, so it is usually in the open or in the company of other short-stature plants. On the heavily agriculturalized landscape of today, it is perhaps easiest to find it in sandpits that were abandoned when excavations hit the water table, or in wet ditch bottoms. It also does well where rainwater ponds on compacted clay soils and drains slowly.

Stems are slender, rigid, and firm.

Dominating a wet depression, Lake County—August 8.

Distinctive sheaths.

A cone approaching maturity.

Silica deposits on ridges of stem.

Stem cross-section.

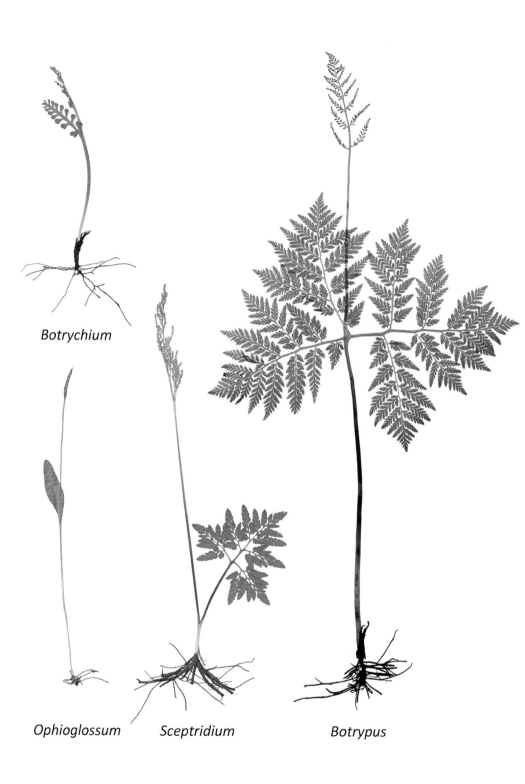

Botrychium

Ophioglossum *Sceptridium* *Botrypus*

Chapter 5

The Fern Order Ophioglossales (Adder's-Tongue Ferns)

The order Ophioglossales consists of a single family, Ophioglossaceae (adder's-tongue family). Worldwide the family has perhaps 10 genera and an estimated 112 species. In Minnesota, there are 4 genera with a total of 20 species. Members of this order are considered the oldest, most primitive of the ferns. In fact, one school of thought would separate them from the ferns altogether.

Members of this order appear to be short-lived, perhaps on the order of 10–20 years, with most of the early years spent underground as a gametophyte. The heart of the plant is the rhizome, a small, underground structure that produces a cluster of fleshy roots and typically a single leaf each year. The leaf is divided into 2 distinct and separate segments. The familiar leaflike segment is photosynthetic and called the trophophore. The sporangia are borne on a much-modified fertile segment called the sporophore. Both segments are attached to a common stalk, which is round in cross-section and somewhat succulent in texture. Most individuals, except those in the genus *Botrychium,* will not produce a sporophore in any given year, just a single trophophore. Hybridization between species is apparently rare, or rarely recognized. There are no named hybrids among the species that occur in Minnesota.

KEY TO OPHIOGLOSSALES

1. Trophophore entire, undivided; veins forming an irregular net pattern (reticulate); sporophore unbranched, about 3 mm wide . . . .*Ophioglossum*

1. Trophophore pinnately divided; veins free and ending at margins of leaf segments; sporophore pinnately branched, significantly wider than 3 mm.

    2. Mature trophophore often appearing ternate (3 equal pinnae joined at base), at least 3-pinnate, 15–42 cm wide; height from ground to top of sporophore 30–80 cm
    . . . . *Botrypus*

    2. Trophophore not ternate, less divided than 3-pinnate, 0.5–20 cm wide; height from ground to top of sporophore 2–30 cm.

        3. Trophophore and sporophore joined to a common stalk belowground; trophophore 4–20 cm wide, leathery, evergreen . . . . *Sceptridium*

        3. Trophophore and sporophore joined to a common stalk aboveground; trophophore 0.5–6 cm wide, herbaceous, dying back before winter . . . .*Botrychium*

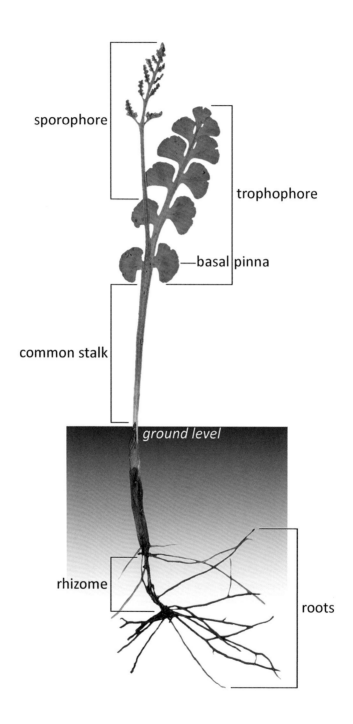

sporophore

trophophore

basal pinna

common stalk

ground level

rhizome

roots

BOTRYCHIUM (MOONWORTS)

There are believed to be about 35 species of *Botrychium* in the world. There are about 30 species in North America and 14 (plus one variety) in Minnesota. The diversity of *Botrychium* in Minnesota is among the highest in the world. It is not unheard of to find *Botrychium* communities where 5 or even 6 species occur together.

Without doubt, no genus of ferns elicits a more excited (and troubled) response among botanists than the moonworts. They are notoriously hard to find and even harder to identify. The gross structure of a *Botrychium* plant is quite simple, wherein lies the problem. Their simplicity has the unfortunate consequence of making it extraordinarily difficult to tell one species from another. Identification relies almost entirely on features of the trophophore, even though such features are highly variable. Each segment of the trophophore is a pinna (*pl.* pinnae). It is defined as the primary, stand-alone (separate and distinct) division of a fern leaf. But the pinnae of *Botrychium* can be very small and appear rudimentary.

Among the 1-pinnate species of *Botrychium* (the species that key-out by following the first choice of the first dichotomy), pinnae seem to come in 5 basic shapes: spoon-shaped (spatulate), squarish or rhombic (quadrilateral), wedge-shaped (cuneate), fan-shaped (flabellate), and mushroom-shaped (pileiform). Spoon-shaped means widened at the tip like a spoon, although the spoon may be notched at the tip. Squarish or rhombic means broad where it attaches at the base and flattened at the far end. Wedge-shaped means the sides are shaped like the letter *V*. Fan-shaped looks like an old-fashioned handheld fan with straight diverging sides and a rounded end. Mushroom-shaped means the sides curve outward, resulting in a shape like the cap of a mushroom.

The following key and descriptions were derived from specimens that were morphologically mature. Individual specimens that are young, perhaps only their first year aboveground or those that have been found early in the growing season, are likely to be smaller and have poorly developed features. Avoid such plants if possible.

The images on the comparison plates are of pressed specimens selected to illustrate the ideal morphology of mature, fully grown individuals. In many cases, the leaf was pressed with the sporophore bent downward to better show the trophophore. It should also be known that characteristic color, as seen in living plants, was lost in the process.

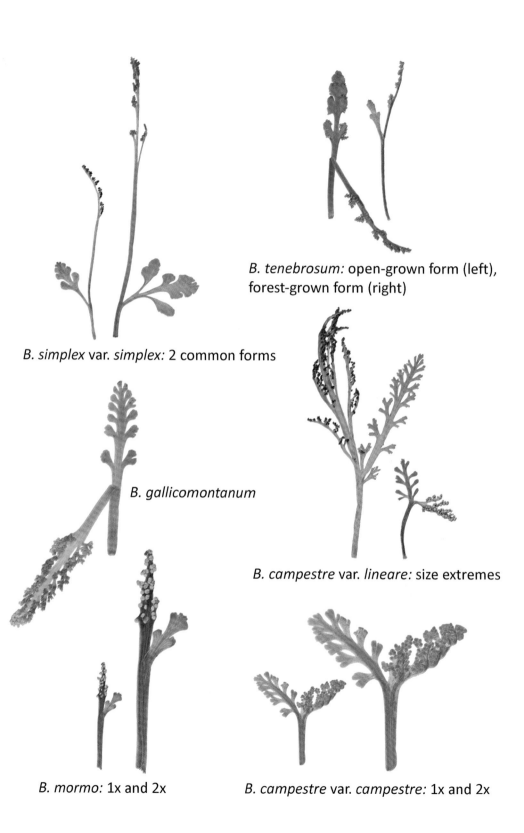

B. tenebrosum: open-grown form (left),
forest-grown form (right)

B. simplex var. simplex: 2 common forms

B. gallicomontanum

B. campestre var. lineare: size extremes

B. mormo: 1x and 2x

B. campestre var. campestre: 1x and 2x

1. The trophophore merely 1-pinnate (i.e., the side margins of the individual pinnae undivided, although the tips may be notched); common stalk uniformly green or greenish.

  2. Basal pinnae differing from the others by being conspicuously larger, having a narrower base and/or ascending at a steeper angle.

    3. Sporophore stalk (at the time of spore release) 3–8 cm long, longer than the aboveground portion of the common stalk and longer than the trophophore; pinnae usually lacking supernumerary sporangia, or if present then usually on basal pinnae only . . . . *B. simplex* var. *simplex* (in part)

    3. Sporophore stalk (at the time of spore release) 0.5–3 (usually 1–2) cm long, shorter than the aboveground portion of the common stalk and shorter than or equal in length to the trophophore; pinnae of robust specimens usually with at least a few supernumerary sporangia, and not limited to basal pinnae
. . . . *B. tenebrosum* (in part)

  2. Basal pinnae not distinctly different from the others.

    4. Middle pinnae rhombic or squarish in general outline; distal margins curved or straight, not notched; attachment to rachis broad and strongly decurrent.

      5. Plants stout; trophophore fleshy, whitish to pale green; distal margins of pinnae ± straight; sporangia partially sunken into the sporophore. . . . . *B. mormo*

      5. Plants comparatively slender; trophophore thin, yellow-green; distal margins of pinnae wavy to roundish; sporangia attached on the surface of the sporophore.

        6. Sporophore stalk (at the time of spore release) 3–8 cm long, longer than the aboveground portion of the common stalk and longer than the trophophore; pinnae usually lacking supernumerary sporangia, or if present then usually on basal pinnae only . . . . *B. simplex* var. *simplex* (in part)

        6. Sporophore stalk (at the time of spore release) 0.5–3 (usually 1–2) cm long, shorter than the aboveground portion of the common stalk and shorter than or equal in length to the trophophore; robust pinnae usually with at least a few supernumerary sporangia, and not limited to basal pinnae
. . . . *B. tenebrosum* (in part)

    4. Middle pinnae not rhombic or squarish in general outline; distal margins curved, sometimes notched; attachment to rachis is comparatively narrow and not strongly decurrent.

      7. Basal pinnae widening comparatively little as approaching the distal end, their side margins diverging at an angle ≤ 45 degrees.

        8. Trophophore stalk 4–8 mm long; sporophore stalk 1–2.5 cm long
. . . . *B. gallicomontanum*

        8. Trophophore sessile or with a stalk no more than 2 mm long; sporophore stalk 0–1 cm long.

          9. Distal margins of larger pinnae lobed or cleft into somewhat rounded segments. . . . . *B. campestre* var. *campestre*

          9. Distal margins of larger pinnae deeply cleft into 2–4 linear or angular segments. . . . . *B. campestre* var. *lineare*

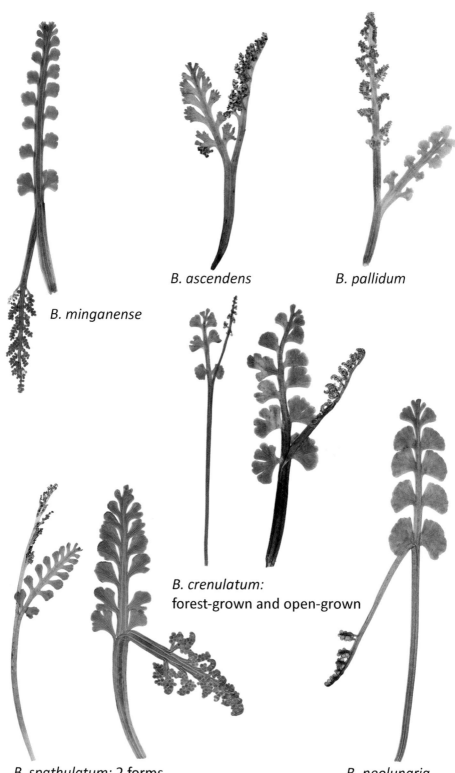

B. minganense

B. ascendens

B. pallidum

B. crenulatum:
forest-grown and open-grown

B. spathulatum: 2 forms

B. neolunaria

7. Basal pinnae widening noticeably toward the distal end, their side margins diverging at an angle ≥ 45 degrees.

    10. Basal pinnae wedge-shaped to broadly spoon-shaped in general outline (ignoring notches), the margins diverging at an angle of 45–120 degrees.

        11. Trophophore sessile; the lowest pinnae often folded over (clasping) the sporophore stalk . . . .*B. spathulatum*

        11. Trophophore with a distinct stalk; the lowest pinnae not folded over the sporophore stalk.

            12. Basal pinnae usually not cleft, notched, or toothed . . . . *B. minganense*

            12. Basal pinnae often cleft, notched, or toothed.

                13. Plants green; pinnae wedge-shaped to spoon-shaped; middle pinnae undivided or symmetrically cleft, distal margins uniformly toothed . . . .*B. ascendens*

                13. Plants silvery gray-green in life (changing to green following pressing and drying); pinnae broadly spoon-shaped to mushroom-shaped; middle pinnae undivided or asymmetrically cleft into a larger upper and smaller lower lobe, distal margins smooth or scalloped . . . .*B. pallidum*

    10. Basal pinnae fan-shaped, the margins diverging at 120–180 degrees.

        14. Pinnae green to dark green, somewhat fleshy, distal margins entire to scalloped; trophophore stalk 0–8 mm long . . . . *B. neolunaria*

        14. Pinnae light green, herbaceous (not fleshy), distal margins notched or blunt toothed; trophophore stalk 1–17 mm long . . . .*B. crenulatum*

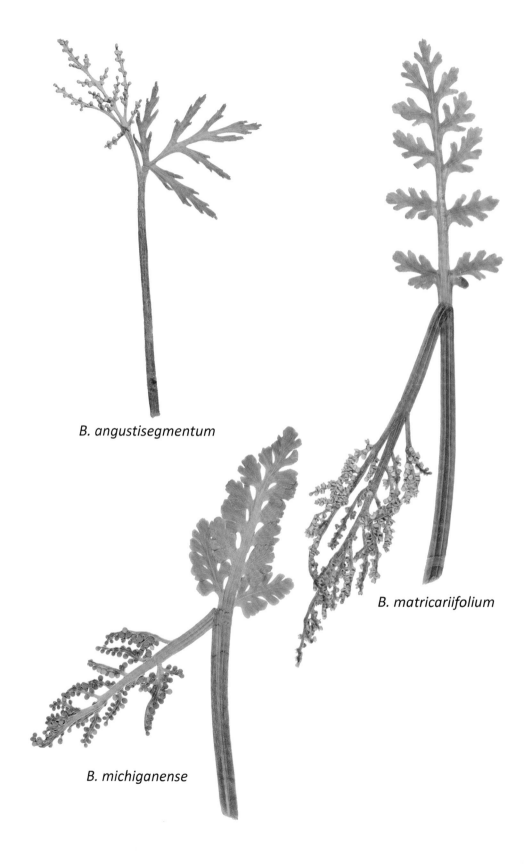

B. angustisegmentum

B. matricariifolium

B. michiganense

1. Trophophore 1-pinnate-pinnatifid to 2-pinnate-pinnatifid (i.e., side margins of the lowest pair of pinnae divided at least halfway to the midline); common stalk often reddish tinged near base.

    15. Trophophore about as long as wide, producing the shape of an equilateral triangle, sessile, oriented parallel to the ground; sporophore stalk ¼–½ the length of the entire trophophore. . . . . *B. angustisegmentum*

    15. Trophophore significantly longer than wide, producing the shape of a narrow triangle, rectangle or oblong, sessile or stalked, oriented vertically; sporophore stalk ¼ to fully as long as the entire trophophore.

        16. Trophophore sessile; the lowest pinnae 1.5–2.5 times as long as the pinnae immediately above, and more deeply incised . . . . *B. michiganense*

        16. Trophophore sometimes sessile but more often with a distinct stalk; the lowest pinnae 1–1.5 times as long as the pinnae immediately above, and about equally incised . . . . *B. matricariifolium*

Botrychium angustisegmentum (Pease & Moore) Fernald
Narrow Triangle Moonwort

[*B. lanceolatum* subsp. *angustisegmentum* (Pease & Moore) Clausen]

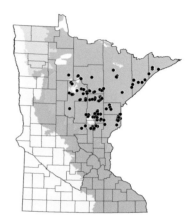

PLANTS deciduous, 8–20 cm in height. **COMMON STALK** (the portion aboveground) 3–10 cm long, often reddish tinged toward base. **TROPHOPHORE** sessile; shiny, triangular in shape, 1.5–4 cm long, 2–5 cm wide, 1-pinnate-pinnatifid to 2-pinnate or nearly 2-pinnate-pinnatifid. **PINNAE** in 2–4(5) pairs, decreasing evenly in size from the lowest to the uppermost; ultimate segments smooth, scalloped, toothed, or notched; venation imperfectly pinnate. **SPOROPHORE** divided into 2 or more equally long branches, the stalk ¼ to ½ the length of the trophophore. **PHENOLOGY:** Plants emerge in late May to early June, reach full size by the end of June, release spores in July, remain green and intact through the rest of summer, and fade (senesce) in autumn.

IDENTIFICATION: Perhaps dainty best describes the first impression of *B. angustisegmentum*. It does not have the otherworldly appearance of most moonworts, but it is definitely a moonwort. The outline of the trophophore (laid flat) very nearly forms an equilateral triangle regardless of the size or age of the plant, and it is the only Minnesota moonwort shaped that way. The trophophore of all the other moonworts will be clearly longer than wide. Also, the trophophore of *B. angustisegmentum* is sessile, it has no stalk, and it tends to be oriented parallel to the ground, growing at a right angle to the sporophore. The trophophore of other moonworts tends to be upright, growing side by side with the sporophore.

NATURAL HISTORY: *Botrychium angustisegmentum* is endemic to temperate forests of eastern North America. In Minnesota, it is found in undisturbed forest interiors, usually in deep shade under mature hardwood trees. Most often, the canopy will be dominated by sugar maple and basswood, often with black ash, red oak, and paper birch. Expect the terrain to be level or gently rolling, often with shallow wetlands or vernal pools in the low areas. Soils are typically moist loam formed of noncalcareous glacial till, uncompacted and worm-free. Little is known about how *Botrychium* interacts with the belowground ecosystem, yet the quality of the soil appears to be of utmost importance for this species. It is a frequent companion of *B. mormo* but is less rare and more widely distributed.

Sporophore is erect; branches near base.

Stands about 10 cm high—August 9.

Trophophore is sessile, held horizontally.

Botrychium ascendens W. H. Wagner
Upswept Moonwort

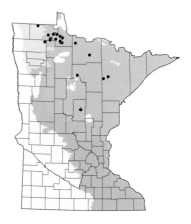

PLANTS deciduous, 4–10 cm in height, exceptionally to 15 cm. **COMMON STALK** (the portion aboveground) typically 1.5–5 cm long, exceptionally to 10 cm. **TROPHOPHORE:** Stalk 2–15 mm long; blade 1-pinnate, narrowly rectangular to oblong in outline, normally 1.5–4 cm long and 0.7–1.5 cm wide, rarely larger. **PINNAE** ascending and well separated, in 3–6 pairs, wedge-shaped to broadly spoon-shaped; sides diverging at an angle of 45–70 degrees, sometimes more in larger pinnae; distal margins uniformly toothed, or if notched in such a way as to create 2, 3, or 4 distinct lobes, then the lobes ± symmetrical in size and shape; veins appearing roughly parallel. **SPOROPHORE** 2–6 cm long; the stalk portion 0.7–2.5 cm long. **PHENOLOGY:** Plants emerge in mid to late May (in a normal spring), mature during June, shed spores in July, and senesce in late summer or early autumn.

IDENTIFICATION: The name *B. ascendens* implies pinnae that angle upward, which is true but not unique to this species. The main feature of the pinnae is the row of small teeth that line the ends. The teeth are in addition to the somewhat irregular notches that cut much deeper than the teeth. Compared with *B. spathulatum,* the trophophore of *B. ascendens* has a short stalk; that of *B. spathulatum* has no stalk. Another similar species is *B. minganense,* which, at its best, is a taller plant with more pinnae, and the individual pinnae tend to be more rounded and the outer margins smooth or wavy.

NATURAL HISTORY: *Botrychium ascendens* occurs primarily in western North America, with isolated occurrences in central and eastern North America. It appears to be quite rare in Minnesota, or at least rarely found. Most discoveries are from the northwest region of the state, in a landscape characterized by open-canopy woodlands and jack pine savannas—strongly influenced by prairies to the west and boreal forest to the east. This is an area of about 35,000 square km. Settlers arrived there in the early twentieth century, but farming attempts largely failed. By 1930, much of the land had been abandoned, leaving the landscape scarred by small fields and derelict homesteads. For unknown reasons, the scarred land in this region is rich in *Botrychium.*

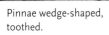

Pinnae wedge-shaped,
toothed.

Note stalked trophophore.

Releasing spores.

Botrychium campestre var. *campestre* W. H. Wagner & Farrar
Prairie Moonwort

PLANTS deciduous, 3–8 cm in height.
COMMON STALK (the portion aboveground)
typically 2–4 cm long. **TROPHOPHORE**
sessile or on a barely recognizable stalk
1–2 mm long; blade 1-pinnate, narrowly
oblong in outline, 1.5–5 cm long, 0.75–1.5
cm wide. **PINNAE** in 3–7 pairs (usually
fewer than 5); narrowly wedge-shaped to
narrowly spoon-shaped, sometimes peg-
shaped on smaller specimens; ascending;
side margins diverging at an angle of 15–
45 degrees; distal margin scalloped or
blunt-toothed, or larger pinnae with 1–3
deep notches resulting in 2–4 thumb-like

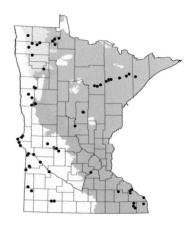

lobes; veins few, dichotomously branching. **SPOROPHORE** (at time of spore
release) 1–3.5 cm long; the stalk portion 0–5 mm long. **PHENOLOGY:** Plants
emerge in late April or early May (in a normal spring), mature and release spores
in June, senesce in late June, and are gone by early July.

IDENTIFICATION: *Botrychium campestre* var. *campestre* is very small, even for a
Botrychium. The aboveground portion is often less than 4 cm tall. The individual
pinnae are especially small and notably narrow. The side margins of the pinnae
diverge at an angle no greater than 45 degrees. This results in narrowly wedge-
shaped pinnae. Although the smaller pinnae may appear unformed, the ends
of larger pinnae will usually have 2–4 short lobes with rounded ends. Lobes of
B. campestre var. *lineare* are usually longer and with squared-off ends.

NATURAL HISTORY: To the best of everyone's knowledge, *B. campestre* var. *campestre*
is endemic to dry prairies, grasslands, and other nonforested habitats in
midcontinent North America. In Minnesota, it is found primarily in dry hill
prairies composed of coarse-textured glacial till, and in bluff prairies where
limestone bedrock is near the surface. Within historic times, it has found its way
to long-abandoned mine sites on the Mesabi and Cuyuna iron ranges in forested
regions of the northeast. By all reckonings, *B. campestre* var. *campestre* is the
earliest of the moonworts to emerge in the spring and the quickest to complete its
annual cycle. Its duration aboveground is about one month—reputed to be among
the briefest of any terrestrial fern. It is also notable as the first species of fern that
was discovered to produce gemmae on its rhizome.

Sporophore and trophophore emerging together.

The size of a golf tee, 5 cm high.

Searching a bluff prairie two weeks after a burn, Winona County—May 24.

Botrychium campestre var. *lineare* (W. H. Wagner) Farrar
Slender Prairie Moonwort

[*B. lineare* W. H. Wagner]

PLANTS deciduous, 4–15 cm in height.
COMMON STALK (the portion aboveground)
typically 2.5–4 cm long. **TROPHOPHORE**
sessile or with a stalk to 1 cm long; blade
1-pinnate, extreme examples appearing
1-pinnate-pinnatifid, oblong in outline,
2–7 cm long, 1–2 cm wide. **PINNAE** in
3–7 pairs (usually fewer than 5), wedge-
shaped; distal margin shallowly notched to
deeply divided, the resulting segments
with parallel sides (linear) and truncate
ends; veins of segments few, parallel.
SPOROPHORE (at time of spore release)
2–8 cm long, the stalk portion 0.5–1 cm

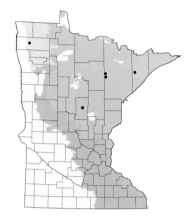

long. **PHENOLOGY:** Poorly known for Minnesota. Believed to emerge in May,
mature and release spores in June, and senesce in late June or early July.

IDENTIFICATION: This species was described in 1994 as *B. lineare*. A careful
genetic study subsequently concluded it was better treated as a variety of
B. campestre. The name *lineare* refers to the pinnae, which are the narrowest of all
moonworts. A typical specimen of var. *lineare* will look much like var. *campestre*
except the pinnae will be deeply divided into 2–4 linear segments. Linear, in this
case, means the sides of the individual segments are parallel, creating a
recognizable rectangle, and the ends tend to be straight rather than rounded. In
comparison, var. *campestre* has shorter, broader pinnae that are less deeply divided,
and the divisions are usually shorter, with rounder ends.

NATURAL HISTORY: *Botrychium campestre* var. *lineare* has been found at widely
scattered and isolated locations across much of North America, particularly at
high elevation and northern latitudes. Habitats have been variously described as
limestone ledges, meadows, native prairie remnants, and gravely roadsides. It is
considered rare or at least uncommon wherever it occurs and it is unpredictable,
at best. This is especially true in Minnesota, where discoveries, to date, have been
in long-term openings and clearings in forested regions. These have been human-
created habitats, including an inactive mine site, a perpetually maintained
clearing under an electrical transmission line, and an abandoned one-track
roadbed. There are so few records from Minnesota that a clear pattern is not
apparent. There is still much to learn about this rare and unique moonwort.

An exemplary specimen, rarely seen; note linear divisions of pinnae.

Botrychium crenulatum W. H. Wagner
Crenulate Moonwort

[*Botrychium lunaria* var. *crenulatum*
(W. H. Wagner) Stensvold]

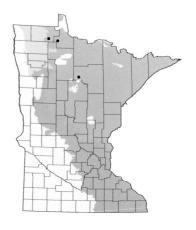

PLANTS deciduous, 6–16 cm in height.
COMMON STALK (the portion aboveground)
4–10 cm long. **TROPHOPHORE:** Stalk
1–17 mm long; blade roughly oblong in
shape, gradually tapering to a rounded
apex, 2.5–6 cm long, 1–2 cm wide,
1-pinnate. **PINNAE** in 2–5(6) pairs; the
larger pinnae fan-shaped, 3–12 mm long, ±
evenly spaced and not usually overlapping;
side margins creating an angle of 70 to 180
degrees; distal margins notched, scalloped,
or blunt-toothed; veins roughly parallel,
dichotomously branched, midvein lacking.
SPOROPHORE 2.5–9.5 cm long. **PHENOLOGY:** Plants emerge in May, mature
during June, shed spores in July, and senesce in late summer or early autumn
(estimates for Minnesota).

IDENTIFICATION: *Botrychium crenulatum* was first recognized (described by
science) in 1981, based on morphology of specimens from California. At that
time, *B. crenulatum* was not known to occur anywhere near Minnesota.
Amazingly, it was discovered in Minnesota in 2011. Its identity has been
genetically verified by a leading expert. At least two additional occurrences have
been confirmed by morphology. Plants from Minnesota resemble a rather small,
delicate *B. neolunaria* but with rather ragged-looking pinnae margins and a
trophophore that is more distinctly stalked. *Botrychium crenulatum* is also said to
average fewer pinnae per leaf than *B. neolunaria,* and have a paler green color and
a thinner texture. Some of those differences might be obscured by growing
conditions, and need further field testing in Minnesota.

NATURAL HISTORY: *Botrychium crenulatum* has been reported from most of the
western states, but Minnesota is one of the few places it has been found east of
the Rocky Mountains. To date, specimens from Minnesota have been found at
three sites. The first is an ecotonal habitat along the edge of a mesic hardwood
forest where it grades into a sedge meadow. Plants were growing in undisturbed
loamy soils in partial shade of mature black ash trees. The two other sites were
forests of jack pine that had been cleared and briefly used for agriculture but were
long-since abandoned. After abandonment, the habitats became home to young
trees and a mix of native and adventive herbaceous plants.

Basal pinnae often have ragged edges.

Pinnae are typically fan-shaped.

Fully grown at
10 cm tall—June 22.

Habitat along the edge of a forest, Itasca County.

Botrychium gallicomontanum Farrar & Johnson-Groh
Frenchman's Bluff Moonwort

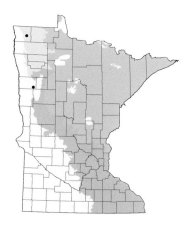

PLANTS deciduous, 5–12 cm in height.
COMMON STALK (the portion aboveground)
3–7 cm long. TROPHOPHORE: Blade
1-pinnate, narrowly rectangular to oblong
in outline, 1.4–3.5 cm long, 0.6–1.5 cm
wide; stalk 4–8 mm long. PINNAE in 3–6
pairs, ascending, broadly to narrowly
spoon-shaped; side margins diverging at
an angle of 25–45 degrees; distal margins
entire or the larger pinnae irregularly
notched or incised; veins dichotomously
branching, appearing roughly parallel.
SPOROPHORE often described as massive,
3–8 cm long; the stalk portion 1–2.5 cm
long, roughly half the length of the trophophore at time of spore release.
PHENOLOGY: Most plants emerge in late April or early May, mature and release
spores in late May and early June, and senesce by early July.

IDENTIFICATION: The trophophore of *B. gallicomontanum* most resembles that of
B. campestre. It differs most consistently in having a definite stalk. Also, the
sporophore of *B. gallicomontanum* compared to that of *B. campestre* is larger in all
regards and can appear massive in comparison. Sometimes the individual pinnae
of *B. gallicomontanum* will look much like those of *B. minganense* or *B. pallidum*.
But in the case of *B. gallicomontanum*, there is a conspicuously greater gap
between the lowest pinnae and the others. The pinnae of *B. minganense* and
B. pallidum are more evenly spaced.

NATURAL HISTORY: *Botrychium gallicomontanum* was discovered in 1986 on
Frenchman's Bluff in Norman County, Minnesota. It was described as a new
species in 1991. A handful of additional locations have subsequently been
discovered at scattered sites in the northern Great Plains, but it remains an
extremely rare species. Most *Botrychium* occur in association with forests; few
appear to be prairie specialists. *Botrychium gallicomontanum* is one of the latter.
To date, all known occurrences in Minnesota are in prairies in two northwestern
border counties. Soils appear to be moderately dry, sandy or gravely, glacial till,
or morainic deposits. The vegetation is sparse in places, dense in others, to which
B. gallicomontanum seems indifferent. The habitat suggests *B. gallicomontanum* is
adapted to periodic drought and frequent wildfire, but such resilience has not
been tested.

Gap separates the lowest pinnae.

Sporophore is outsized compared to similar species.

Botrychium matricariifolium (Döll) A. Braun ex Koch
Daisy-Leaved Moonwort

[*B. acuminatum* W. H. Wagner]

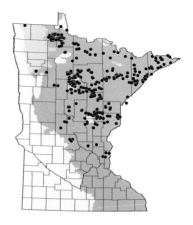

PLANTS deciduous, 5–20(25) cm in height.
COMMON STALK (the portion aboveground)
3–8 cm long, often reddish tinged toward
base. **TROPHOPHORE:** Stalk 0–1.5 cm long;
blade 2–10 cm long, 1–6 cm wide,
1-pinnate-pinnatifid to 2-pinnate. **PINNAE**
in 3–7 pairs, gradually decreasing in size
from the lowest or the second lowest pair
to the uppermost pair; margins of pinnae
segments entire, scalloped, toothed, or
notched; venation imperfectly pinnate.
SPOROPHORE stalk from ¼ to nearly equal
in length to the trophophore. **PHENOLOGY:**
Plants emerge in mid to late May, reach
full size by the end of June, release spores in July, and senesce in autumn.

IDENTIFICATION: The pinnae of *B. matricariifolium* will have notches along the
sides, not just at the ends. This is a critical distinction, but caution is needed.
Pinnae of small, poorly developed *B. matricariifolium* may show only one or two
shallow notches along their sides. If the notches are not recognized, such a plant
could easily be confused with just about every other species of *Botrychium,* even
those to which it is not closely related. If the notches are shallow, the leaf is said to
be 1-pinnate-pinnatifid. If the notches go all the way to the middle of the pinnae,
the leaf is said to be 2-pinnate. Both cases will lead to the second branch of the
first dichotomy (p. 97), which narrows the possibilities to 3 species: *B.
matricariifolium, B. angustisegmentum,* and *B. michiganense.* These 3 species share
another unique feature: the base of the common stalk will be reddish tinged.

NATURAL HISTORY: *Botrychium matricariifolium* is found in eastern and north-
central North America and parts of Europe. It is by far the most frequently
encountered moonwort in Minnesota. It occurs in forest interiors, forest edges,
grassy upland meadows, long-term forest clearings, and along lightly maintained
forest roads. Marginal populations can sometimes be found in stable, disused
mine sites and shallow borrow pits that have been left to recover on their own, but
only in northern forested regions. It has not been found in prairie regions, and
not in the southern third of the state. It prefers mesic, noncalcareous soils but
seems indifferent to sun or shade.

Margins of pinnae are notched or lobed.

The tip of a typical leaf.

This leaf is fully 2-pinnate.

Botrychium michiganense W. H. Wagner ex Gilman, Farrar & Zika
Michigan Moonwort

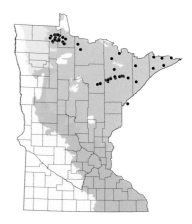

PLANTS deciduous, 5–15 cm in height.
COMMON STALK (the portion aboveground)
3–8 cm long, often reddish tinged toward
base. **TROPHOPHORE** sessile, 2–5 cm long,
1.5–3.5 cm wide, 1-pinnate-pinnatifid to
nearly 2-pinnate at base. **PINNAE** in
4–7 pairs; basal pinnae 1.5–2.5 times as
long as the pinnae immediately above,
usually pinnatifid with roundish or
squarish segments; nonbasal pinnae with
fewer and shallower segments and roughly
uniform in size or gradually decreasing in
size upward; veins imperfectly pinnate.
SPOROPHORE stalk ⅓ to fully as long as
the entire trophophore. **PHENOLOGY:** Plants emerge in mid to late May, reach full
size by the end of June, release spores in July, and senesce in autumn.

IDENTIFICATION: The idealized form of *B. michiganense* is quite distinctive
although rarely seen. It will have greatly oversized and deeply divided basal
pinnae that jut out to the sides. The other pinnae will be smaller and less divided.
Most specimens, however, will not have the ideal form and will look much like
B. matricariifolium. But even when the basal pinnae are not conclusively longer,
they should exhibit a greater degree of incising compared to the other pinnae
of the leaf. Also, the trophophore of *B. michiganense* is always sessile; that of
B. matricariifolium may be sessile but more often it will have a noticeable stalk.

NATURAL HISTORY: *Botrychium michiganense* ranges across North America in a
rather narrow band at about the latitude of northern Minnesota. Habitats in
Minnesota are loosely associated with forests. But rather than forest interiors, it is
usually found in open or partially open habitats where human activities have
removed the tree cover and the damage is slowly healing. This includes small,
long-abandoned fields; overburden from inactive open-pit mines; log landings;
and utility corridors. However, it would be wrong to consider *B. michiganense* a
ruderal species. It is a native species exploiting habitat opportunities where it
finds them. Soils are sometimes the residue of mining activities or land grading
but more often coarse, noncalcareous, glacial till, moist to somewhat dry. Expect
to find it in the company of other moonworts such as *B. pallidum, B. simplex* var.
simplex, and the common look-alike, *B. matricariifolium.*

Sporophore still developing.

Sporophore releasing spores—July 14.

The idealized form with greatly enlarged basal pinnae—July 14.

Botrychium minganense Victorin
Mingan Moonwort

PLANTS deciduous, 5–20 cm in height.
COMMON STALK (the portion aboveground)
2.5–6 cm long. TROPHOPHORE stalk
3–15 mm long; blade narrowly oblong in
shape, 2.5–11 cm long, 1–2.5 cm wide,
1-pinnate. PINNAE in 4–8 pairs, spoon-
shaped to roundish or nearly fan-shaped;
side margins diverging at an angle of
60–120 degrees; distal margin entire or
scalloped, or less often notched to a depth
of about ⅓ the length of the pinna;
venation like ribs of a fan, not pinnate.
SPOROPHORE 3–10 cm long; the stalk
portion 2–5 cm long. PHENOLOGY: Plants

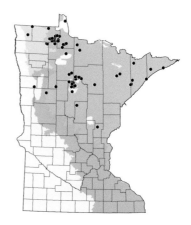

emerge around mid-May (in a normal spring), mature during June, shed spores in
July, and senesce in late summer or early autumn.

IDENTIFICATION: *Botrychium minganense* typically has 4–8 pairs of widely spaced
pinnae. All except the topmost are about equal in size, shape, and spacing. In fully
developed plants, the individual pinnae widen quite a bit as approaching the tip,
giving them a broad spoon-shaped outline. In smaller individuals, the pinnae may
be fewer in number and narrower in shape. The end of each pinna is usually
smooth or scalloped, although the lowermost pinnae of robust specimens may
have a shallow notch or two. The rare specimen of *B. minganense* that has reached
a pinnacle of development may have large, nearly fan-shaped pinnae that might
look like those of *B. neolunaria*. But the span of the basal pinnae will be less
than 120 degrees for *B. minganense* and more than 120 degrees for *B. neolunaria*.
Also, the trophophore of *B. minganense* has a stalk 3–15 mm long, while that of
B. neolunaria has a shorter stalk or no stalk at all.

NATURAL HISTORY: *Botrychium minganense* is found in a wide swath across the
central part of North America and into Alaska. *Botrychium* specialists consider it
one of the most widespread and common of the moonworts, which may qualify as
faint praise. In Minnesota, it is best described as an uncommon forest species. It
is found primarily in northern conifer and hardwood forests, in noncalcareous
glacial till. It occurs in undisturbed, old-growth forests as well as openings in
fragmented forests that are recovering from past wounds.

Pinnae numerous, widely spaced.

Pinnae margins are usually smooth, not notched.

Botrychium mormo W. H. Wagner
Little Goblin

PLANTS deciduous, 2–10 cm in height, somewhat succulent. **COMMON STALK** (the portion aboveground) 1–5 cm long. **TROPHOPHORE:** Stalk 0.2–1.5 cm long or indistinct; blade 1-pinnatifid or 1-pinnate, 1–4 cm long, 0.4–0.8 cm wide, whitish to pale green. **PINNAE** most often in 1–3 pairs, small and indistinct, ascending, decurrent, rhombic or squarish, all roughly the same size and shape; side margins parallel or converging distally; veins often appearing parallel. **SPOROPHORE** (at the time of spore release) irregularly and sparsely branched, 3–5(7) cm long; the stalk

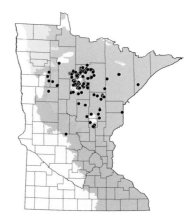

portion 0.5–2(3) cm long; sporangia large, partially sunken into the sporophore, relatively few in number and widely spaced. **PHENOLOGY:** Most plants emerge in June or early July. A few may emerge later, even into September, or may not emerge at all in a given year or at a given location; spores are not shed until senescence in late September or October.

IDENTIFICATION: A fully developed *B. mormo* (somewhat of an oddity) is about the size of a matchstick. Plants are so small that even at maturity they may not emerge above the leaf litter. The only reasonable look-alike is a forest-grown *B. tenebrosum*. When pressed flat, the trophophore of both species have stubby, rhombic-shaped pinnae that merge imperceptibly into the rachis (decurrent). Of the two, *B. mormo* is somewhat more succulent with a thicker, shorter sporophore and partially embedded sporangia. Note that *B. tenebrosum* is generally found in the first half of summer while *B. mormo* appears in the second half.

NATURAL HISTORY: *Botrychium mormo* is endemic to the Upper Great Lakes region of North America. In Minnesota, it has been found only in the interior of mature forests, in habitats undisturbed by human activities. The forest canopy is usually dominated by sugar maple and American basswood, with lesser amounts of paper birch, northern white cedar, or balsam fir. Soils are loamy, moist but well drained. It is safe to consider *B. mormo* a member of the belowground ecosystem. As such, most of its life history goes unseen. And yet there is evidence that the invasion of nonnative earthworms has taken a heavy toll on *B. mormo* by consuming the humus layer of the soil where *B. mormo* and its symbiont live.

Mature hardwood forest; typical habitat, Cass County.

Appears succulent, with few sporangia—August 10.

MALCOLM MACFARLANE

Full size at 5 cm, the size of a matchstick.

Botrychium neolunaria Stensvold & Farrar
New World Moonwort

PLANTS deciduous, 7–20 cm in height.
COMMON STALK (the portion aboveground)
3–7 cm long. **TROPHOPHORE** sessile, or on
a stalk to about 8 mm long; blade roughly
oblong in shape, 2.5–7 cm long, 1–3 cm
wide, 1-pinnate. **PINNAE** in 4–7 pairs,
broadly fan-shaped, side margins diverging
at 90–180 degrees; larger pinnae 5–15 mm
long, 6–20 mm wide, ± evenly spaced;
distal margins entire to scalloped,
infrequently notched; venation like ribs of
a fan. **SPOROPHORE** 6–15 cm long,
narrowly and uniformly pinnate, the stalk
portion (at time of spore release) usually

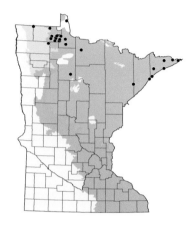

exceeding the length of the trophophore. **PHENOLOGY:** Plants emerge in May,
mature during June, shed spores in July, and senesce in late summer or early
autumn.

IDENTIFICATION: In many ways, *B. neolunaria* is the archetypical moonwort. To
find one with the classic form as it is often represented in books can be a
transcendent experience for a botanist. The pinnae are comparatively large,
typically fan-shaped, and closely spaced, sometimes overlapping. The lower
pinnae are almost a half circle in shape, the upper pinnae about a quarter circle.
The closest in appearance is probably the very rare *B. crenulatum*. The pinnae of
B. crenulatum have a thinner texture, are usually notched along the outer margins,
and are not quite as broadly fan-shaped as *B. neolunaria*. Also, the trophophore of
B. crenulatum typically has a short stalk; that of *B. neolunaria* has little if any stalk.

NATURAL HISTORY: As a point of clarification, *B. neolunaria* was separated
(taxonomically) from the worldwide *B. lunaria* in 2016. Its current name is meant
to signify this as the "New World" version of the "Old World" *B. lunaria*. It appears
that *B. neolunaria* occurs in a wide band across boreal and subboreal regions of
North America. Although its range includes the northern third of Minnesota, it is
uncommon and sporadic in the state. It has been found most often in gravely or
rocky exposures in full sunlight or partial shade. It also occurs in stable forest
clearings of human origin, including forests recovering from small-scale clear-
cuts. Similarly, it has been found along minimally maintained forest roads and in
utility corridors kept clear of encroaching trees and shrubs.

Pinnae fan-shaped; trophophore sessile.

The archetypic moonwort, Lake of the
Woods County—June 26.

Botrychium pallidum W. H. Wagner
Pale Moonwort

PLANTS deciduous, 3–15 cm in height.
COMMON STALK (the portion aboveground)
1.5–7 cm long. **TROPHOPHORE:** Stalk
2–15 mm long; blade 1-pinnate, narrowly
rectangular to oblong in outline, 1.2–4 cm
long and 0.6–1.5 cm wide, ± folded
longitudinally (trough-like) in life. **PINNAE**
in 3–6 pairs; broadly spoon-shaped to
roughly fan-shaped or mushroom-shaped;
side margins diverging at an angle of
60–120 degrees; distal margins entire,
scalloped, or blunt-toothed, or if notched
in such a way as to create 2 lobes, then the
upper lobe the largest; venation like ribs of

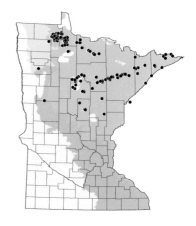

a fan. **SPOROPHORE** 3–8 cm long, the stalk portion 0.5–1.5 times as long as the
trophophore. **PHENOLOGY:** Plants emerge in mid to late May (in a normal spring),
mature during June, shed spores in July, and senesce in late summer or early
autumn.

IDENTIFICATION: The silvery gray-green (pallid) color of B. pallidum is a
distinctive trait but not always pronounced, and seen only in the living plant. The
trophophore is typically small, with pinnae best described as spoon-shaped,
although sometimes the sides may be recurved, causing the pinnae to look like a
mushroom cap. It has been suggested that B. pallidum resembles a very pale,
dwarf form of B. minganense. However, the pinnae of B. minganense tend to have
straighter sides, and the ends are usually unnotched. The pinnae of B. pallidum
are likely to be notched at the end, resulting in 2 unequal lobes, the upper lobe
usually larger than the lower lobe.

NATURAL HISTORY: Botrychium pallidum is found in cool temperate habitats in the
north-central United States and adjacent parts of Canada. It was described as a
species new to science in 1990. Upon its discovery in Minnesota in 1992, it was
thought to be very rare, but now it is considered more overlooked than rare. It is
generally a species of forest habitats, including associated thickets and edges. In
Minnesota, it is easiest to find in small-scale forest openings, including human-
created clearings near abandoned farmsteads, as well as "mine dumps" associated
with iron ore mining. This does not appear to represent a migration into ruderal
habitats, since the limited dispersal potential of B. pallidum prevents it from
moving far or fast.

MALCOLM MACFARLANE

MALCOLM MACFARLANE

Sporangia have turned brown, indicating maturity.

Clumps of plants and "pallid" color; typical of *B. pallidum*.

MALCOLM MACFARLANE

A long-abandoned farmstead in Roseau County; excellent habitat.

Botrychium simplex var. *simplex* E. Hitchc.
Least Moonwort

PLANTS deciduous, 3–15 cm in aboveground height. **COMMON STALK** (the portion aboveground) 1–3 cm long. **TROPHOPHORE:** Stalk 0–2 cm long; blade 1-pinnate, ovate in outline, 1–5 cm long, 0.7–3.5 cm wide. **PINNAE** in 1–5 pairs (usually 1–2), wedge-shaped to spoon-shaped or squarish, strongly decurrent; side margins forming an angle of 30–90 degrees; distal margin typically entire, sometimes scalloped or shallowly notched; basal pinnae strongly ascending, often larger than the others; veins pinnate or fanlike. **SPOROPHORE** slender, 3–14 cm long (at the time spores are released); stalk portion 3–8 cm long, 1–4 times as long as the trophophore. **PHENOLOGY:** Plants emerge in May, mature during June, shed spores in late June and July, and senesce in August and September.

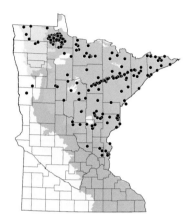

IDENTIFICATION: The most common configuration of *B. simplex* var. *simplex* in Minnesota is a simple plant. There are few pinnae, typically just 1 or 2 lateral pairs plus a large terminal pinna. If there is more than one pair of lateral pinnae, the basal pair will usually be the largest and they will be growing upward at a steeper angle than the others, and each will have a narrower base. In some cases, the basal pinnae are so greatly enlarged that each one may match the terminal portion of the blade in size and shape, giving the impression that there are 3 separate leaf blades attached at the base. In essentially all cases, the common stalk is very short, and the stalk of the sporophore is very long.

NATURAL HISTORY: *Botrychium simplex* var. *simplex* occurs across the northeastern United States and southern Canada, including the northeastern half of Minnesota, as well as parts of Europe and Asia. We refer to it as var. *simplex* because there is a var. *compositum* that occurs to the west of Minnesota. *Botrychium simplex* var. *simplex* is likely the most common *Botrychium* in Minnesota, but because of its small size it is easily overlooked. It occurs in a variety of habitats but seems to favor forest openings that might resemble meadows or prairies. Some openings are quite natural looking; some are clearly of human origin. It is also found on raised hummocks in forested swamps, and in lakeside and streamside vegetation.

Long sporophore and short trophophore—
June 6.

Sporophore and trophophore joined
near ground level.

Open-grown "squatters."

Botrychium spathulatum W. H. Wagner
Spatulate Moonwort

PLANTS deciduous, 8–20 cm in height.
COMMON STALK (the portion aboveground)
2.5–6(10) cm long. **TROPHOPHORE** sessile
or essentially so; blade 1-pinnate, narrowly
rectangular to oblong in outline, 3–7 cm
long, 1.5–3 cm wide. **PINNAE** in 4–7 pairs,
generally spoon-shaped or wedge-shaped;
basal pinnae somewhat fan-shaped and
commonly clasping the sporophore stalk;
side margins diverging at an angle of
45–90 degrees; distal margins scalloped,
blunt-toothed, or lobed; with 2 or 3 major
veins entering pinna base. **SPOROPHORE**
3–6 cm long; the stalk portion 0.5–1.5 cm

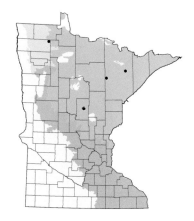

long. **PHENOLOGY:** Poorly known for Minnesota. Believed to emerge in May,
mature during June, shed spores in July, and senesce in late summer or early
autumn.

IDENTIFICATION: In most cases, the pinnae of *B. spathulatum* are indeed spatulate
(spoon-shaped), as the name implies. This is useful to know, but pinnae of other
Botrychium have a similar shape, most notably *B. pallidum* and *B. minganense*.
Importantly, the trophophore of *B. spathulatum* is consistently without a stalk, and
the lowest pinnae often clasp the stalk of the sporophore. The trophophore of both
B. minganense and *B. pallidum* will have a short but distinct stalk, and the lowest
pinnae do not clasp the sporophore.

NATURAL HISTORY: *Botrychium spathulatum* is widespread but scattered in
southern Canada and adjacent parts of the United States. It is quite rare in
Minnesota, with too few records to get a good sense of its habitat or distribution.
It seems it could be found wherever other *Botrychium* might be found, such as
partial openings and brushy edges in northern forested regions. Known habitats
include long-abandoned mining sites that are reverting to forest, powerline
corridors being kept clear of trees, and long-deserted farmsteads of early settlers.
Habitats seem limited to historically forested areas, with forest soils but only
sparse tree cover. It has not been found in prairies, or anything that floristically
resembles prairies, or areas that were originally prairie. Although the difference
between forest soils and prairie soils might not seem critical, *Botrychium* are
basically underground organisms that interact with the soil ecosystem in
unknown ways.

The trophophore lacks a stalk—June 27.

Basal pinnae clasp the sporophore.

Pinnae are spoon-shaped or wedge-shaped.

Botrychium tenebrosum A. A. Eat.
(common name not standardized)

[*B. simplex* var. *tenebrosum* (A. A. Eat.) Clausen]

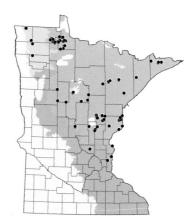

PLANTS deciduous, 6–12 cm in aboveground height. **COMMON STALK** (the portion aboveground) 1–4 cm long. **TROPHOPHORE:** Stalk 0–1.5 cm long; blade 1-pinnate, 1–4 cm long, 0.5–1.5 cm wide. **PINNAE** most often in 2 or 3 pairs, sometimes 4; irregularly shaped, often squarish or indistinct; side margins forming an angle of 45–90 degrees; distal margins entire to scalloped; basal pinnae often larger and more ascending than the others, but not consistently so; veins roughly pinnate or somewhat parallel. **SPOROPHORE** slender, 2–8 cm long; the stalk portion (at the time spores are released) 0.5–3 cm long, 0.3–1 times as long as the trophophore. **PHENOLOGY:** Emerges in May, matures during June, sheds spores in late June and July, and senesces in July and August.

IDENTIFICATION: *Botrychium tenebrosum* is similar to *B. simplex* var. *simplex*. Distinguishing the two species is often an issue. Perhaps the best character concerns the aboveground portion of the common stalk. In *B. tenebrosum*, it is longer than that of *B. simplex* var. *simplex*, especially in relation to the stalk of the sporophore. Also, the trophophore of *B. tenebrosum* is often folded lengthwise, with a noticeable keel along the fold, and the middle pinnae are often wider than long. Forest-grown *B. tenebrosum* tends to be smaller, and may resemble *B. mormo* in some characteristics. But *B. mormo* has a stiffer, stouter, more succulent appearance, and the sporangia are partially sunken into the sporophore. Also, the phenology is opposite: *Botrychium tenebrosum* will be found in the first half of the summer, *B. mormo* in the second half.

NATURAL HISTORY: The global distribution of *B. tenebrosum* is poorly known, probably because of lingering taxonomic issues. Reliable records are primarily from eastern and central North America. In Minnesota, it has been found in a variety of places, mostly in northern forested habitats, or in stable open habitats that were previously forested. There is nothing obvious to set it apart from other *Botrychium* habitats. Soils are typically derived from noncalcareous glacial till. On the iron range, in the northeastern part of the state, it can be found in the overburden discarded by open-pit iron ore mines.

Typical forest-grown plant.

MALCOLM MACFARLANE

Open-grown plants are "beefier"; these are extremes.

Supernumerary sporangia.

Forest opening habitat, Sherburne County—May 29.

B. virginianus

BOTRYPUS (RATTLESNAKE FERN)

Worldwide, there is just one species in the genus *Botrypus,* usually referred to as *B. virginianus.* For much of the past century, it had been placed in the genus *Botrychium* but was never a good fit. It differs in a number of easy-to-see characters and in chromosome number. The current preference is to return it to an older name, *Botrypus virginianus,* which was first proposed in 1803.

It has a unique distinction among plants that may help explain its success. It seems that at some time in the distant past, it was the beneficiary of horizontal gene transfer from a root parasite in the mistletoe family (Loranthaceae). This is the only known instance of genes being transferred from a flowering plant to a fern (parasite to host). It seems that soon after the event, *B. virginianus* quickly expanded its range to become nearly worldwide.

Botrypus virginianus (L.) Michx.
Rattlesnake Fern

[*Botrychium virginianum* (L.) Swartz]

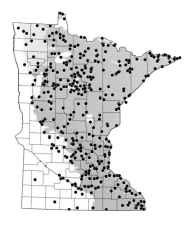

PLANTS deciduous. **RHIZOMES** to about 3 cm long, vertical. **TROPHOPHORES** sessile, 2-pinnate-pinnatifid to 3-pinnate-pinnatifid; large ternate specimens questionably 4-pinnate at base; 10–30 cm long, 15–42 cm wide; pinnae in 8–12 pairs, thin, herbaceous; ultimate segments deeply toothed or notched; veins pinnate, ending at the margin in a tooth. **SPOROPHORES** much reduced, 1- to 3-pinnate, 10–50 cm long; the sporangia-bearing portion 3–15 cm long, 2–7 cm wide. **PETIOLE** (common stalk) round in cross-section, the aboveground portion to 30 cm long. **PHENOLOGY:** Plants emerge from the ground in late April or early May and reach full size by June; the sporophore sheds spores in June or early July, then shrivels; the trophophore senesces in September.

IDENTIFICATION: The sporangia of *B. virginianus* are found at the very top of a tall, straight stalk that easily reaches knee height. This structure is called the sporophore. The green leafy blade, called the trophophore, appears at about the middle of the plant and grows outward or obliquely upward. If both sporophore and trophophore are present, then identification is simple. Small (young) plants may not produce a sporophore, just a trophophore, leaving few clues to its identity. Note that the petiole of *B. virginianus* is round in cross-section and rather succulent. Most ferns have a channel running the length of the petiole and are not succulent. The petioles of grape ferns (*Sceptridium*) are an exception, but the leaf of a grape fern is smaller than that of *B. virginianus,* more coarsely divided, and leathery in texture.

NATURAL HISTORY: *Botrypus virginianus* is a wide-ranging species found across North America and much of the world. In Minnesota, it is common in a variety of forest settings throughout the state, associated with either hardwood or coniferous trees and loamy soil. It is sometimes found in swampy woods, growing in wet peat or moist humus. Although *B. virginianus* favors habitats with stable native vegetation and undisturbed soil, conditions are sometimes less than pristine. Individual plants tend to be solitary and are short-lived, perhaps on the order of 8–12 years. It reproduces only by spores and does not establish long-lasting colonies. And yet it is not hard to find in any sizeable tract of mesic forest.

Releasing spores, Winona County—
July 10.

Sporophore still green, Isanti County—
June 10.

Young *Botrypus* resemble a *Sceptridium*—
October 16.

Ripening sporangia—June 19.

O. pusillum

OPHIOGLOSSUM (ADDER'S-TONGUE FERNS)

There are believed to be about 41 species of *Ophioglossum* in the world. They occur worldwide from the tropics to the arctic. About 7 species occur in the United States, mostly in the southeastern states, with 1 species occurring in Minnesota.

The rhizome of an *Ophioglossum* is a short, fleshy, underground structure that gives rise to long, unbranched roots and one or two leaves each year. The leaf is divided into a sterile trophophore (the blade) and a separate sporophore, which is a slender unbranched structure bearing the sporangia.

Members of this genus are notable for many curious things. One of the most curious is the large number of chromosomes in each cell. *Ophioglossum pusillum* is reported to have at least 960 somatic chromosomes—the highest of any North American plant (humans have 46). The significance of this is not apparent, but no denying it is curious. Also, the world's smallest terrestrial fern is reputed to be an Indian species of *Ophioglossum* (*O. malviae*), reaching an average height of only 1–1.2 cm, about the size of an insect.

Ophioglossum also has very unusual roots. They have the ability to form new plants some distance from the parent plant (root proliferation). Sprouting new plants is something roots normally have no role in. That is typically what rhizomes do. This proliferation in *O. pusillum* can result in 10 or more distant plants interconnected by a single root system. Such root systems may be a meter or more across.

Ophioglossum pusillum Raf.
Northern Adder's-Tongue

[*Ophioglossum vulgatum* var. *pseudopodum* (Blake) Farw.]

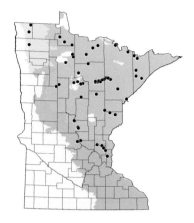

PLANTS deciduous. **RHIZOMES** erect, to 2 cm long. **ROOTS** fleshy, unbranched, creating new rhizomes along their length. **LEAVES** 1–3 (usually 1) per rhizome; trophophore and sporophore joined to a common stalk 1–10 cm long (aboveground portion). **TROPHOPHORE** entire, 3–15 cm long, 1–3.5 cm wide, imperfectly elliptic, ± erect, pale green, dull; base tapered, partially clasping; apex rounded or blunt; venation reticulate. **SPOROPHORE** slender, 10–25 cm long at maturity; bearing 10–40 pairs of embedded sporangia arranged in 2 parallel rows. **PHENOLOGY:** Plants emerge aboveground in mid to late May; the trophophores reach full size by the end of June, but the sporophores continue to lengthen until late July or early August, and shed spores in August. The entire leaf dies back by winter.

IDENTIFICATION: *Ophioglossum pusillum* generally produces one leaf at a time (three at the most). The leaf (trophophore) is said to be entire, meaning it has no lobes, segments, or divisions. In the absence of the sporophore, the leaf of *O. pusillum* is most likely to be confused with the leaf of an orchid, such as *Malaxis monophyllos* (white adder's-mouth orchid). Visible differences involve the veins of the leaf. The veins of *O. pusillum* form a closed network, like a fishing net, and there is no midvein. The veins of an orchid leaf run parallel to each other and have a distinct midvein.

NATURAL HISTORY: *Ophioglossum pusillum* is an uncommon fern that ranges sporadically across cool temperate regions of North America. In Minnesota, it is decidedly scarce and very hard to find. Any discovery is notable. It is most often found in shallow, treeless wetlands, such as wet meadows, wet prairies, and shrubby fens, typically among scattered willows, dogwoods, or alders. It will not likely be found in permanently standing water but on slightly raised hummocks with grasses or sedges. In spite of its small size, it is quite competitive in dense vegetation. It has also been found in early successional wetlands such as disused gravel pits, lightly managed roadsides, and revegetating mine sites. There are a few records from uplands some distance from wetlands, particularly long-term forest openings and abandoned forest roads.

Ground-level view, Anoka County—July 20.

Sporophore has more growing to do—June 28.

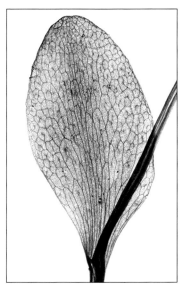

Veins form a closed network.

Tip of mature sporophore—August 31

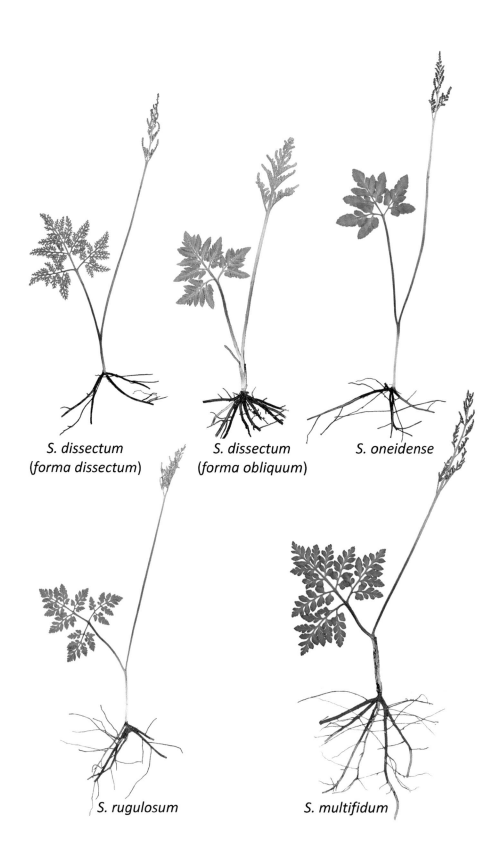

S. dissectum
(*forma dissectum*)

S. dissectum
(*forma obliquum*)

S. oneidense

S. rugulosum

S. multifidum

SCEPTRIDIUM
(EVERGREEN GRAPE-FERNS)

There are believed to be about 25 species of *Sceptridium* in the world, 6 in North America and 4 in Minnesota. *Sceptridium* normally produce a single leaf each year. It is divided just below ground into a sporophore and a trophophore. Each rises aboveground on a separate stalk. Most plants will not produce a sporophore every year. Fortunately, it is the trophophore that is used for identification. It is somewhat thick and leathery in texture, and shaped in predictable ways, or so we tell ourselves. The variability in shape between individuals of the same species, even within the same population, can be baffling. There is far more variability and uncertainty than can possibly be incorporated into the key. Clearly, a foolproof way to identify every specimen has eluded science, leading many to conclude that identifying grape-ferns is perhaps more art than science.

KEY TO *SCEPTRIDIUM*

1. Ultimate segments of trophophore deeply and conspicuously incised; the smallest divisions only about 1 mm wide, with parallel sides (rectilinear) and mostly 1–2 veinlets .... *S. dissectum (forma dissectum)*

1. Ultimate segments of trophophore entire or toothed but not deeply incised; the smallest divisions significantly wider than 1 mm, sides convex or tapered (not parallel), with several veinlets.

   2. Terminal segment of most pinnae (and larger pinnules) smaller than the preceding pair; the terminal segment 2–8 mm wide.

      3. Margins of segments smooth or shallowly scalloped; terminal segment of pinnae mostly 4–8 mm wide .... *S. multifidum*

      3. Margins of segments lined with pointed teeth; terminal segment of pinnae mostly 2–5 mm wide. .... *S. rugulosum*

   2. Terminal segment of most pinnae (and larger pinnules) larger than the preceding pair; the terminal segment 5–16 mm wide.

      4. Terminal segment 5–10 mm wide (mostly 7–9 mm), lanceolate, the sides nearly straight as they taper evenly to a pointed tip at an angle of 20–30 degrees .... *S. dissectum (forma obliquum)*

      4. Terminal segment 8–16 mm wide (mostly 9–12 mm), somewhat ovate, the sides convex as they curve slightly to a blunt or broadly angled tip at an angle of 30–45 degrees. .... *S. oneidense*

Sceptridium dissectum (Spreng.) Lyon
Cutleaf Grape-Fern

[*Botrychium dissectum* Spreng.]

(includes both *forma dissectum* and *forma obliquum*)

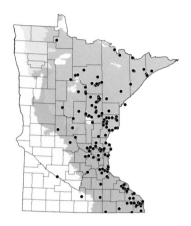

RHIZOMES upright, to about 2 cm long, unbranched. **LEAF** solitary, consisting of an evergreen trophophore (living 14–16 months) and a seasonal sporophore. **TROPHOPHORE** 5–25 cm long; the stalk portion 2–10 cm long; the blade portion 3–12 cm long, 4–15 cm wide; *forma obliquum* 2-pinnate to 2-pinnate-pinnatifid, margins finely toothed; *forma dissectum* 2-pinnate-pinnatifid to 3-pinnate, margins incised. **SPOROPHORE** 10–30 cm long, consistently overtopping the trophophore, sometimes by a factor of 2 or 3. **PHENOLOGY:** New leaves appear aboveground in early June. Sporangia mature and release their spores in October and the sporophore soon withers. The trophophore survives over winter, remaining functional until the new leaf is nearly developed the following summer.

IDENTIFICATION: Even though the two forms of *S. dissectum* look quite different, they cannot be distinguished genetically. And there are many gradations, often within the same population. The lacy form (*f. dissectum*) is easy to identify, but the non-lacy form (*f. obliquum*) can be difficult to separate from *S. oneidense*. Compared to *S. oneidense*, the leaf segments of *S. dissectum f. obliquum* are on average more numerous, smaller, less rounded, and more distinctly pointed. Both *S. dissectum* and *S. oneidense* sometimes grow mixed together, and not all specimens will fall neatly into one or the other branch of the dichotomy.

NATURAL HISTORY: *Sceptridium dissectum* is found in the eastern half of the United States and adjacent portions of southern Canada. In Minnesota, it is basically a species of the forested region, but it is rather eclectic in choice of habitat. It seems most at home in deciduous forests. It is also found in forest openings and clearings, but usually not far from trees, and not in wetlands. Substrates are typically moist, noncompacted, loamy soils derived from noncalcareous glacial till. It is also found in bedrock-influenced habitats and in sandy outwash soils. In Minnesota, *forma obliquum* seems to be more common than *forma dissectum* by perhaps 2 to 1, but there appears to be no geographic or habitat preference expressed by either form. In fact, just about every large population of the species will have both forms intermixed.

A lucky shot: *forma dissectum* and *forma obliquum* side by side.

Isanti County—September 19.

Leaves of *forma dissectum* are deeply incised.

Segments of *forma obliquum* are pointed and lined with "teeth."

Sceptridium multifidum (S. G. Gmel.) Nashida ex Tagawa
Leathery Grape-Fern

[*Botrychium multifidum* (S. G. Gmel.)
Ruprecht]

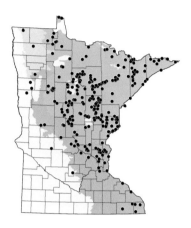

RHIZOMES upright, to 3 cm long,
unbranched. **LEAF** solitary, consisting of an
evergreen trophophore (living 14–16
months) and a seasonal sporophore.
TROPHOPHORE 8–22 cm long; the stalk
portion 3–10 cm long; the blade portion
4–15 cm long, 5–20 cm wide, partially
1-pinnate-pinnatifid to 2-pinnate-
pinnatifid, margins smooth to shallowly
scalloped. **SPOROPHORE** to 30 cm long,
1.5–2.5 times the length of the
trophophore. **PHENOLOGY:** New leaves
typically appear aboveground beginning in May. The trophophore reaches full size
sometime before July; the sporophore reaches maturity and releases spores in late
September and October. The trophophore survives over winter and remains
functional until sometime in August or September.

IDENTIFICATION: *Sceptridium multifidum* is, on average, the largest *Sceptridium* in
Minnesota, but it comes in all sizes. Despite the common name, it is not
noticeably more leathery than the other grape-ferns. Compared to similar species,
the leaf segments of *S. multifidum* tend to be numerous and roundish; at least that
is the ideal form botanists always look for. Margins of the leaf segments are
smooth or wavy; they do not have rows of pointed teeth as seen on other
Sceptridium. This is a nearly foolproof way to tell *S. multifidum* from the other
grape-ferns and should be the first thing to check.

NATURAL HISTORY: *Sceptridium multifidum* is the most widespread of all
Sceptridium. It occurs in subarctic, boreal, and north temperate regions across
North America and Eurasia. In Minnesota, it is fundamentally a forest species,
dividing its habitat choices about equally between coniferous forests and broadleaf
forests. It is also found in forest clearings and brushy edges, even small prairie
habitats in otherwise forested areas. It is also known to exploit opportunities in
disused sand/gravel pits, old mine sites, and long-abandoned farmland, especially
where such habitats are small inclusions within forested land and have been left
to revegetate on their own. However, *S. multifidum* should not be considered a
ruderal species. Native soils are typically noncalcareous and somewhat sandy but
not exclusively so. The critical habitat factors are hard to pinpoint and likely
involve the underground environment favored by the gametophyte and its
associated mycorrhizal fungi.

Sherburne County—
August 1.

Leaf segments are often numerous, rounded.

Leaf margins are smooth or scalloped.

Sceptridium oneidense (Gilbert) Holub
Blunt-Lobed Grape-Fern

[*Botrychium oneidense* (Gilbert) House]

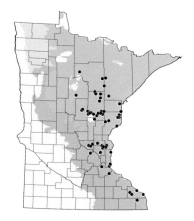

RHIZOMES upright, to about 2 cm long, unbranched. **LEAF** solitary, consisting of an evergreen trophophore (living 14–16 months) and a seasonal sporophore. **TROPHOPHORE** 10–25 cm long; the stalk portion 4–8 cm long; the blade portion 4–13 cm long, 6–20 cm wide, with finely toothed margins; lower portion of large leaves 2-pinnate to sparingly 3-pinnate. **SPOROPHORE** consistently overtopping the trophophore, to 40 cm long (usually 20–25 cm). **PHENOLOGY:** New leaves typically appear aboveground in the middle of May. Sporangia mature and release their spores in September and October and the sporophore soon withers. The trophophore survives over winter and remains functional until sometime the following summer.

IDENTIFICATION: The key character used to identify *S. oneidense* is the shape and size of the terminal segment of the pinnae and of the larger pinnules. They are comparatively large and undivided in comparison with *S. multifidum* or *S. rugulosum,* and somewhat broader and more rounded in comparison with *S. dissectum.* There can be a lot of confusing variability, especially with a small plant that may have only one or two well-developed pinnae and no distinct pinnules. Also, the terminal segment of a pinna is rarely distinct. It is often overlapped by the pair of segments immediately preceding it. In fact, a single plant may have 10 or more pinnae, each with a slightly different terminal segment. With a difficult specimen, try to determine an average or representative tip shape.

NATURAL HISTORY: *Sceptridium oneidense* is endemic to the eastern United States and adjacent parts of southern Canada. In east-central Minnesota, it is an infrequent forest species that seems to favor moist, loamy soil at the margins of woodland ponds or vernal pools. It seems to never be found on steep hillsides but sometimes appears on low rises. Soils tend to be deep, noncalcareous glacial till. In the southeastern counties, *S. oneidense* has been found on dry ridgetops, shaded by oak trees and various shrubs, a seemingly different habitat entirely. The integrity of the soil is a consistent feature. It must provide a healthy biotic environment: not having been compacted by cattle, invaded by earthworms, or turned over by a plow. Taking everything into account, *S. oneidense* appears to be the rarest and most habitat-sensitive of Minnesota's grape-ferns.

Resembles *S. dissectum*, but segments are more rounded.

Margins lined with jagged "teeth."

Tip of pinnae are large, rounded.

Sceptridium rugulosum (W. H. Wagner) Skoda and Holub
Laurentian Grape-Fern

[*Botrychium rugulosum* W. H. Wagner]

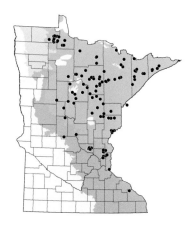

RHIZOMES upright, to about 2 cm long, unbranched. **LEAF** solitary, consisting of an evergreen trophophore (living 14–16 months) and a seasonal sporophore. **TROPHOPHORE** 5–18 cm long; the stalk portion 2–8 cm long; the blade portion 3–10 cm long, 4–12(16) cm wide, 2-pinnate-pinnatifid to 3-pinnate; margins with sharp teeth, regular in distribution but irregular in form. **SPOROPHORE** to 24 cm long, 1.5–2.5 times the length of the trophophore. **PHENOLOGY:** New leaves typically appear aboveground in late May or early June. The trophophores reaches full size sometime before July, and the sporophores release spores in late September and October. The trophophores survives the winter and are replaced sometime during the following summer.

IDENTIFICATION: In the case of *S. rugulosum,* each pinna and the larger pinnules are divided into pairs of successively smaller and simpler units going from the base to the tip. The very tip is capped by a single (unpaired) segment smaller than the rest. This is the same basic structure as *S. multifidum.* The structure of *S. dissectum* and *S. oneidense* is different in that the terminal segment is not the smallest segment. In fact, it might be the largest. When comparing *S. rugulosum* to *S. multifidum,* check the margins of the leaf segments (a hand lens may be needed). Those of *S. rugulosum* will be lined with small, pointed teeth. Those of *S. multifidum* will be smooth, slightly roughened, or shallowly scalloped.

NATURAL HISTORY: *Sceptridium rugulosum* occurs primarily in the Great Lakes region of the United States and adjacent Canada. Its occurrence in Minnesota is widespread but spotty, and known habitats vary quite a bit. They are usually associated with forests, including a variety of early successional forest types. It may occur in forest interiors, but it is far easier to find in forest clearings, disused log landings, and openings along forest roads. It is sometimes found in long-abandoned fields and homesteads carved from forests, but only where time has restored at least some of the ecological process associated with forest recovery. It has not been found in active agricultural regions, urban areas, or industrial sites. It is hard to think of *S. rugulosum* as a long-term resident of any habitat.

Wadena County—September 24.

Segments of leaf are typically small and numerous.

Margins lined with irregular but distinct "teeth."

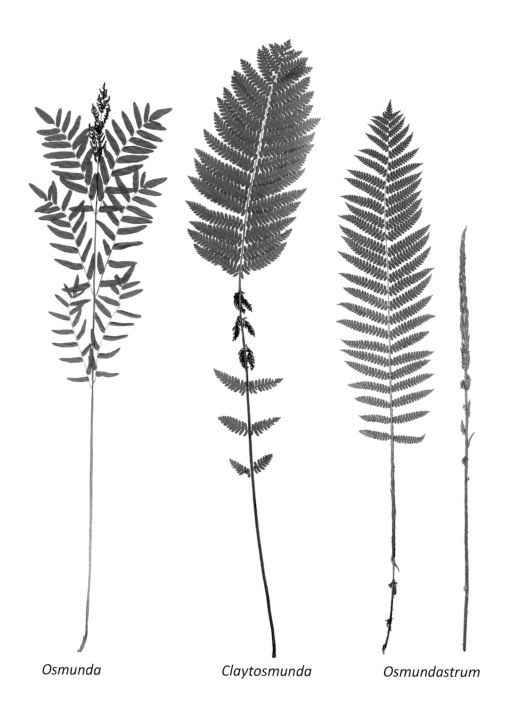

Osmunda   *Claytosmunda*   *Osmundastrum*

Chapter 6

The Fern Order Osmundales (Royal Ferns)

Worldwide, the order Osmundales consists of just one family, Osmundaceae. The family has a total of 6 genera and about 18 species. Minnesota has 3 genera, each with a single species.

The Osmundales is one of the smallest order of ferns but also one of the most ancient. Fossil representatives are known from the Permian nearly 300 million years ago. Members of this order are perhaps better known as fossils than as living plants.

Although species in the order Osmundales are not obviously different from other ferns, there are a number of unusual features that make them unique: all have massive rhizomes with a highly distinctive anatomy, sporangia that are not organized into sori, and spores that are green. All these features are biologically significant but too technical for easy use in the field. The 3 species in Minnesota are most easily recognized as large leafy ferns with sporangia set apart in a dedicated portion of the leaf, or in an entirely separate leaf. That last feature is also seen in the common, but unrelated, *Matteuccia struthiopteris* var. *pensylvanica* (ostrich fern, p. 250) and *Onoclea sensibilis* (sensitive fern, p. 258), which are in a different, more recently derived order, the Polypodiales. In reality, all these species are most easily learned individually by a few simple visual characteristics set out in the key.

KEY TO *OSMUNDALES*

1. Leaves 2-pinnate; ultimate segments of the leaf attached to the rachilla by short stalks; sporangia found on highly modified pinnae at the top of an otherwise ordinary green leaf
.... *Osmunda regalis* var. *spectabilis*

1. Leaves 1-pinnate-pinnatifid; ultimate segments of the leaf attached to the rachilla by broad, sessile bases; sporangia found on a few highly modified pinnae near the middle of an otherwise ordinary green leaf, or on a separate cinnamon-colored structure dedicated entirely to sporangia.

    2. Sporangia found on a few highly modified pinnae near the middle of an otherwise ordinary green leaf; margins of sterile pinnae glabrous; leaf tips somewhat rounded
    .... *Claytosmunda claytoniana*

    2. Sporangia found on a separate cinnamon-colored structure dedicated entirely to sporangia; margins of sterile pinnae lined with short crinkly hairs; leaf tips somewhat pointed.. *Osmundastrum cinnamomeum*

C. claytoniana (sterile)   *C. claytoniana* (fertile)

CLAYTOSMUNDA (INTERRUPTED FERN)

The genus *Claytosmunda* was established as a monotypic subgenus of *Osmunda* in 2005, then as a separate and distinct genus in 2016. It contains only one species, *C. claytoniana* (interrupted fern). It is native to the eastern half of North America and eastern Asia. Fossils of *C. claytoniana,* which are numerous, are known from the Triassic, more than 200 million years ago. It currently grows wild in Minnesota, essentially unchanged since the time of the dinosaurs.

The rhizomes are very thick and coarse, and heavily armored with persistent petiole bases. They grow slowly and are very long-lived, perhaps on the order of centuries. The common name comes from the fertile pinnae that bear the sporangia. These are highly modified pinnae that develop near the middle of an otherwise normal leaf. They seem to "interrupt" the symmetry of the leaf. Many leaves will not have any fertile pinnae; then they look surprisingly like the leaves of *Osmundastrum cinnamomeum* (cinnamon fern). The two species often grow together where their habitats overlap in low damp woods or at the edge of a marsh or wooded pond, but they are not known to hybridize.

Claytosmunda claytoniana (L.) Metzgar & Rouhan
Interrupted Fern

[*Osmunda claytoniana* L.]

RHIZOMES horizontal, massive, to 32+ cm long, infrequently branching. LEAVES partially dimorphic, 1-pinnate-pinnatifid, elliptic, 80–170 cm long, 15–40 cm wide, dying back before winter. PETIOLE 20–50 cm long, greenish or straw-colored, glabrous at maturity. STERILE PINNAE green, glabrous or sparsely hairy near base; ultimate segments 1–2 cm long, 0.6–1.2 cm wide; base broad; margins entire and glabrous; apex rounded; veins pinnate, lateral veins bifurcate. FERTILE PINNAE (when present) occurring near the middle of the leaf; consisting of size-reduced, non-green, sporangia-bearing segments. SORI AND INDUSIA absent. PHENOLOGY: First leaves (fertile and sterile) emerge in late April or early May in the south, 1 to 2 weeks later in the north. Fertile pinnae release spores from late May through June, and usually persist until late summer or autumn. All leaves die back before winter.

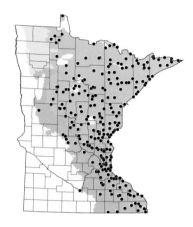

IDENTIFICATION: The fertile portion of this plant is near the middle of the leaf and consists of small, dark, oddly shaped pinnae; that is where the sporangia are. Cinnamon fern (*Osmundastrum cinnamomeum*, p. 158) is similar but dedicates an entire leaf to sporangia, which is cinnamon colored and very slender. If only sterile leaves are present, look at the margins of the leaf segments. Those of interrupted fern will be smooth, without hairs. Those of cinnamon fern will be lined with small, crinkly hairs. The rounded versus pointed feature of the leaf (dichotomy 2) is real but works best in side-by-side comparison. Sterile leaves of both species will look very much like those of ostrich fern (*Matteuccia struthiopteris* var. *pensylvanica*, p. 250). Resolve any uncertainty by checking the lateral veins of the leaf segments. Those of interrupted fern and cinnamon fern are bifurcated; those of ostrich fern are not.

NATURAL HISTORY: *Claytosmunda claytoniana* occurs in subboreal regions of eastern North America and eastern Asia. It is found commonly in mesic forests throughout the forested region of Minnesota, often on sheltered hillsides in well-drained, noncalcareous soil, and in similar situations on level terrain. Well-established populations sometimes persist in the open in utility corridors cut through forests. It is occasionally found in wet forests that might be called swamps, although it does not grow in permanently wet soils.

Abundant in ideal habitat, Washington County—July 23.

Large and proud, Sherburne County—May 27.

Fiddleheads—April 29.

Fertile pinnae ready to release spores—May 25.

O. regalis (sterile leaf)   *O. regalis* (fertile leaf)

OSMUNDA (ROYAL FERNS)

The genus *Osmunda,* as it is currently recognized by most fern biologists, consists of about 4 species. Only 1 species occurs in Minnesota, *O. regalis.* It is found in forested regions of the Americas as well as parts of Europe, Africa, and Asia. A number of varieties have been described for plants occurring in various parts of the world, but only one variety is recognized in North America. It is *O. regalis* var. *spectabilis.*

As in all Osmundales, the sporangia of *O. regalis* var. *spectabilis* are not organized into sori and are not covered by indusia. They are clustered in separate, small, exclusively sporangia-bearing pinnae at the very top of the leaf. In season, it may resemble a brown tassel. In that regard, it is unique among Minnesota ferns.

Osmunda regalis var. *spectabilis* (Willd.) Gray
Royal Fern

RHIZOMES horizontal or sometimes vertical, massive, to 20+ cm long, infrequently branched. **LEAVES** partially dimorphic, 2-pinnate, broadly ovate or elliptic, 60–130 cm long, 20–55 cm wide, dying back before winter. **PETIOLE** 20–65 cm long, glabrous at maturity. **STERILE PINNAE** glabrous; pinnules 3–5.5 cm long, 0.8–1.8 cm wide, short-stalked, oblong to oblong-lanceolate; base asymmetrically rounded to somewhat truncate; margins serrulate; apex blunt to rounded; veins pinnate, lateral veins bifurcate. **FERTILE PINNAE** restricted to the

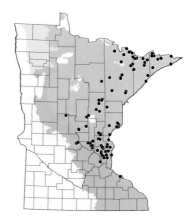

distal 10–30 cm of the leaf, greatly reduced in size, exclusively sporangia-bearing, brown except for the rachis and costae, withering by autumn. **SORI AND INDUSIA** absent. **PHENOLOGY:** Emerges aboveground from mid-May (south) to early June (north). Fertile portions develop and shed spores during the summer and soon wither. The remaining green portion of the leaf turns yellow and dies with the first hard frost of autumn.

IDENTIFICATION: Royal fern emerges from the ground late in the spring, perhaps not until June in the north. It grows erect, and at first is a ghoulish orange color, gradually becoming green. In any given year, most leaves will be sterile, meaning there will be no spore-producing structures at the top of the plant. Even without the brown tassel at the top, royal fern is quite distinctive. The pinnules of the leaf are rather large, widely spaced, and attach to the rachis with a short stalk. This makes the leaf 2-pinnate. The leaves can be quite large, often more than waist high, and nearly half that in width. They look much like the leaf of a black locust tree, or perhaps something in the pea family.

NATURAL HISTORY: The typical variety of *O. regalis* occurs in Africa and across Eurasia. Variety *spectabilis* is found in the eastern United States and adjacent parts of Canada, including Minnesota. In Minnesota, habitat requirements are closely linked to soil moisture and sunlight; it needs a fair amount of both. It is found most often along marshy or rocky lakeshores and riverbanks, as well as in forested swamps, shrubby marshes, and wet meadows. It is sometimes found on level uplands where the water table is near the surface, even though there may be no standing water nearby.

Brown sporangia, Sherburne County—
June 24.

In a wet meadow, Anoka County—June 14.

Sterile leaves still developing—May 24.

Fall leaves show venation—September 27.

O. cinnamomeum
(sterile leaf)

O. cinnamomeum
(fertile leaf)

OSMUNDASTRUM (CINNAMON FERN)

The genus *Osmundastrum* is believed to be composed of one extant species, *O. cinnamomeum*. It occurs widely in Minnesota and much of the Americas and Asia. It is given the common name cinnamon fern because the highly modified fertile leaf resembles a quill of cinnamon, as it is commonly sold in stores.

Fossil evidence indicates that *O. cinnamomeum* has been present, virtually unchanged, in North America for at least 70 million years and possibly as long as 180 million years.

Osmundastrum cinnamomeum (L.) C. Presl
Cinnamon Fern

[*Osmunda cinnamomea* L.]

RHIZOMES horizontal, massive, to 23+ cm long, infrequently branching. **LEAVES** dimorphic, 1-pinnate-pinnatifid, dying back before winter. **STERILE LEAVES** green, elliptic to narrowly elliptic, 50–160 cm long, 15–40 cm wide; pinnae with persistent tuft of crinkly hairs at base (on dorsal surface); ultimate segments 10–17 mm long, 6–8 mm wide, base broad, apex rounded or broadly angled, margins entire, lined with short crinkly hairs especially at sinuses; veins pinnate, lateral veins bifurcate. **PETIOLE** 20–35 cm long; initially covered with patches of loose, woolly, pale-brown felt that may persist into summer. **FERTILE LEAVES** 40–125 cm long, 2–5 cm wide, with greatly reduced pinnae; petiole and rachis with woolly, orangish-brown hairs; withering soon after spore release. **SORI AND INDUSIA** absent. **PHENOLOGY:** The first leaves emerge in May. Fertile leaves release spores in late May or June, then wither. Sterile leaves reach full size in late June and survive until winter.

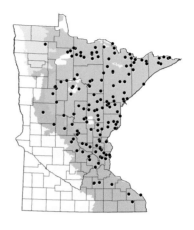

IDENTIFICATION: In late May and early June, the tall spire-like fertile leaves of cinnamon fern are very distinctive and stand out at a distance. The color is not seen elsewhere in the woods. This is the signature feature of cinnamon fern. By July, the fertile leaves will have released their spores and withered. They disintegrate rapidly and leave no trace. By then the green sterile leaves will have reached full size and remain green through autumn. The sterile leaves of cinnamon fern look very much like those of interrupted fern (*Claytosmunda claytoniana*, p. 150), except for the row of fine hairs along the margin of the leaf segments.

NATURAL HISTORY: *Osmundastrum cinnamomeum* occurs in eastern North America as well as Central and South America and Asia. In Minnesota, it is fairly common in forested wetlands, especially conifer swamps, black ash swamps, and alder swamps. Soils are often saturated but relatively firm. It does not seem to occur in uplands except where the water table is within reach of its roots. In such habitats, it may grow intermixed with interrupted fern. Although the two species are related, they do not seem to hybridize. The best habitats offer direct sunlight for a portion of the day, although continual shade is not an impediment.

Fiddleheads—May 24.

Spire-like cinnamon fronds bear the sporangia—June 15.

Lined with tiny, crinkly hairs

Tufts of hairs where rachilla meet rachis.

Marsilea vestita (x 0.65)

Azolla microphylla (x 3.5)

Chapter 7

The Fern Order Salviniales (Water Ferns)

Worldwide, the order Salviniales consists of just 2 families: Salviniaceae with 2 genera and about 20 species, and Marsileaceae with 3 genera and about 60 species. In Minnesota, we have just 2 species, one from each family.

Ferns in this order are often called water ferns, and they are deserving of the name. Despite their outward appearance and peculiar biology, these plants are thoroughly ferns, although very special ferns. They are the only heterosporous ferns, meaning they produce separate male spores (microspores) and female spores (megaspores), which result in separate male and female gametophytes. All other ferns are homosporous. They produce just one type of spore, which will germinate and produce a bisexual gametophyte, one that is both male and female.

Lycophytes in the orders Selaginellales (p. 57) and Isoetales (p. 49) are also heterosporous, but they developed heterospory independently of the ferns. The biological differences between homosporous and heterosporous plants are profound, but for field identification such knowledge is not needed; species can be identified by general appearance.

KEY TO GENERA OF SALVINIALES

1. Plants partially aquatic, rooted in soil beneath the water; leaves 2–4 cm across, each divided into 4 lobes, resembling a clover leaf. . . . . *Marsilea vestita*

1. Plants fully aquatic, free-floating on the surface of water; leaves about 1 mm across, not resembling a clover leaf. . . . . *Azolla microphylla*

mass of *Azolla microphylla* (x 4)

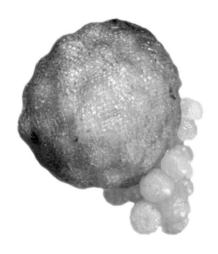

megasporocarp (x 20)

microsporocarp with microsporangia (x 20)

AZOLLA (MOSQUITO FERNS)

The genus *Azolla* is one of only 2 genera in the family Salviniaceae, the other being *Salvinia,* a largely tropical genus. There are believed to be 7–9 species of *Azolla* scattered around the world, with 3 species native to North America and 1 species known to occur in Minnesota. A second species, most often referred to as *A. caroliniana* (Carolina water fern), is sometimes said to have a range that includes Minnesota, but conclusive evidence of it occurring in Minnesota is elusive.

Individual *Azolla* plants are only a few centimeters long, yet they tend to clump together and form continuous mats on the surface of water if wind or current does not disperse them. When growing in full sunlight, particularly in late summer and fall, *Azolla* will produce reddish anthocyanin in the leaves, giving the whole colony a dull, brick-red or pinkish color. Few people have ever seen this phenomenon in Minnesota. The species, and its trademark display of red, is quite rare in the state.

The stems of *Azolla* readily break apart into fragments, which continue to grow at an astonishing rate. Entire ponds and muddy banks may be completely covered by a carpet of velvety green or pink in a matter of weeks if not days. Not only does *Azolla* reproduce by fragmentation; it also reproduces sexually. It is heterosporous, meaning it produces two kinds of spores: male spores, called microspores; and separate female spores, called megaspores. These are produced in structures called sporocarps on the undersides of the branches.

Azolla is reputed to be one of the fastest-growing plants in the world, and it has a secret. Each leaf has a specialized cavity that houses a nitrogen-fixing cyanobacterial symbiont (*Anabaena azollae*). It is passed down through generations of *Azolla* in the female spores, creating a "super-organism." This symbiotic relationship has existed since the Late Cretaceous Period, when dinosaurs roamed the earth. In other words, *Azolla* and *Anabaena* have not been apart for 70 million years.

Azolla microphylla Kaulf.
Mexican Mosquito Fern

[*A. mexicana* C. Presl]

PLANTS aquatic, free-floating and mat-forming on water surface but subsisting on mud or wet silt, dying back in winter (in Minnesota). **STEMS** horizontal, to about 3 cm long, extensively branching and readily fragmenting. **ROOTS** emerging singly, unbranched, descending 3–5 cm into the water column. **LEAVES** sessile, alternate, overlapping, 1–1.5 mm long; upper surface with stout, multicelled hairs. **MEGASPOROCARPS** roughly ovoid, 0.5–0.7 mm long, containing a single megasporangium that produces a single megaspore; megaspore spherical, pitted,

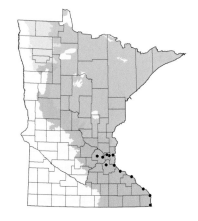

and sparsely covered with a few long filaments. **MICROSPOROCARPS** spherical, 1–2 mm across; containing up to 130 microsporangia, each producing 32 or 64 microspores. **PHENOLOGY:** Herbaceous portions are seasonal, thriving in summer, dying back before winter. Sporocarps are released in late autumn as plants senesce, and survive winter (perhaps as gametophytes) in bottom sediments.

IDENTIFICATION: *Azolla* floats on the surface of still water with roots that hang downward into the water column. It looks nothing like a fern but is, in fact, the world's smallest fern, about the size of a dime. A solitary *Azolla* might be mistaken for a duckweed (such as *Lemna* or *Spirodela*) or an aquatic liverwort (such as *Ricciacarpa*), or overlooked entirely. But growing en masse, they form a carpet of red or pink and are hard to miss.

NATURAL HISTORY: There appears to be just one species of *Azolla* in Minnesota; it is called *A. microphylla* or *A. mexicana*. It appears to be widespread in North America and beyond, but there is much uncertainty about the identification of specimens. It seems tolerant of the climate in southern Minnesota since it sometimes appears in the same pond for consecutive years, indicating a resident population. A suitable pond does not need to be pristine. In fact, inhabited ponds are often urban storm-water catchment basins, or filled with phosphorus-laden runoff from agricultural fields. It seems that *Azolla* could be found in just about any pond, but it rarely is. It can also be found in placid stretches of backwater along the Mississippi River. Normal river currents prevent plants from congregating in great numbers like they do in ponds. Instead, they will be scattered among emergent vegetation such as reeds and cattails and the floating leaves of water lilies.

A small pond, Ramsey County—
October 10.

With duckweed (*Lemna*)—September 1.

Turning color—October 10.

Underwater view of dangling roots.

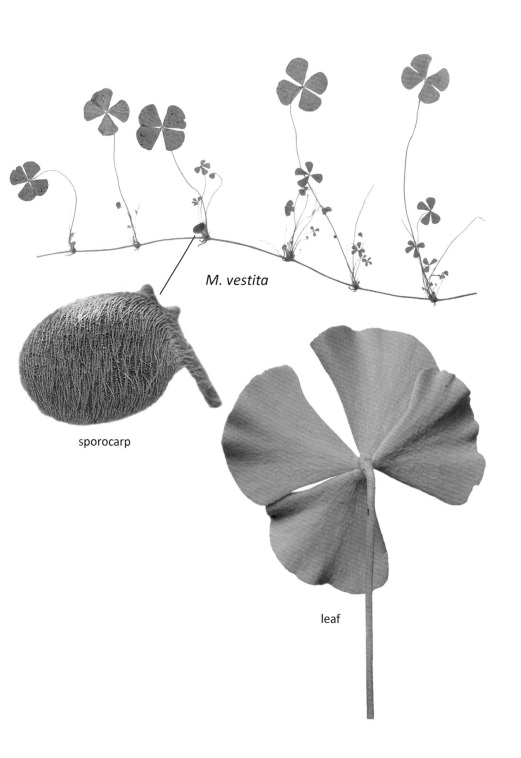

M. vestita

sporocarp

leaf

MARSILEA (WATER-CLOVERS)

The genus *Marsilea* is one of three genera in the family Marsileaceae. There are about 55 species of *Marsilea* in the world, occurring in tropical and temperate regions. Five species are native to the United States, and one species is native to Minnesota. It is *M. vestita* (hairy water-clover), which occupies the largest continuous range of any New World *Marsilea*.

Marsilea is one of the very few heterosporous ferns, meaning it produces separate male spores called microspores and much larger female spores called megaspores. Both are borne in a single structure called a sporocarp. Sporocarps are usually easy to find (in season). They are solid, dark objects about the size of a pea. They grow on a short stalk at the base of a leaf petiole.

Sporocarps are extremely durable, surviving years, even decades, of desiccation (up to 100 years, by some accounts). The sporocarp contains both the male and female spores, making it a self-contained dispersal unit, similar to the fruit of a seed plant. They can be transported long distances by migrating shorebirds.

There has been unfortunate and unnecessary confusion surrounding where this species has been found in Minnesota. In a 1986 monograph on the New World species of *Marsilea* (Johnson 1986), the author cited a specimen of *M. vestita* from 10 miles north of Crookston, Polk County, Minnesota. However, the label on the specimen clearly states Crookston, Nebraska, a small town in Cherry County. The monograph also cites a specimen of *M. vestita* from Roscoe, Stearns County, Minnesota. The label on that specimen indicates it was collected near Roscoe, Nebraska, a small town in Keith County. Another specimen was cited as having been collected near Gary in Norman County, Minnesota. That specimen has not been located yet, but it is provisionally discounted because no suitable habitat is known to occur in Norman County. All currently known and verified populations of *M. vestita* in Minnesota are represented on the following map.

Marsilea vestita Hook. & Grev.
Hairy Water-Clover

[*M. mucronata* A. Brown]

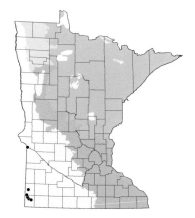

PLANTS semiaquatic, forming diffuse or dense colonies. **RHIZOMES** (stolons) superficial, slender, annual, branching freely, to 1+ m long. **ROOTS** arising at nodes. **LEAVES** arising singly or a few together at intervals of 1–5 cm, deciduous, floating or emergent; petioles filiform, 2–20 cm long, thinly hairy; blade palmately divided into 4 equal pinnae. **PINNAE** fan-shaped, to 1.9 cm long and 1.6 cm wide, thinly to densely hairy on one or both surfaces; margins entire; veins parallel with occasional cross-partitions. **SPOROCARP** elliptic in lateral view, to 7 mm long and 6 mm wide, about 2 mm thick; initially covered with coarse, appressed hairs, becoming smooth; stalk (peduncle) erect, unbranched, to 2.5 cm long, attached to the base of the petiole. **PHENOLOGY:** Leaves and sporocarps are produced in spring through fall (environmentally dependent).

IDENTIFICATION: Leaves of *M. vestita* are not complicated: just a petiole and a single blade with 4 nearly identical leaflets that spread widely during the day and fold together at night. They bear an uncanny resemblance to that of a true clover, especially the common white clover (*Trifolium repens*). But the leaves of *M. vestita* have stiff, coarse hairs on the surface, and parallel veins with no midvein. Leaves of true clover are hairless and have pinnate venation and a strong midvein.

NATURAL HISTORY: *Marsilea vestita* is found in southern and western parts of the United States and adjacent parts of Canada. In Minnesota, it is found on low, nearly level stretches of exposed crystalline bedrock within a prairie matrix in the southwest corner of the state. Suitable habitat will have shallow rainwater pools that develop in depressions of the rock and just as quickly evaporate, leaving behind a thin layer of sediment. Rhizomes of *M. vestita* will root in the sediments when they are underwater or only wet, and creep over bare rock and through vegetation. The pools may cycle between dry and wet multiple times during the course of a summer, a cycle to which *M. vestita* is supremely adapted. It is seemingly ephemeral, easy to find some years, and hard to find other years, depending on weather patterns. Yet it is known to have persisted at sites in Minnesota for at least 80 years and counting.

Leaves floating on rainwater pool, Rock County.

Leaves resemble those of true clover.

Sporocarps: the reproductive structure.

Rhizomes root in mud but can climb over rocks.

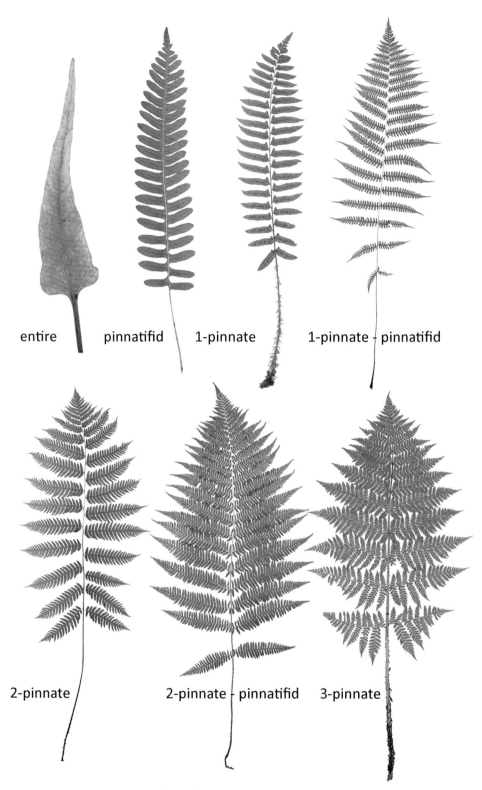

entire pinnatifid 1-pinnate 1-pinnate - pinnatifid

2-pinnate 2-pinnate - pinnatifid 3-pinnate

Examples of leaf structure in the *Polypodiales*

Chapter 8

The Fern Order Polypodiales ("True Ferns")

The order Polypodiales contains 6 suborders, 26 families, 253 genera, and an estimated 8,714 species, about 80 percent of extant ferns. It is the youngest of all the spore-bearing orders of plants, having arisen just 100 million years ago. Members of this order occur worldwide, with the highest diversity in the tropics.

In Minnesota, we have representatives of 3 suborders, 11 families, 19 genera, and 43 species (not counting named and unnamed hybrids). This amounts to only about half of 1 percent of the worldwide species diversity, which reflects Minnesota's decidedly nontropical climate.

Families in the order Polypodiales are not emphasized in this book because they are not easily recognized by beginners, and not totally agreed upon by experts. Genera seem to be a more logical place to start. Yet the technical differences that distinguish the genera are often rather obscure or cryptic, and sometimes require expert knowledge of fern anatomy and morphology, which is impractical for most users. For that reason, the following key attempts to use simple, easily seen characters as much as possible. Leaf structure is fundamental in this process, making pattern recognition paramount.

KEY TO GENERA OF POLYPODIALES

1. Leaf blades possessing minimal structural complexity: either undivided (without segments), pinnatifid (divided into segments that are connected at their base), or 1-pinnate (divided into one series of separate segments).
    2. Leaf blades undivided; tapering from the base to a long, whiplike tip
        . . . .*Asplenium rhizophyllum*, p. 184
    2. Leaf blades variously pinnatifid or 1-pinnate; not tapering to a long, whiplike tip.
        3. Leaf blades 1-pinnate (individual segments separate).
            4. Leaf blades 1–12 cm wide; individual pinnae appearing to be attached to the rachis off-center of an asymmetrical base.
                5. Leaf blades 6–12 cm wide; teeth along margins of pinnules tipped with spines
                    . . . . *Polystichum acrostichoides*, p. 278
                5. Leaf blades 1–5 cm wide; teeth not tipped with spines
                    . . . . *Asplenium* (in part), p. 181
            4. Leaf blades 10–22 cm wide; individual pinnae attached to the rachis at the center of a symmetrical base. . . . . *Homalosorus pycnocarpos*, p. 246
        3. Leaf blades predominately pinnatifid (individual segments connected by leaf tissue along the rachis and/or costae).

6. Leaf blades predominately 1-pinnatifid (may be pinnate at base); lateral veins forming a closed netlike pattern or veins obscurely pinnate; margins of segments lacking cilia.

    7. Leaves 2–7 cm wide; monomorphic (all leaves alike); primary segments entire, shallowly toothed, or scalloped; lateral veins obscurely pinnate . . . .*Polypodium virginianum,* p. 274

    7. Leaves 15–40 cm wide; dimorphic (sporangia-bearing leaves separate, and distinct in appearance); primary segments with broad, rounded lobes; lateral veins forming a closed netlike pattern . . . . *Onoclea sensibilis,* p. 258

6. Leaf blades 2-pinnatifid; veins clearly pinnate; margins of segments ciliate . . . . *Phegopteris* (in part), p. 267

1. Leaf blades possessing greater structural complexity: at a minimum 1-pinnate-pinnatifid (leaf divided into at least 2 series of increasingly smaller segments, the first series separate, the second series connected at their bases).

8. Rachis split at base, each branch curving away in a helicoid fashion, causing the leaf blade to appear circular or semicircular . . . . *Adiantum pedatum,* p. 178

8. Rachis intact, ± straight; the leaf blade ± elongate.

    9. Basal pinnae disproportionately large, each one 50–90 percent as large as the portion of the blade above the basal pinnae, giving the impression the leaf blade is divided into three separate and ± equal parts (ternate); blade roughly the shape of an equilateral triangle.

        10. Leaf blades 25–85 cm wide, stiff and leathery; margins of leaf segments inrolled and lined with small crinkly hairs. . *Pteridium aquilinum* subsp. *latiusculum,* p. 284

        10. Leaf blades 5–25 cm wide, thin and herbaceous; margins of leaf segments not inrolled; sori appearing as separate round dots on the underside of the segments; margins lacking hairs . . . .*Gymnocarpium,* p. 237

    9. Basal pinnae not disproportionately large, not giving the impression the leaf blade is divided into three separate parts; blade triangular or otherwise.

        11. Margins of pinnules or ultimate leaf segments toothed or scalloped.

            12. Leaves dimorphic; sori forming a continuous line along the margins of the fertile segments and covered by the inrolled margins (false indusium); small delicate rock ferns . . . .*Cryptogramma,* p. 193

            12. Leaves ± monomorphic; sori separate and distinct, each fully or partially covered by an individual indusium; ferns of various sizes and habitats.

                13. Sori elongate (oblong); lowest pair of pinnae often jutting forward and downward, out of plane with the other pinnae.

                    14. Leaf blades 1-pinnate-pinnatifid; margins of ultimate leaf segments with shallow teeth or crenations, or essentially entire; petiole and rachis with abundant slender segmented (multicellular) hairs . . . .*Deparia acrostichoides* (in part), p. 214

                    14. Leaf blades 2-pinnate or 2-pinnate-pinnatifid; margins of leaf segments deeply toothed or lobed; petiole and rachis with few if any slender segmented hairs . . . . *Athyrium filix-femina* var. *angustum,* p. 190

13. Sori ± round; lowest pair of pinnae in ± the same plane as the other pinnae.
    15. Teeth along the margins of the segments spine-tipped.
        16. Leaf blades tapering equally at both ends; petiole 2–8 cm long
        . . . . *Polystichum braunii*, p. 280
        16. Leaf blades tapered more toward the tip than the base; petiole
        > 8 cm long. . . . . *Dryopteris* (in part), p. 217
    15. Teeth not spine-tipped.
        17. Leaves with tiny, stalked glands (often most visible on the rachis and undersides of the costae).
            18. Leaf typically 40–90 cm long; the blade widest at the base, tapering gradually to a long, slender tip; bulblets often present on undersides of leaves. . . . . *Cystopteris bulbifera*, p. 200
            18. Leaf rarely exceeding 40 cm in length; the blade widest near the middle, tapering more abruptly to a shorter tip; bulblets lacking.
                19. Petiole and rachis with broad, orangish, papery scales; indusia ± entire, large and overlapping, persistent; dried leaves of previous season conspicuously retained on rhizome . . . . *Dryopteris fragrans*, p. 228
                19. Petiole and rachis with sparse, narrow scales or none at all; indusia jaggedly fringed, small and ephemeral; dried leaves of previous season not retained on rhizome
                . . . . *Woodsia* (in part), p. 291
        17. Leaves lacking stalked glands (or a few scattered glands on three species of *Cystopteris*).
            20. Petioles slender ≤ 1.5 mm wide, glabrous or with few scales/hairs at base; leaf blade 2-pinnate-pinnatifid, normally 3–12 cm wide. . . . . . . *Cystopteris* (in part), p. 199
            20. Petioles > 1.5 mm wide, lower portions with broad orange scales up to 10 mm long; leaf blade 1-pinnate-pinnatifid to 2-pinnate, normally 12–36 cm wide
            . . . . *Dryopteris* (in part), p. 217
11. Margins of pinnules or ultimate leaf segments entire or indistinctly scalloped.
    21. Comparatively small, slender rock plants, leaves usually < 30 cm long.
        22. Upper pinnae entire, elongated; pinnules (where present on lower pinnae) stiff and leathery, 0.5–4 cm long . . . . *Pellaea*, p. 261
        22. All pinnae divided or lobed; pinnules (or corresponding division of the pinnae) not stiff or leathery, less than 0.5 cm long.
            23. Leaf blade 2-pinnate-pinnatifid to 4-pinnate; lower surfaces uniformly and densely covered with long, tangled hairs; petiole not jointed
            . . . . *Myriopteris gracilis*, p. 254
            23. Leaf blade no more than 2-pinnate; lower surface with narrow, flattened scales or glabrous; petiole jointed . . . . *Woodsia* (in part), p. 291

21. Comparatively large, terrestrial or wetland plants, leaves typically > 30 cm long.

24. Leaves strongly dimorphic; the sporangia borne on separate slender, unexpanded leaves that becomes black and somewhat woody and persists through winter; lateral veins of leaf segments unbranched
.... *Matteuccia struthiopteris* var. *pensylvanica*, p. 250

24. Leaves essentially monomorphic; the sporangia borne on fully expanded green leaves not significantly different from sterile leaves; lateral veins of segments various.

25. Only the lowest pair of pinnae distinctly separate, the others connected by a narrow strip of leaf tissue that runs along the rachis; rachis and costae with broad brown scales
.... *Phegopteris* (in part), p. 267

25. All pinnae separate and distinct; rachis and costae with slender hairs but not broad brown scales.

26. Sori elongate; leaf blade 15–30 cm wide, tapered evenly to a narrow base; tips of pinnae attenuate; lateral veins of segments ending in hydathodes before reaching margins; found in upland forests .... *Deparia acrostichoides* (in part), p. 214

26. Sori ± round; leaf blade 6–18 cm wide, tapered very little to a broad base; tips of pinnae merely acute; lateral veins of segments ending at margins, hydathodes absent; found in wetland habitats
.... *Thelypteris palustris* var. *pubescens*, p. 288

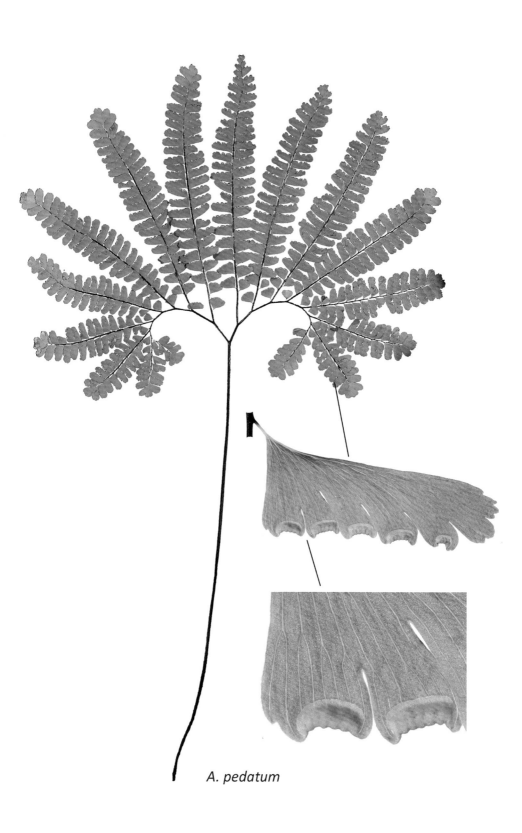

A. pedatum

ADIANTUM (MAIDENHAIR FERNS)

There are about 225 species of *Adiantum* worldwide. They are currently placed in the subfamily Vittarioideae of the family Pteridaceae. They occur mostly in the tropics and subtropics, in both the Old World and the New World. There are about 10 species in the United States, primarily occupying small ranges in the southern and western states. Only 1 species is found in Minnesota. It is the familiar northern maidenhair fern *Adiantum pedatum*.

The feature shared by all species of *Adiantum* is the false indusium. An indusium is typically a small flap of tissue covering each sori during matura-tion of the sporangia. In one form or another, it is present in most ferns. The shape and configuration of the indusium are often diagnostic of a genus. In the case of *Adiantum,* the indusium is called false because it is not a distinct struc-ture but rather the margin of the pinnule that folds inward to cover the sporan-gia. This "false indusium" is not unique to *Adiantum* but is unusual in the fern world.

Adiantum pedatum L.
Northern Maidenhair

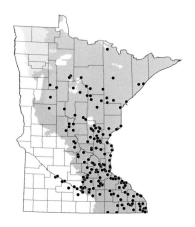

RHIZOMES horizontal, to 16+ cm long, branching often, covered with persistent golden-brown scales. **LEAVES** monomorphic, dying back in winter, 30–75 cm long. **PETIOLE** scaly at base, otherwise glabrous; dark brown to blackish, shiny, erect. **BLADE** split at base of rachis into 2 helically diverging branches forming a nearly circular blade, oriented horizontally, 2-pinnate, 15–30 cm long, 15–40 cm wide, glabrous. **PINNAE** each with 5–25 pairs of pinnules; rachis similar to petiole. **PINNULES** oblong to rectangular or triangular, 1–2.5 cm long and about half as wide; acroscopic margin shallowly to deeply incised; stalk 0.5–1.5 mm long, attached at the basiscopic corner. **VEINS** dichotomously forking. **INDUSIA** false, formed by the infolded margins of the pinnules. **PHENOLOGY:** The first leaves emerge in late April or May and reach full size in June. They die back with the first frost and release spores from dried leaves during the winter and the following spring.

IDENTIFICATION: Nothing else in Minnesota resembles *A. pedatum*. It is a common and familiar fern in the forests of Minnesota. The helicoid or spiraled structure of the leaf blade is unmistakable from almost any distance. It is composed of numerous delicate, closely spaced pinnules, each attached by a slender stalk. Leaves are often closely spaced and precisely interlayered. Each held horizontally to maximize exposure to the few rays of sunlight reaching the forest floor.

NATURAL HISTORY: *Adiantum pedatum* is believed to be limited to temperate forests in the eastern half of North America, but confusion with closely related species obscures many of the details of its occurrence. It is common in Minnesota, within certain habitat parameters. Favored habitats include heavily forested, north-facing hillsides, and steep, wooded ravines, under a canopy of sugar maple, basswood, oak, aspen, or ash. It also occurs in the interior of forests on level terrain, but the leaves are fragile and need to be sheltered from wind and direct sunlight. The rooting zone tends to be composed of loose, loamy, noncalcareous soil. The rhizomes are tough but do not run deep, so it also does well in thin, rock soil if moist and shaded. It does not do well where the soil becomes dry during periods of low rainfall.

On a hillside in Washington County—July 23.

Fiddlehead—April 17.

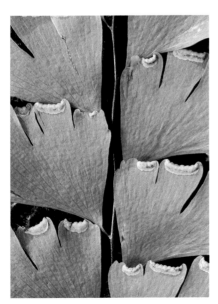

Margins of pinnules fold over sporangia—August 29.

Looking down from above, Winona County.

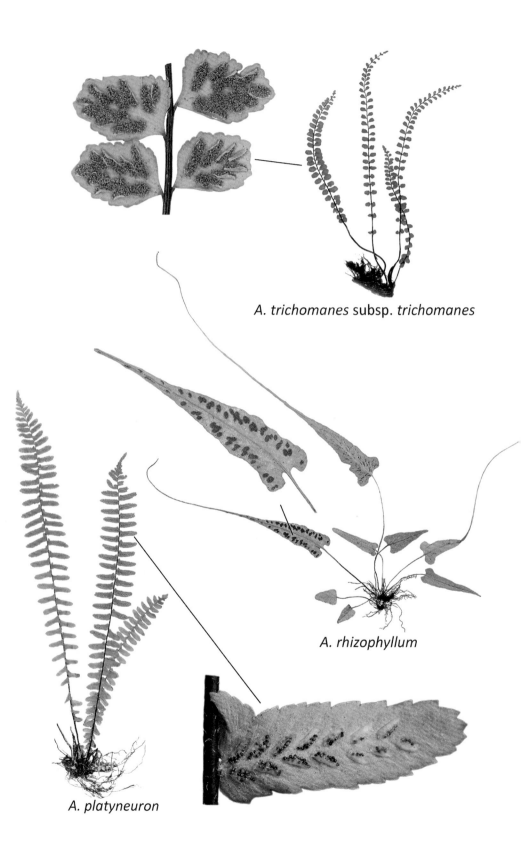

A. trichomanes subsp. *trichomanes*

A. rhizophyllum

A. platyneuron

ASPLENIUM (SPLEENWORTS)

The genus *Asplenium* is often considered the sole genus of the family Aspleniaceae. It is a huge and diverse genus with at least 700 species, making it the largest genus of ferns in the world. Most are tropical epiphytes or cliff dwellers, but in total they occupy a wide variety of habitats and climates, absent only from deserts, grasslands, and far northern regions. There are 28 species reported in the United States and 3 in Minnesota.

The spleenworts are notorious for hybridizing wherever two or more species occur together. However, the species of *Asplenium* that occur in Minnesota are generally kept separate by geography, rarity, and habitat and are not known to have formed hybrids within the state.

KEY TO *ASPLENIUM*

1. Leaf blades undivided, narrowly triangular in shape; tapering from the base to a long, slender, whiplike tip . . . . *A. rhizophyllum*

1. Leaf blades divided into numerous repeating segments (1-pinnate), linear in shape; tapering gradually at both ends.

   2. Individual leaf segments (pinnae) elongate, those near the middle of the leaf 10–30 mm long, 2–4.5 times longer than wide. . . . . *A. platyneuron*

   2. Individual leaf segments (pinnae) roundish or squarish, those near the middle of the leaf 4–9 mm long, 1–2 times longer than wide . . . . . . *A. trichomanes* subsp. *trichomanes*

Asplenium platyneuron (L.) Britton, Stearns & Poggenb.
Ebony Spleenwort

RHIZOMES horizontal, to about 5 cm long. **LEAVES** somewhat dimorphic; fertile leaves longer and more erect than sterile leaves. **PETIOLE** reddish brown to reddish black, shiny, 1–10 cm long, glabrous or sparsely hairy. **BLADE** ± linear, tapering gradually at both ends, 1-pinnate, 5–50 cm long, 2–5 cm wide; rachis similar to petiole. **PINNAE** in 15–50 pairs, oblong to narrowly and asymmetrically triangular; medial pinnae 10–30 mm long, 3–7 mm wide, 2–4.5 times longer than wide; margins serrate; apex acute to obtuse or rounded; base asymmetrically truncate, usually with

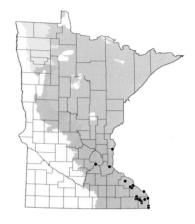

an auricle on the acroscopic (upper) side, attached by a minute stalk. **SORI** oblong, borne on veins. **INDUSIA** originating along one margin of the sori. **PHENOLOGY:** Fertile leaves die back in winter, sterile leaves survive winter, and spores are released in autumn and winter.

IDENTIFICATION: The fertile leaves of *A. platyneuron* stand stiffly erect. They are somewhat brittle and easily broken, and typically die back in the winter. The sterile leaves are greater in number, smaller, more pliable, and not nearly so erect. Most established plants will have both types of leaves. The closest look-alike in Minnesota is probably Christmas fern (*Polystichum acrostichoides,* p. 278). The teeth that line the pinnae of Christmas fern are tipped with slender spines; those of *A. platyneuron* are not.

NATURAL HISTORY: *Asplenium platyneuron* is found primarily in the eastern United States and adjacent parts of Canada, although several disjunct populations are known elsewhere on the continent, even in southern Africa. In Minnesota, it appears to be a habitat generalist within a forested context. But if we knew more about it, we might discover it has specialized skills. It is usually found in rather dry sandy soil in the shade of trees; often in secondary forests, including pine plantations; and sometimes in long-abandoned pastures reverting to forests. It has not been found in urban areas or places in active use. Perhaps more than most ferns, *A. platyneuron* is adept at establishing populations through long-range dispersal of its spores. Although small founder populations may not survive long, it does explain how plants seem to pop up in unexpected places. These solitary and isolated individuals might be called "fringe dwellers" or the advance guard.

On a steep hillside in Fillmore County—July 11.

Fertile leaves stand erect; tips curve.

Leaves are 1-pinnate.

Petiole is smooth, reddish black.

Sori on underside of leaf.

Asplenium rhizophyllum L.
Walking Fern

[*Camptosorus rhizophyllus* (L.) Link]

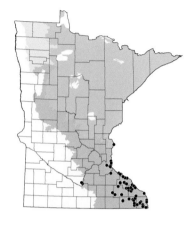

RHIZOMES short, seldom more than 1 or 2 cm long. **LEAVES** monomorphic, oriented horizontally, often hugging the mossy substrate; both sterile and fertile leaves remain green through winter. **PETIOLE** greenish or becoming reddish brown near base, 1–10 cm long; with small, dark, club-shaped glands distally. **BLADE** narrowly triangular, undivided, 2–30 cm long, 0.5–5 cm wide, leathery; surface with small, dark, club-shaped glands; base auriculate; margins entire to sinuate; apex attenuate and blunt-tipped or very long-attenuate and rooting at tip. **SORI** ± elongate, scattered somewhat irregularly over the lower surface of the blade. **INDUSIA** originating along one margin of sori. **PHENOLOGY:** Fertile leaves are produced through the summer and into the fall. They remain green over winter and release spores during the winter and the following spring.

IDENTIFICATION: The leaves of walking fern are quite distinctive but not particularly fernlike. They are rather thick and leathery, allowing them to survive winter and drought. The basic shape is roughly triangular, with ear-shaped lobes (auricles) at the base, and they tend to mingle freely with the mosses in their habitat. The tips of larger leaves are drawn out to a slender whiplike extension that will burrow into the moss and take root. Each new root crown will produce a new plant some distance from the parent plant. This is how it gained its common name, "walking fern." No other plant in Minnesota even remotely resembles walking fern.

NATURAL HISTORY: *Asplenium rhizophyllum* is endemic to the eastern and central United States and adjacent part of southeastern Canada. In Minnesota, it occurs almost exclusively on sheltered, moss-covered boulders and bedrock outcrops of dolomite and limestone. These are cool, damp habitats shaded by mature forest trees. Such conditions are found most often in steep, forested ravines and narrow, rock-walled stream valleys. It is highly specific to its habitat, and that habitat is rather rare in Minnesota. Under ideal conditions, *A. rhizophyllum* can be abundant, forming colonies 1–2 m across, which is an impressive achievement for such a small fern. Individual plants are evergreen but seem not to be long-lived, yet it reproduces by tip-rooting so quickly and reliably that colonies are semipermanent.

At home on a moss-covered boulder, Winona County—May 8.

Leaf tips grow long, then take root in mossy substrate—November 19.

Asplenium trichomanes subsp. *trichomanes* L.
Maidenhair Spleenwort

RHIZOMES compact, with short branches; older portions not retained. **LEAVES** monomorphic, evergreen or partially deciduous, erect or stiffly arching. **PETIOLES** reddish brown or blackish, shiny, 1–8 cm long, minutely winged, glabrous or with scattered hairs. **BLADES** linear, gradually tapered at both ends, 1-pinnate, 5–25 cm long, (0.7)1–2 cm wide, glabrous or with scattered hairs; rachis similar to petiole. **PINNAE** irregularly oblong to ovate or roundish; medial pinnae 4–9 mm long, 3–6 mm wide, 1–2 times longer than wide; margins with shallow blunt-tipped teeth or rounded crenulations; base truncate to broadly tapered, sometimes with a low, rounded auricle on the acroscopic side; attached basiscopically. **SORI** elongate, borne on veins. **INDUSIA** attached along one margin of sori. **PHENOLOGY:** Sporangia release spores in later summer, autumn, and over winter.

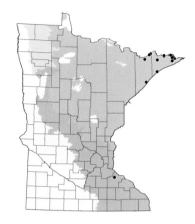

IDENTIFICATION: *Asplenium trichomanes* subsp. *trichomanes* L. is a rather delicate cliff fern with slender leaves that tend to radiate stiffly in random directions. Each leaf has numerous small, roundish pinnae evenly spaced along a dark rachis. By way of comparison, the pinnae of *A. platyneuron* are consistently larger and more elongated.

NATURAL HISTORY: Worldwide, *A. trichomanes* is said to be a common species with diploid, tetraploid, and hexaploid races. The races do not interbreed and are usually recognized as distinct subspecies. The subspecies that occurs in Minnesota is diploid and is designated subspecies *trichomanes*. It occurs mostly in mountainous areas of North America and Europe. It is considered quite rare in Minnesota—rare by way of having very specific and habitat-limited requirements. It occurs primarily in crevices of noncalcareous rock, including sandstone, basalt, diabase, and granite, most often on somewhat dryish east-facing cliffs and near the tops of associated talus. It is generally positioned so it is shaded for most of the day, thereby remaining cool and out of the desiccating sun. Suitable conditions tend to be in remote, hard-to-reach habitats in the northeast corner of the state. The record from Goodhue County in southeastern Minnesota is based on a specimen collected somewhere near Vasa in 1895. The exact location was never recorded. Repeated attempts to find this species in the vicinity of Vasa have failed, although much potential habitat remains to be explored.

Amid diabase talus.

Sheltered in rocky crevice, Lake County—
September 6.

OTTO GOCKMAN

MICHAEL D. LEE

Leaves are 1- pinnate, partially evergreen.

Sori borne on undersides of leaves.

A. filix-femina var. *angustum*

ATHYRIUM (LADY FERNS)

Athyrium is one of 5 genera in the family Athyriaceae. The genus has about 230 species and occurs worldwide. The greatest number of species occur in Asia. Only 2 species occur in the United States, and 1 in Minnesota.

Our species, *A. filix-femina,* is not so much a species as a species complex, which fern biologists have not entirely sorted out. Members of this complex are found in temperate forests over much of the Northern Hemisphere, including Europe and Asia and, by some interpretations, extending into South America. All answer to the common name "lady fern."

There are likely as many as 5 recognizable entities involved in the complex, each with overlapping geographies and morphologies. It seems likely that all the plants occurring in Minnesota belong to a single taxonomic entity, which is most often called *Athyrium filix-femina* var. *angustum* and referred to as "northern lady fern." *Athyrium filix-femina* var. *asplenioides* is the corresponding "southern lady fern," which is found in the southeastern United States.

Athyrium filix-femina var. *angustum* (Willd.) G. Lawson
Northern Lady Fern

[*A. filix-femina* var. *michauxii* (Spreng.) Farwell; *A. angustum* (Willd.) K. Presl]

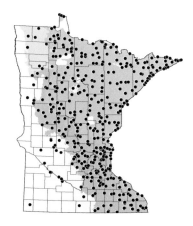

RHIZOMES horizontal, to 32 cm long, infrequently branching. **LEAVES** monomorphic, dying back by winter, 40–125 cm long, 15–45 cm wide. **PETIOLE** 15–50 cm long, predominately straw-colored with proximal portion dark red-brown or black; glabrous or with brown to dark-brown scales. **BLADE** ovate to elliptic-ovate, 2-pinnate to 2-pinnate-pinnatifid, broadest near or just below the middle, narrowed to base; apex short-acuminate. **PINNAE** sessile to short-stalked; apices acuminate. **RACHIS AND COSTAE** with tiny gland-tipped hairs. **PINNULES** incised to pinnatifid, margins toothed. **VEINS** pinnate. **SORI** oblong, ± straight, or curved at distal end, arranged along veins. **INDUSIA** attached laterally. **PHENOLOGY:** Typically appears aboveground in late April in the south, mid-May in the north; leaves reach full size in about a month, release spores in late summer and autumn, and die back with the first hard frost.

IDENTIFICATION: There are 3 ferns in Minnesota that look similar to *A. filix-femina* var. *angustum*: *Dryopteris carthusiana* (spinulose wood fern, p. 220), *Thelypteris palustris* var. *pubescens* (marsh fern, p. 288), and *Deparia acrostichoides* (silvery spleenwort, p. 214). Two characters, oblong sori and pointed teeth along the margins of the pinnae, should be enough to confirm *A. filix-femina* var. *angustum*. If sori are absent, then check that the leaf blade is 2-pinnate and the individual pinnae are widest at their middle, not at their base. Another useful character involves the lowest pair of pinnae. Those of *A. filix-femina* var. *angustum* are reduced in size and tend to jut downward and outward.

NATURAL HISTORY: *Athyrium filix-femina* var. *angustum* may be the most common and abundant fern in Minnesota. If there is only one species of fern in a forest, it is usually this one. It occurs in all types of upland forests and along the margins of swamp forests. It grows in a wide variety of soils, even calcareous soils and heavy clay soils, which surprisingly few ferns can do, and it can survive in deeper shade than almost any other fern. It is long-lived and tenacious, growing from a seemingly eternal rhizome that can reach the size of a man's forearm. It is also the most commonly chosen fern for urban Minnesota shade gardens.

A common and abundant fern, Sherburne County—June 24.

Leaf gets narrower toward base.

Fiddleheads—April 29.

Sori on undersides of leaves—August 29.

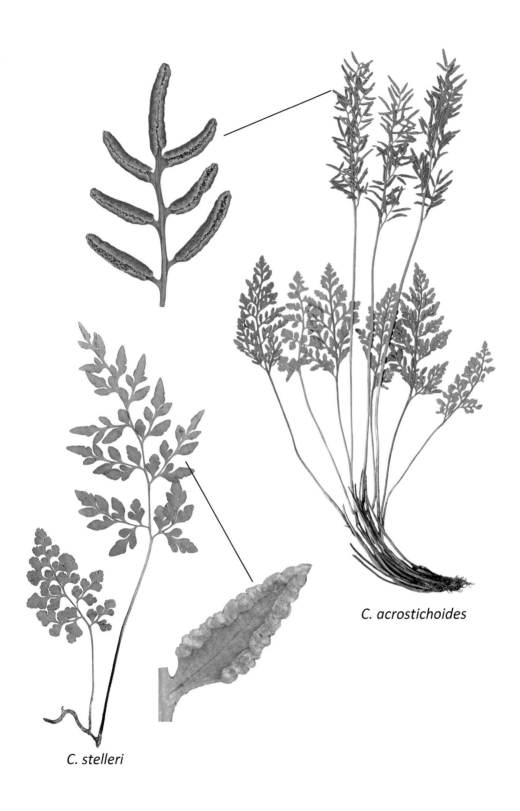

C. acrostichoides

C. stelleri

CRYPTOGRAMMA (ROCK-BRAKE FERNS)

There are believed to be about 10 species in the genus *Cryptogramma*. There is 1, or perhaps 2, species in Minnesota. Current taxonomic thinking places the genus in the superfamily Pteridaceae, which has 5 subfamilies, 53 genera, and an estimated 1,211 species worldwide.

All *Cryptogramma* ferns have dimorphic leaves. The fertile leaves are longer and stiffer than the sterile leaves and have differently shaped pinnae. The pinnae of fertile leaves have sori along their margins that are covered by the inrolled margin of the leaf. This forms a "false indusium." Fertile as well as sterile leaves of both species can be identified with the following key.

KEY TO *CRYPTOGRAMMA*

1. Leaves few (1–2 per rhizome), lacking hydathodes, spaced along a slender succulent rhizome 1–1.5 mm in diameter; petioles dark brown on the lower half, not persisting after the leaf senesces . . . . *C. stelleri*

1. Leaves many (3–10+ per rhizome), with conspicuous hydathodes (seen on upper surface near outer margins of ultimate segments), clustered at the tip of a stout woody rhizome > 2 mm in diameter; petioles straw-colored throughout, lower portions persisting on rhizome for several years. . . . . *C. acrostichoides*

Cryptogramma acrostichoides R. Brown
American Rock-Brake

[*C. crispa* subsp. *acrostichoides* (R. Brown) Hultén]

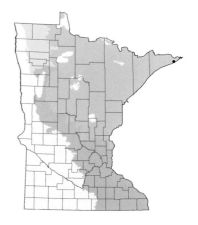

RHIZOMES horizontal, to about 7 cm long, > 2 mm wide, short-branched, woody, long-lived. **LEAVES** dimorphic, ± erect, glabrous; sterile leaves 5–25 cm long, remaining green through winter; fertile leaves 15–35 cm long, senescing in late summer. **PETIOLE** straw-colored, essentially glabrous; lower portions persisting on rhizome for several years. **BLADE** lanceolate to ovate-lanceolate, 2-pinnate to 2-pinnate-pinnatifid, with conspicuous hydathodes. **ULTIMATE SEGMENTS OF STERILE LEAVES** roundish to elongate, 3–10 mm long; margins toothed, scalloped, or lobed, broadly attached. **ULTIMATE SEGMENTS OF FERTILE LEAVES** linear, 5–15 mm long, 2–3 mm wide, narrowly attached. **INDUSIA** false, formed by the inrolled margins of the ultimate leaf segments. **PHENOLOGY:** Unknown for Minnesota.

IDENTIFICATION: *Cryptogramma acrostichoides* is larger and more robust than *C. stelleri* and differs in a few important features. The leaves arise from a coarse, woody rhizome that retains the lower portions of the petioles from year to year. The rhizome will likely be wedged deep within a rocky crevice and hard to see. Yet it is an important feature that should not be overlooked. Also, the fertile leaves of *C. acrostichoides* are larger and more prominent than those of *C. stelleri,* standing erect and turning brown by midsummer.

NATURAL HISTORY: *Cryptogramma acrostichoides* occurs primarily in mountainous and rocky habitats in western North America, with isolated occurrences as far east as Lake Superior. It tends to occur on dry, exposed, noncalcareous rocks, such as flat, open stretches of bedrock. Habitats in Minnesota will most likely be found along the shore of Lake Superior and be dominated by lichens in the genera *Cladonia* (reindeer lichens) and *Cetraria* (Iceland lichens). The actual evidence for *C. acrostichoides* occurring in Minnesota is rather sketchy. It is based on a specimen in the University of Michigan Herbarium, collected by J. C. Jones (probably around 1865) from "Farquhar Point," Minnesota. Potential habitat in that area has been searched, but *C. acrostichoides* was not found. However, it is known to occur on Isle Royale, in Lake Superior (Michigan), about 50 km (31 miles) to the east. Lacking any recent confirmation, it is far from certain that *C. acrostichoides* still occurs in Minnesota.

Among the lichen *Cladonia mitis* in early season, Isle Royale in Lake Superior.

Fertile leaves turn brown in late season, Isle Royale in Lake Superior.

Cryptogramma stelleri (S. G. Gmel.) Prantl
Slender Rock-Brake

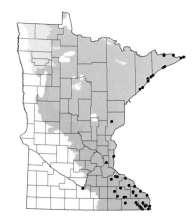

RHIZOMES horizontal, to about 8 cm long, 1–1.5 mm wide, succulent, brittle, smooth, frequently branching, living 1–2 years. LEAVES weakly dimorphic, glabrous, tending to droop, dying back in late summer; sterile leaves 7–20 cm long; fertile leaves 10–25 cm long. PETIOLE dark-brown proximally, greenish distally, essentially glabrous, not persisting on rhizome. BLADE lanceolate to ovate-lanceolate, 1-pinnate-pinnatifid to 2-pinnate-pinnatifid. ULTIMATE SEGMENTS OF STERILE LEAVES roundish to fan-shaped, 4–8 mm long and nearly as wide; outer margin scalloped; base broadly or narrowly attached. ULTIMATE SEGMENTS OF FERTILE LEAVES lanceolate to linear, 8–25 mm long, 2–4 mm wide, narrowly attached. INDUSIA false, formed by the inrolled margins of the ultimate segments. PHENOLOGY: The first leaves develop early, reach full size in May, release spores during summer, and senesce in late August or September, usually before the first frost.

IDENTIFICATION: The alternative common name "parsley fern" is not far off the mark; the leaves of *C. stelleri* do look something like parsley. They may seem rather flaccid and randomly constructed, and are always small. Fertile leaves are similar to the sterile leaves but somewhat larger. Also, fertile leaf segments are more elongated, and the margins are rolled inward to cover the sporangia. The leaves, both fertile and sterile, are structurally similar to those of the larger *C. acrostichoides* but differ in lacking hydathodes. The rhizome of *C. stelleri* is the biggest difference, being slender and succulent rather than coarse and woody.

NATURAL HISTORY: *Cryptogramma stelleri* is a fern of mountainous and cold temperate regions of North America and Eurasia. In Minnesota, it occurs in damp to wet crevices in sheltered rocks and cliffs, or sometimes in damp soil between rocks. The type of rock includes metamorphic and sedimentary rock such as dolomite, slate, sandstone, and occasionally limestone. Habitats are typically shaded by a north-facing aspect or overhanging trees. The best conditions are often found in steep, narrow stream gorges. The whole plant, including the fragile rhizome, might almost be considered ephemeral. No part of the rhizome lives more than a year or two, and it will have only 1 or 2 leaves. It persists by branching frequently and constantly burrowing deeper into the narrowest of fissures.

In a rocky gorge along the Zumbro River, Dodge County—June 9.

Fertile leaf (*left*); sterile leaf (*right*), Cook County—
July 31.

Underside of fertile leaf.

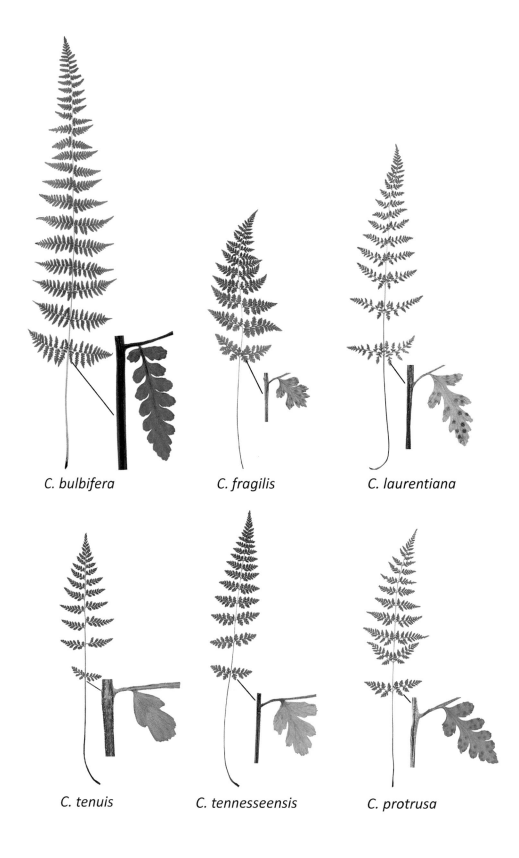

C. bulbifera

C. fragilis

C. laurentiana

C. tenuis

C. tennesseensis

C. protrusa

CYSTOPTERIS (BLADDER FERNS)

The genus *Cystopteris* is one of 3 genera in the family Cystopteridaceae. There are at least 26 species in the genus, with 9 species in the United States and 6 in Minnesota. They are renowned for their taxonomic complexity, reticulate evolution, and morphological variability. Putting a name on every specimen may not be practical.

KEY TO *CYSTOPTERIS*

1. Leaves widest at the lowest pair of pinnae; leaves often tapered to a long, drawn-out tip; tiny, unicelled, stalked glands often present and abundant; bulblets often present on rachis and/or costae; basal basiscopic pinnules of the lowest pair of pinnae 10–25 mm long and less than half as wide, each with 4–8 pairs of lateral lobes . . . . *C. bulbifera*

1. Leaves widest at the second or third pair of pinnae from the base; leaves tapered to an acute tip; tiny, unicelled, stalked glands few or absent; bulblets absent; basal basiscopic pinnules of the lowest pair of pinnae 4–15 mm long and more than half as wide, each with 1–4 pairs of lateral lobes.

    2. Tiny, unicelled, stalked glands usually present in low numbers on the indusia and/or rachis; aborted (malformed) bulblets sometimes present along the rachis.

        3. Spores 0.038–0.042 mm across; basal basiscopic pinnules of the lowest pair of pinnae 7–14 mm long (mostly 8–10 mm), 5–10 mm wide (mostly 6–8) . . . . *C. tennesseensis*

        3. Spores 0.049–0.06 mm across; basal basiscopic pinnules of the lowest pair of pinnae 10–20 mm long (mostly 11–14 mm) and 9–13 mm wide. . . . . *C. laurentiana*

    2. Tiny, unicelled, stalked glands absent (ignore any long, multicelled hairs); aborted bulblets absent.

        4. Stalk of basal pinnae 1.5–5 mm long; petiole pale green or straw-colored throughout; basal basiscopic pinnule of the lowest pair of pinnae 10–15 mm long, 7–14 mm wide; rhizome early and fast-growing, the tip often extending 1 cm beyond where the leaves are attached by the beginning of June, extending 2–4 cm by July . . . . *C. protrusa*

        4. Stalk of basal pinnae 0.2–1.5 mm long; petiole predominately brown (especially on proximal portion); basal basiscopic pinnule of the lowest pair of pinnae 4–12 mm long, 3–9 mm wide; rhizome not growing before June, and growing no more than 1–2 cm by the end of July.

            5. Basal basiscopic pinnule of the lowest pair of pinnae 3–7 mm wide, the 2 sides of the narrowly tapered base forming an angle of 70–100 degrees; pinnule margins typically scalloped or with rounded teeth; uppermost 10 cm of leaf blade tapered 30–40 degrees. . . . . *C. tenuis*

            5. Basal basiscopic pinnule of the lowest pair of pinnae 4.5–9 mm wide, the 2 sides of the broadly tapered base forming an angle of 100–180 degrees; pinnule margins typically with broadly pointed teeth; uppermost 10 cm of leaf blade tapered 40–50 degrees. . . . . *C. fragilis*

Cystopteris bulbifera (L.) Bernh.
Bulblet Bladder Fern

RHIZOMES horizontal, glabrous, to about 6 cm long, occasionally branched. **LEAVES** monomorphic, dying back in winter, to 90 cm long and 15 cm wide. **PETIOLE** reddish when young, becoming yellowish or straw-colored. **BLADE** 2-pinnate to 2-pinnate-pinnatifid, widest at the lowest pair of pinnae; apex acuminate to long-attenuate; often with very small, unicelled, stalked glands, especially along the rachis; bulblets often present near axils of upper pinnae. **PINNAE:** The lowest pair on stalks ≤ 0.5 mm long; margins of pinnules toothed. **BASAL BASISCOPIC PINNULES OF**

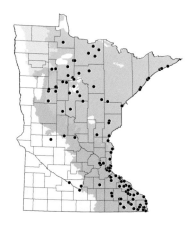

THE LOWEST PAIR OF PINNAE 10–25 mm long, 4–7 mm wide, with 4–8 pairs of lateral lobes; the 2 sides of the broadly tapered base forming an angle of 120–180 degrees. **VEINS** ending in small notches at margins of segments. **INDUSIA** hoodlike or bladderlike, usually glandular. **PHENOLOGY:** Leaves normally emerge in late April or early May in the south, somewhat later in the north, reach full size in July, shed spores and bulblets in late summer and autumn, and die back with the first frost.

IDENTIFICATION: The long, slender tip of well-developed leaves makes this species instantly recognizable. The eponymous bulblets are essentially tiny plants curled up in a ball about the size and color of a pea, but they are not always present. Two other features to check: the lowest pair of pinnae are consistently the largest pinnae of the leaf; and the basal basiscopic pinnules of the lowest pair of pinnae are long and narrow, with numerous lobes along the margins. Spotting the stalked glands (dichotomy 1) is the final check. They are usually present somewhere on the rachis, costae, midribs, or most consistently the indusia. But they are very small and not evenly distributed. It may take a while to find them.

NATURAL HISTORY: *Cystopteris bulbifera* is a forest species of eastern and central North America. In southeastern Minnesota, it is found mostly in steep, forested ravines, rocky north-facing wooded slopes, and mossy talus. It is especially abundant among sheltered limestone outcrops and ground-water seeps. The habitat in northern Minnesota is somewhat different. There it occurs most often in minerotrophic swamps under conifers or hardwoods. The terrain will be level, poorly drained, with no exposed bedrock, and often with rivulets of groundwater.

At the bottom of a rocky gorge, Cook County.

Note gradual taper of the leaves.

Dotted with tiny glands—
July 28.

Many sori and a single bulblet—July 30.

Cystopteris fragilis (L.) Bernh.
Fragile Bladder Fern

RHIZOMES horizontal, glabrous, to about
14 cm long, occasionally branched.
LEAVES monomorphic, dying back in
winter, to 45 cm long (mostly 20–30 cm)
and 11 cm wide (mostly 6–9 cm).
PETIOLE brown, or greenish to straw-
colored distally. BLADE 1- or 2-pinnate-
pinnatifid; usually widest at the third pair
of pinnae above the base, sometimes the
second; unicelled stalked glands absent;
bulblets absent. PINNAE: The lowest pair
on stalks ≤ 1.5 mm long; margins of
pinnules with somewhat regularly spaced
and shaped teeth. BASAL BASISCOPIC

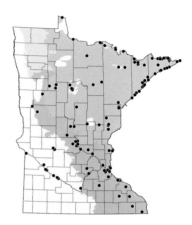

PINNULES OF THE LOWEST PAIR OF PINNAE 4–12 mm long, 4.5–9 mm wide, with
1–3 pairs of distinct lateral lobes; the 2 sides of the broadly tapered base forming
an angle of 100–180 degrees. VEINS ending in points and notches at margins of
pinnules. INDUSIA hoodlike or bladderlike, without glands. PHENOLOGY: Leaves
normally emerge in late April or early May in the south, somewhat later in the
north, and survive until winter, or sometimes senesce early in dry years; sporangia
develop in June.

IDENTIFICATION: Confusion between *C. fragilis* and *C. tenuis* can usually be
settled by looking at the shape of the basal basiscopic pinnule of the basal pinnae.
This is the first discrete segment of the leaf encountered while moving upward
along the petiole. There are actually two: one on either side of the petiole. It
will have either a broad, flattish bottom (*C. fragilis*) or a narrow, tapered bottom
(*C. tenuis*). Differences between *C. fragilis* and the rock-dwelling *C. tennesseensis*
and *C. laurentiana* are very slight, and may require a careful search for the
presence of tiny, stalked glands on the rachis or indusia (dichotomy 2).

NATURAL HISTORY: *Cystopteris fragilis* occurs throughout North America, including
boreal and arctic habitats. It also occurs in South America and Eurasia. Habitats
of *C. fragilis* in Minnesota are not so different from those of *C. tenuis,* and the two
species sometimes grow side by side. It is usually found in forested ravines, on
steep, shaded riverbanks and well-stabilized and sheltered roadcuts. It seems to
always be in the shade of trees and usually rooted in soil rather than rock. The
exception seems to be in the northeast, where it is closely associated with bedrock-
influenced habitats.

Growing among mosses on a sheltered cliff face, Cook County—July 31.

Basal pinnules of basal pinnae.

At peak development—August 1.

Cystopteris laurentiana (Weath.) Blasdell
Laurentian Bladder Fern

RHIZOMES horizontal, glabrous, to about
7 cm long, branching occasionally.
LEAVES monomorphic, to 48 cm long
(mostly 30–40 cm) and 12 cm wide (mostly
8–10 cm). **PETIOLE** usually some shade of
brown. **BLADE** narrowly ovate (sides
somewhat convex), 2-pinnate to
2-pinnate-pinnatifid, widest at the second
or third pair of pinnae from the base; apex
narrowly acute to short-attenuate; rachis
and costae often with very small,
unicellular, stalked glands; bulblets absent
(rarely small and misshapen abortive
bulblets seen along rachis). **PINNULE**
margins with variable but usually recognizable teeth. **BASAL BASISCOPIC**
PINNULES OF THE LOWEST PAIR OF PINNAE 10–20 mm long (mostly 11–14 mm),
9–13 mm wide, with 3–4 pairs of lateral lobes; the 2 sides of the broadly tapered
base forming an angle of 90–140 degrees. **INDUSIA** hoodlike or bladderlike, often
glandular. **PHENOLOGY:** Leaves normally emerge in late April or early May and die
back before winter.

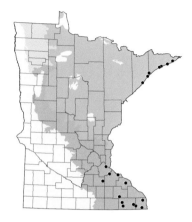

IDENTIFICATION: It can be tedious, but look carefully for tiny, stalked glands;
there are usually a few on the indusia or the rachis. Also look for abortive bulblets.
They are only 1 or 2 mm across, with numerous spidery arms. They might be
mistaken for a very small insect nest. If either glands or abortive bulblets are
found, it will lead to *C. laurentiana* and *C. tennesseensis*. Unfortunately, these two
species do not separate well, a problem for experts and beginners alike. A more
common look-alike is *C. fragilis*. It lacks glands and abortive bulblets but is
otherwise similar to *C. laurentiana*. The basal basiscopic pinnules of the lowest
pair of pinnae of *C. laurentiana* are larger and more deeply lobed than those of
C. fragilis. They are usually 10–20 mm long and 9–13 mm wide, with 3–4 pairs of
lateral lobes.

NATURAL HISTORY: *Cystopteris laurentiana* inhabits a rather restricted region in
north-central and northeastern portions of the United States and adjacent Canada.
It appears to be rare in Minnesota, but field recognition is so difficult it is hard to
know for sure. It occurs on sheltered rock ledges and crevices in vertical exposures
of sedimentary bedrock. It might also be found on mossy talus and in moist soil
among rocks, always within a forested environment.

On a sheltered rock ledge in a deep gorge, Cook County—August 1.

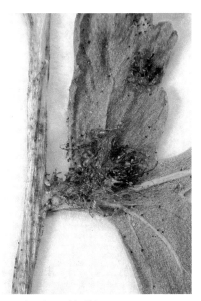

An aborted bulblet.

Leaves taper evenly to the tip.

Cystopteris protrusa (Weath.) Blasdell
Lowland Bladder fern

[*C. fragilis* var. *protrusa* Weatherby]

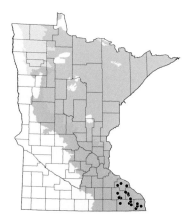

RHIZOMES horizontal, glabrous or with
sparse yellow hairs, to about 20 cm long,
occasionally branched. **LEAVES**
monomorphic, dying back in winter, to 46
cm long (mostly 25–35 cm) and 10 cm
wide (mostly 6–9 cm). **PETIOLE** pale green
or straw-colored. **BLADE** 1- or 2-pinnate-
pinnatifid; usually widest at the third
pinnae pair above the base, sometimes at
the second pair; single-celled stalked
glands absent; bulblets absent. **PINNAE:**
The lowest pair of pinnae on stalks ≥ 1.5
mm long; margins of pinnules with
somewhat regularly spaced pointed teeth.

BASAL BASISCOPIC PINNULES OF THE LOWEST PAIR OF PINNAE 10–15 mm long,
7–14 mm wide, with 1–4 lateral lobes; the 2 sides of the broadly tapered base
forming an angle of 90–140 degrees. **VEINS** primarily ending in points, sometimes
notches. **INDUSIA** hoodlike or bladderlike; lacking glands. **PHENOLOGY:** Leaves
normally emerge in late April or early May and survive until winter, or sometimes
senesce early in dry years. Sporangia develop in June.

IDENTIFICATION: The best character to separate *C. protrusa* from all other
Minnesota *Cystopteris* is the stalk that attaches the lowermost pinnae to the rachis.
It will be at least 1.5 mm long, and often 3–5 mm. The corresponding stalk on
other Minnesota *Cystopteris* will be no more than 1.5 mm long. The petioles of
C. protrusa are typically pale green, yellowish, or straw-colored, although
occasionally some will look brown near the base. The epithet *protrusa* refers to
the rhizome, which grows longer and more quickly than that of other *Cystopteris,*
causing it to protrude beyond where the leaves are attached. The fast-growing
rhizome can lead to the formation of clonal patches but not large ones.

NATURAL HISTORY: *Cystopteris protrusa* is endemic to portions of the east-central
United States. It is rather uncommon in Minnesota, found in mesic hardwood
forests in the Blufflands region of the southeastern counties. It seems to prefer
shade and loamy soil, on moderate hillsides or bottom land along streams—
but not active floodplains, and not directly on rocks. Reports of *C. protrusa*
growing farther northwest in Minnesota than is indicated on the accompanying
map are based on misidentified herbarium specimens.

In a mesic forest, Wabasha County—June 7.

A typical leaf of C. *protrusa*.

The growing tip of the rhizome—
June 15.

Basal pinnules of the basal pinnae.

Cystopteris tennesseensis Shaver
Tennessee Bladder Fern

RHIZOMES horizontal, glabrous, to about 8 cm long, branching occasionally. **LEAVES** monomorphic, to 50 cm long (mostly 25–40 cm) and 11 cm wide. **PETIOLE** some shade of brown, or straw-colored distally. **BLADE** narrowly deltate to lanceolate (margins straight), 1-pinnate-2-pinnatifid to 2-pinnate, widest at the first or more often the second pair of pinnae above the lowest, apex narrowly acute to short-attenuate; rachis and costae often sparsely glandular; bulblets absent (rarely small and misshapen abortive bulblets seen along rachis). **PINNAE:** The lowest

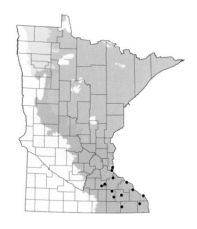

pinnae on stalks ≤ 1.5 mm long; pinnule margins with variable but usually recognizable teeth. **BASAL BASISCOPIC PINNULES OF THE LOWEST PAIR OF PINNAE** 7–14 mm long (mostly 8–10 mm), 5–10 mm wide (mostly 6–8), with 3–4 pairs of lateral lobes; the 2 sides of the broadly tapered base forming an angle of 90–140 degrees. **VEINS** ending either in points or notches or both. **INDUSIA** hoodlike or bladderlike, often with a few glands. **PHENOLOGY:** Leaves normally emerge in late April or early May and die back by winter.

IDENTIFICATION: Most people who are botanically inclined get to dichotomy 2 in the key and then get stuck. At that point, look closely for very small, stalked glands, especially on the indusia and rachis, and for abortive bulblets along the rachis. If neither can be found, then look again more carefully. They probably will not be found without a second look. If even one gland or one hint of an abortive bulblet is found, then it is down to *C. tennesseensis* or *C. laurentiana*. Most differences between the two species reside at the molecular level, which is not to say differences are not real, just hard to see, even for a specialist.

NATURAL HISTORY: *Cystopteris tennesseensis* is endemic to the east-central United States. It is rare in Minnesota, or at least it is very hard to find and identify. It is associated primarily with exposures of sandstone and limestone bedrock within a forest setting. These are most often found in deep gorges and forested ravines where there are crevices and shallow ledges on vertical rock faces. Although bedrock is the primary habitat, it has also been found rooted in soil on sheltered north-facing forested slopes but never far from bedrock.

C. tennesseensis looks very much like *C. fragilis* and *C. laurentiana.*

In a forested ravine, Washington County—June 30.

Aborted bulblet.

Stalked glands are present but very small and sparse.

Cystopteris tenuis (Michx.) Desv.
Upland Bladder Fern

[*C. fragilis* var. *mackayi* G. Lawson]

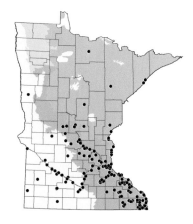

RHIZOMES horizontal, glabrous, to about 10 cm long, occasionally branched. **LEAVES** monomorphic, dying back by winter, to 45 cm long (mostly 15–35 cm) and 10 cm wide (mostly 4–7 cm). **PETIOLE** golden brown on proximal ⅔, greenish or straw-colored on distal ⅓. **BLADE** 1- to 2-pinnate-pinnatifid, usually widest at the third pair of pinnae above the base; unicelled stalked glands absent; bulblets absent. **PINNAE:** The lowest pair on stalks ≤ 1.5 mm long; pinnule margins with irregularly rounded or blunt teeth. **BASAL BASISCOPIC PINNULES OF THE LOWEST PAIR OF PINNAE** 4–12 mm long, 3–7 mm wide, with 1–3 distinct lateral lobes per side; the 2 sides of the narrowly tapered base forming an angle of 70–100 degrees. **VEINS** ending in both points and notches. **INDUSIA** hoodlike or bladderlike, without glands. **PHENOLOGY:** Leaves normally emerge in late April or early May in the south, somewhat later in the north; leaves survive until winter or sometimes senesce early (weather dependent).

IDENTIFICATION: *Cystopteris tenuis* is generally smaller than the other *Cystopteris* and more slender, but there is considerable overlap. The most useful character relates to the basal basiscopic pinnules of the lowest pair of pinnae (dichotomy 5). They are small, with only 1 or 2 (sometimes 3) pairs of lateral lobes, and the base is tapered, not flat. This works against all species of *Cystopteris* that occur in Minnesota. But the pinnules can be variable. There can even be differences between leaves that come from the same rhizome. Look at pinnules from as many leaves as possible before coming to a conclusion.

NATURAL HISTORY: *Cystopteris tenuis* is found mostly in the eastern and central United States and adjacent parts of Canada. It is a species of temperate and subboreal habitats and is relatively common in Minnesota. It is usually found rooted in soil in forested ravines, on high stream banks, and on moderate to steep slopes, often among exposed tree roots. Soils are usually moist or somewhat dry and range from coarse to fine-textured. The soil surface is sometimes bare, or more often moss-covered. It is also found on cool, shaded cliffs, bedrock exposures, and crevices of large boulders, but always under a forest canopy.

The smallest and simplest of the Minnesota *Cystopteris*, and the most common.

On a steep, mossy slope, Winona County.

Basal pinnules of basal pinnae.

D. acrostichoides

DEPARIA (FALSE SPLEENWORTS)

The genus *Deparia* has about 70 species and is 1 of 3 genera in the family Athyriaceae. They inhabit terrestrial forests in tropical, subtropical, and temperate regions of the world, with the greatest number in Asia. Some species are also found in Africa, Australia, New Zealand, and several Pacific and Indian Ocean islands. Only 1 species is native to North America. It is the familiar *D. acrostichoides* (silvery spleenwort). It is found in forests in the eastern half of the continent, reaching Minnesota at the western limit of its range. It has at various times been placed in the closely related genera *Athyrium* and *Diplazium*. But botanists now believe it is a better fit in *Deparia*.

Deparia acrostichoides (Swartz) Kato
Silvery Spleenwort

[*Athyrium thelypterioides* (Michaux) Desvaux; *Diplazium acrostichoides* (Swartz) Butters]

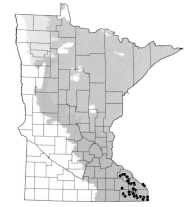

RHIZOMES horizontal, to 30 cm long, branching occasionally. **LEAVES** essentially monomorphic, dying back in winter, 30–90 cm long, 15–30 cm wide. **PETIOLE** 10–40 cm long; straw-colored distally, dark red-brown proximally, with segmented hairs and light-brown lanceolate scales (often sparse). **BLADE** narrowly elliptic to lanceolate, widest near or just below the middle, 1-pinnate-pinnatifid, 30–80 cm long, narrowed at base, acuminate at apex. **PINNAE SEGMENTS** oblong; margins shallowly scalloped to nearly entire; apex round; base broad. **RACHIS AND COSTAE** with segmented hairs. **VEINS** pinnate; lateral veins simple or 1-forked, ending in hydathodes. **SORI** oblong, straight or curved, attached along veins. **INDUSIA** entire. **PHENOLOGY:** Sterile leaves normally emerge in early May and reach full size in early June. Fertile leaves emerge in June, reach maturity in July and August, and release spores before winter.

IDENTIFICATION: In general appearance, *D. acrostichoides* looks much like *Athyrium filix-femina* var. *angustum* (northern lady fern, p. 190), which differs in being 2-pinnate. This means the second series of leaf divisions go all the way to the costae, creating stand-alone segments (pinnules) that are not connected to the other segments. The leaf of *D. acrostichoides* is 1-pinnate-pinnatifid, meaning the corresponding divisions go almost to the costae but not quite, leaving all the segments connected to each other by a narrow strip of leaf tissue that runs along the costae. Another common look-alike is *Thelypteris palustris* var. *pubescens* (eastern marsh fern, p. 288), which has a narrower leaf blade and will be found in wetland habitats. The "silvery" part of the name can be attributed to long, segmented hairs on the petiole.

NATURAL HISTORY: *Deparia acrostichoides* occurs in temperate parts of the eastern United States, adjacent Canada, and possibly Eurasia. In Minnesota, it is found in mesic deciduous forests, usually under a canopy of sugar maple, basswood, or red oak. It is most often on north-facing slopes of stream valleys, where it is sheltered from direct sunlight. Soils are typically moist loam, sometimes with a component of clay. All current records are from the bluff country in the extreme southeastern counties, but there are indications it may also occur in similar habitats along the St. Croix River in the east-central counties.

Compare with *Athyrium filix-femina* var. *angustum*.

In a mesic hardwood forest, Winona County—June 16.

Check for white, segmented hairs on rachis.

Oblong sori; connected leaf segments—July 28.

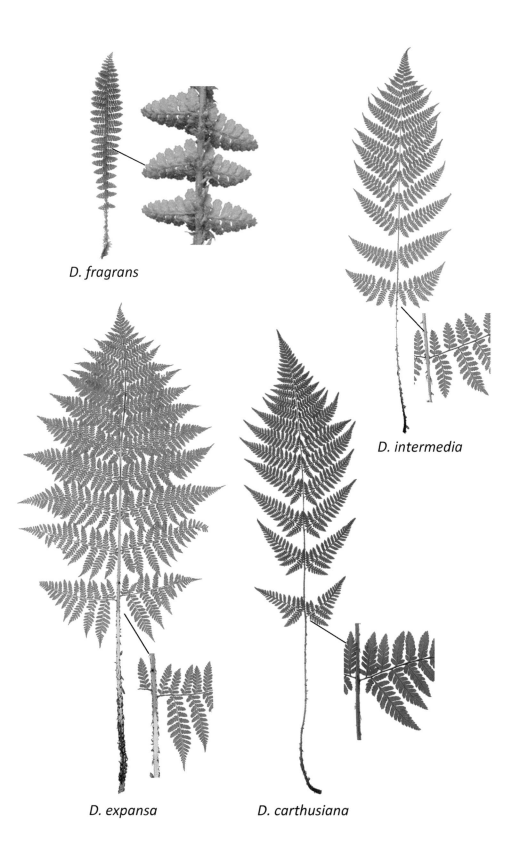

D. fragrans

D. intermedia

D. expansa

D. carthusiana

DRYOPTERIS (WOOD FERNS)

The genus *Dryopteris* is in the superfamily Dryopteridaceae, which, as currently circumscribed, has 3 subfamilies, 26 genera, and an estimated 2,115 species. There are about 400 species in the genus *Dryopteris*. They are mostly Asiatic but also found in Europe, Africa, and the Americas. There are 14 species of *Dryopteris* in North America and 8 in Minnesota.

Hybrids between the species of *Dryopteris* do occur in Minnesota, but they are not common, or at least not commonly recognized, and all are sterile. Hybrids can occur between any 2 species when they are growing closely together. They can usually be identified by their intermediate characters. Only 2 named hybrids have been positively identified in Minnesota, but there are almost certainly others.

KEY TO THE NONHYBRID *DRYOPTERIS*

1. Leaves 6–30 cm long (including the petiole) and 1–6 cm wide; rachis with tiny, yellowish stalked glands . . . . *D. fragrans*

1. Leaves 25–120 cm long (including the petiole) and 7–40 cm wide; rachis sometimes with tiny, clear, stalked glands (*D. intermedia*) but more often without glands.

  2. Leaf blades 1-pinnate-pinnatifid to 2-pinnate; as a result the secondary leaf segments sessile or on broadly attached bases.

    3. Teeth along the margins of the leaf segments spine-tipped.

      4. Each of the lowest pinnae with 3–10 pairs of distinct segments; a typical fully developed leaf 7–13 cm wide. . . . . *D. cristata*

      4. Each of the lowest pinnae with 12–25 pairs of distinct segments; a typical fully developed leaf 20–40 cm wide. . . . . *D. goldieana*

    3. Teeth along the margins of the leaf segments not spine-tipped.

      5. Sori attached at sinuses very near the margins of leaf segments; petiole comprising ¼–⅓ of the leaf; lowermost pinnae ¾ to fully as long as the middle pinnae . . . . *D. marginalis*

      5. Sori attached midway between the margin and the middle of leaf segments; petiole usually comprise less than ¼ of the leaf; lowermost pinnae only ⅓ to ¾ as long as the middle pinnae . . . . *D. filix-mas*

  2. Leaf blades 2-pinnate-pinnatifid to 3-pinnate-pinnatifid; as a result the secondary segments stalked or on narrowly attached bases.

    6. Basal basiscopic pinnules of the basal pinnae shorter than the adjacent pinnules; rachis with very small, clear, stalked glands . . . . *D. intermedia*

    6. Basal basiscopic pinnules of the basal pinnae longer than the adjacent pinnules; rachis lacking glands.

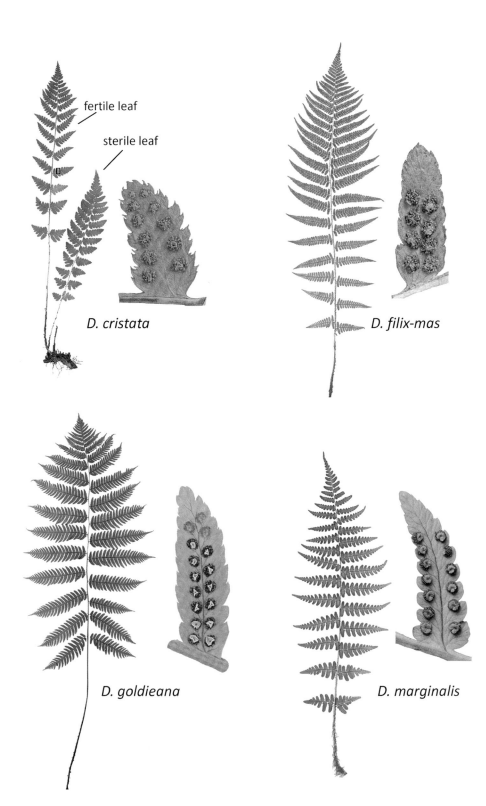

fertile leaf

sterile leaf

D. cristata

D. filix-mas

D. goldieana

D. marginalis

7. Basal basiscopic pinnules of the basal pinnae often attached closer to the basal acroscopic pinnule than to the second acroscopic pinnule, and are perhaps ⅓ wider; leaves 2-pinnate-pinnatifid to 3-pinnate; pinnae at the middle of the leaf blade usually widest at the base . . . . *D. carthusiana*

7. Basal basiscopic pinnules of the basal pinnae attached closer to the second acroscopic pinnule than to the basal acroscopic pinnule, and are about twice as wide; leaves 3-pinnate to 3-pinnate-pinnatifid; middle pinnae usually widest at the middle . . . . *D. expansa*

STERILE HYBRIDS OF *DRYOPTERIS* KNOWN TO OCCUR IN MINNESOTA

D. ×triploidea Wherry is the hybrid between *D. carthusiana* and *D. intermedia*, two very similar-looking species. The features of the hybrid are intermediate between the 2 parents but are not clearly demarcated. The rachis of the hybrid should have at least a few glands, which is a character usually attributed exclusively to *D. intermedia*. The hybrid probably occurs wherever large populations of both parent species intermingle, although it can be very difficult to get a positive identification of suspected hybrids.

   D. ×uliginosa (A. Braun) Druce is the hybrid between *D. carthusiana* and *D. cristata*. It can be found occasionally wherever large populations of both species intermingle or grow in close proximity. Since the parent species look so different from each other, the hybrid is usually easy to identify by the intermediate shape of the leaf.

Dryopteris carthusiana (Vill.) H. P. Fuchs
Spinulose Wood Fern

[*D. spinulosa* (O. F. Mueller) Watt]

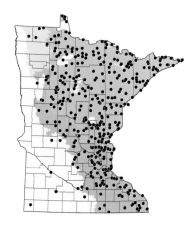

RHIZOMES horizontal, to about 15 cm long, branching occasionally. **LEAVES** monomorphic, inconsistently evergreen, 30–110 cm long, 10–30 cm wide. **PETIOLE** with tan scales, especially near base; lacking glands. **BLADE** light green, 2-pinnate-pinnatifid to 3-pinnate, lanceolate to oblanceolate or narrowly triangular, lacking glands. **PINNAE** usually widest at the base, tapering to the tip. **PINNULES:** Basal basiscopic pinnules of basal pinnae larger than adjacent basiscopic pinnules; margins with spine-tipped teeth. **SORI** attached on veins away from the margins. **INDUSIA** roundish with a narrow sinus, 0.3–0.8 mm across, lacking glands. **PHENOLOGY:** Leaves typically emerge in early May in the south, about 2 weeks later in the north, and release spores in July through autumn and sometimes into winter.

IDENTIFICATION: *Dryopteris carthusiana* is most similar to *D. intermedia,* except it has none of the glands that are so abundant on *D. intermedia.* There is also a critical difference in a single pinnule—the lower-most and inner-most segment of the leaf. It is long in the case of *D. carthusiana* and short in the case of *D. intermedia.* It is perhaps more common for *D. carthusiana* to be confused with the ubiquitous *Athyrium filix-femina* var. *angustum* (northern lady fern, p. 190). Comparing the shape of the sori, those of *D. carthusiana* are round and those of *A. filix-femina* var. *angustum* are elongated. Comparing the shape of the individual pinnae, those of *D. carthusiana* are widest at the base where they attach to the rachis. Those of *A. filix-femina* var. *angustum* are widest at their middle.

NATURAL HISTORY: *Dryopteris carthusiana* occurs in temperate and boreal regions across much of North America and Eurasia. It is seemingly ubiquitous in Minnesota forests, probably among the top 10 most common ferns in Minnesota. It occurs in upland forest of all types. It is also found in wet forests, such as conifer swamps and forested fens, although not in the wettest places. It is usually on well-aerated hummocks or around the somewhat elevated bases of trees. Soils are usually loamy glacial till but sometimes peat or woody humus. The preference is for slightly acidic soils, but it tolerates calcareous soils as well. It is always in moderate to deep shade; it does not seem to survive long in openings or sunlit edges.

Petiole with tan scales near base.

A common sight in Minnesota forests—October 9.

Sori are round, abundant.

Basal pinnae have enlarged basal pinnules.

Dryopteris cristata (L.) Gray
Crested Wood Fern

RHIZOMES horizontal, to about 15 cm long.
LEAVES somewhat dimorphic; fertile leaves
25–95 cm long, 7–13 cm wide, dying back
in winter; sterile leaves somewhat smaller
and remaining green through winter.
PETIOLE with tan to yellowish-brown
scales, lacking glands. **BLADE** green,
narrowly elliptic to narrowly oblong,
1-pinnate-pinnatifid to 2-pinnate,
nonglandular, tapering evenly to an acute
apex, tapering little if at all to the base.
PINNAE of fertile leaves twisted nearly
perpendicular to the plane of the blade;
those of sterile leaves remaining in plane;
margins of segments with spine-tipped teeth. **SORI** attached on veins away from
the margins. **INDUSIA** roundish with a narrow sinus, 0.5–1.5 mm across, lacking
glands. **PHENOLOGY:** Sterile leaves develop before fertile leaves and stay green
over winter; fertile leaves die back; spores are dispersed in late fall and winter.

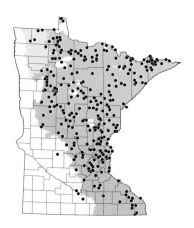

IDENTIFICATION: *Dryopteris cristata* usually has a rather distinctive look. It may be
the short, stubby pinnae that are widely spaced on the rachis. The fertile leaves are
somewhat longer and stiffer than the sterile leaves. They are also darker green
and tend to stand erect with the pinnae curiously twisted out of plane with the
rachis, making them appear somewhat ladderlike. Sterile leaves are smaller, more
abundant, with pinnae oriented in plane with the rachis. A single rhizome can
have both sterile and fertile leaves in any given year. But fertile leaves are
sometimes hard to find.

NATURAL HISTORY: *Dryopteris cristata* is widespread but occurs primarily in north
temperate and boreal regions in the eastern United States, adjacent parts of
Canada, and Europe. In Minnesota, it is common in forested and shrub-
dominated swamps and shallow marshes throughout the forested region of the
state. It does not seem to venture into the prairie region. The long, fast-growing
rhizome is often near the surface, usually in soggy, loamy soil or in soft, mucky
organic material. Scattered individuals are sometimes found in upland forests far
from wetlands, but *D. cristata* does not seem to form long-lived populations in
upland habitats. Typical habitats are in deep to moderate shade of trees,
occasionally in direct sunlight. It commonly occurs adjacent to habitats where
D. carthusiana is found, and the two species hybridize freely.

At the edge of a forested wetland—August 18.

Leaves are 1-pinnate-pinnatifid.

Marginal teeth are spine-tipped.

Pinnae of fertile leaves twist horizontal.

Sterile leaves survive winter—March 17.

Dryopteris expansa (C. Presl) Fraser-Jenkins & Jermy
Spreading Wood Fern

[*D. spinulosa* var. *americana* (Fisch.) Fern.]

RHIZOMES horizontal, to 10+ cm long, branching occasionally. **LEAVES** monomorphic, staying green through early frosts but eventually dying back in winter, 40–120 cm long, 20–40 cm wide. **PETIOLE** scaly, especially near base; lacking glands. **BLADE** green, ovate, 3-pinnate to 3-pinnate-pinnatifid; glands usually absent. **PINNAE:** Medial pinnae usually widest at about the middle. **PINNULES:** Basal basiscopic pinnules of the basal pinnae significantly enlarged; margins with spine-tipped teeth. **SORI** attached on veins away from margins. **INDUSIA** roundish, 0.5–1 mm across, attached at a narrow sinus, usually lacking glands. **PHENOLOGY:** Leaves typically emerge in May, reach full size in June, and shed spores from August through October.

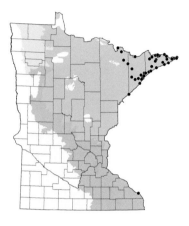

IDENTIFICATION: In Minnesota, *D. expansa* will likely be growing with *D. carthusiana* and possibly *D. intermedia*. At first glance, the three will look much alike. Fortunately, there is a simple way to learn *D. expansa*. At the base of each of the lowest pair of pinnae there is an outsized pinnule that points roughly downward—it may seem oddly out of place. This pinnule is called the basal basiscopic pinnule of the basal pinnae. There is one on either side of the rachis. Each is about twice as wide and at least twice as long as the corresponding pinnule directly above it, which is called the basal acroscopic pinnule. Also, it is usually attached closer to the second acroscopic pinnule than to the basal acroscopic pinnule.

NATURAL HISTORY: *Dryopteris expansa* occurs in boreal and cool temperate regions in eastern and western North America as well as Eurasia. Habitats in Minnesota seem to be limited to the far northeastern corner of the state. Even there it is not common, although not hard to find if looking in the right places. Habitats are in damp, shady spots in forests of coniferous or broad-leaved trees, perhaps most often on steep, rocky, or bouldery slopes or along streams that run through deep gorges. Soils are consistently acidic with a high content of organic matter. The unlikely specimen from Winona County in the southeastern part of the state was collected near La Moille in 1902 by J. M. Holzinger.

A large, prominent fern in the northeastern counties.

A typical leaf—July 19.

Scaly petiole.

The infamous basiscopic basal pinnules.

Sori are round, easy to find.

Dryopteris filix-mas (L.) Schott
Male Fern

RHIZOMES horizontal, to 15+ cm long,
branching occasionally. **LEAVES**
monomorphic, 30–100 cm long, 12–36 cm
wide; fertile leaves die back in winter;
some sterile leaves (those produced in
midsummer) remain green during winter.
PETIOLE scaly, especially near the base;
scales with both broad and hairlike form;
lacking glands. **BLADE** green, narrowly
elliptic to narrowly obovate, 1-pinnate-
pinnatifid to 2-pinnate, nonglandular.
PINNAE: Marginal teeth blunt or broadly
pointed, not spine-tipped. **SORI** attached on
veins away from margins. **INDUSIA**

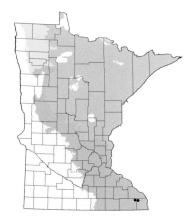

roundish with a narrow sinus, 0.5–1.5 mm across, lacking glands. **PHENOLOGY:**
Sterile leaves emerge in the spring about a week before fertile leaves; fertile leaves
shed spores in midsummer and die back in winter; some sterile leaves stay green
all winter.

IDENTIFICATION: In Latin, *filix* means fern and *mas* means male. Appropriately,
D. filix-mas is commonly called male fern, as a companion to lady fern (*Athyrium
filix-femina,* p. 190). Both species were named long ago when little was known
about fern biology. In reality, the two species are not closely related and are
seldom confused with each other. A fertile specimen of *D. filix-mas* (one with sori)
should go through the key without difficulty, although it might not stand out as
anything unusual in the field. Compared to other species of *Dryopteris* found in
Minnesota, *D. filix-mas* has a rather short petiole and marginal teeth that are not
spine-tipped. The leaves lack glands and are divided only twice.

NATURAL HISTORY: *Dryopteris filix-mas* occurs in scattered temperate and
subboreal habitats in North America and Eurasia. Although not globally rare,
reliable repots of its occurrence are rather spotty, and an overall pattern of
distribution relative to Minnesota is obscure. It was only recently discovered at the
southeastern tip of Minnesota. Little is known about locations or habitats where it
might be found next. It will likely be in woodlands of some sort, probably ravines
or slopes, perhaps tending more to dry than to moist, and possibly associated with
limestone bedrock. The stream-dissected terrain of southeastern Minnesota
seems to offer the best habitats, and more sites will likely be found as botanical
exploration proceeds. When that happens, a clearer picture of its status in
Minnesota may emerge.

In a steep, wooded ravine, Fillmore County.

Leaves are twice divided, with short petioles.

Sori are round; pinna margins are toothed.

Petioles have broad and slender scales.

Dryopteris fragrans (L.) Schott
Fragrant Wood Fern

[*D. fragrans* var. *remotiuscula* Komarov]

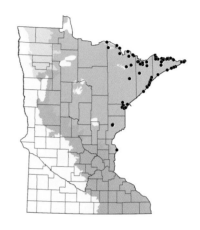

RHIZOMES compact, with few to many short branches. **LEAVES** monomorphic, green through winter, becoming marcescent the second summer, 6–30 cm long, 1–6 cm wide, aromatic when handled. **PETIOLE** coarsely scaly; scales yellow to brown or orange, ovate, 3–6 mm long, 1.5–3 mm wide; with yellow, resinous, stalked glands. **BLADES** dark green, narrowly elliptic to linear-elliptic, 2-pinnate to 2-pinnate-pinnatifid; rachis glandular and scaly in the manner of the petiole. **PINNAE:** Margins of segments bluntly toothed; basal pinnae much reduced. **SORI** attached on veins away from the margins. **INDUSIA** roundish with a narrow sinus, 0.7–1.5 mm across, often overlapping, translucent, persistent.

PHENOLOGY: New leaves appear in spring and remain green through summer and winter, into the following spring. Sporangia develop on nearly all leaves and disperse spores in fall and winter.

IDENTIFICATION: *Dryopteris fragrans* is a small to midsize rock fern common in the northeastern counties. It has slender, dark-green leaves that gradually narrow to the tip and to the base. They are stiff, finely divided, and have the curious habit of remaining attached to the rhizome even after they have died and shriveled. They accumulate over several years and become very conspicuous. The petiole and the rachis are covered with broad, orange, papery scales. The scales should be obvious. There are also small, yellow, resinous glands that might require a hand lens to see but release a distinctive fragrance when handled. At first glance, *D. fragrans* could easily be mistaken for a *Woodsia* or a *Cystopteris*. In fact, all three are sometimes found growing on the same cliff. But the underside of nearly every leaf of *D. fragrans* is covered with large, translucent, overlapping indusia.

NATURAL HISTORY: *Dryopteris fragrans* is found in forests of Eurasia and northern parts of North America, including the northeastern corner of Minnesota. In Minnesota, it is usually found in shaded crevices on cliffs of igneous bedrock, on large boulders, or on bedrock outcrops. It is an arctic species that can survive extreme cold and desiccation. At the comparatively southern latitude of Minnesota, it prefers habitats with a northerly exposure, where it is protected from direct sunlight and the heat of the day.

Leaves are stiff, narrow, tapered at both ends.

The tiny dots are resinous glands.

Broad, orange scales on petiole.

Note the dried leaves clinging to the base, Lake County—September 6.

Dryopteris goldieana (Hooker ex Goldie) Gray
Goldie's Woodfern

RHIZOMES horizontal, to 15+ cm long, branching occasionally. LEAVES monomorphic, dying back late in winter, 40–120 cm long, 20–40 cm wide. PETIOLE scaly, especially near base; scales yellow-brown to brown, or shiny dark brown with paler borders; lacking glands. BLADE green or dull blue-green, oblong to elliptic, narrowed abruptly toward apex, narrowed little if at all toward base, 1-pinnate-pinnatifid to 2-pinnate, nonglandular. PINNAE: Margins of segments with incurved, spine-tipped teeth. SORI attached on veins away from the margins. INDUSIA

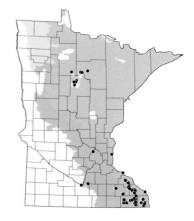

roundish with a narrow sinus, 0.5–1.5 mm across, lacking glands. PHENOLOGY: Leaves typically emerge in early May and reach full size around mid-June; spores are released in late summer and autumn.

IDENTIFICATION: In Minnesota, Goldie's wood fern (usually shortened to Goldie's fern) is a prominent but rather rare fern. The leaves are comparatively large and broad, easily reaching waist high. The individual pinnae are rather rigid and may appear oversized for the plant. They are normally dark green but may appear blue-green in certain lighting. From a distance, Goldie's fern would look most like interrupted fern (*Claytosmunda claytoniana,* p. 150), but the leaves of Goldie's fern are much broader although not consistently longer, and the pinnae have narrow, pointed tips. Also, the leaf segments of Goldie's fern are lined with spine-tipped teeth that curve inward. Interrupted fern has none of those features.

NATURAL HISTORY: Goldie's fern occurs in forested regions of the northeastern United States and adjacent portions of southern Canada. It is broadly distributed in the southeast counties of Minnesota, although it is not at all common. It is usually found in deep stream valleys under a canopy of mature sugar maple and basswood trees. Habitats tend to be ecologically stable forests, if not technically old-growth. In addition, there are small, isolated populations in other forested counties, perhaps most notably on the Otter Tail Peninsula of Leech Lake in Cass County. The geographic disjunction that is apparent on the accompanying map fits no obvious pattern other than that of an adaptable fern finding suitable habitat wherever it can, something ferns are especially good at doing. It is such a conspicuous fern that it is unlikely to have been overlooked in intervening habitats.

A typical forest setting, Winona County—August 16.

Leaves are broad, twice divided.

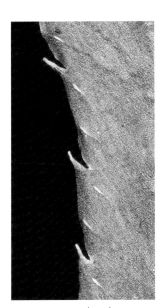

Spine-tipped teeth.

Underside of a pinna.

Brown scales on petiole.

Dryopteris intermedia (Muhl. ex Willd.) Gray
Evergreen Wood Fern

[*D. spinulosa* var. *intermedia* (Muhl. ex Willd.) L. Underwood]

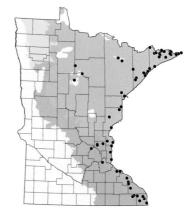

RHIZOMES horizontal, to 15 cm long, branching not observed. **LEAVES** monomorphic, remaining green through winter, 40–100 cm long, 10–25 cm wide. **PETIOLE** scaly; scales ovate, brown or yellow-brown; with small, clear, stalked glands. **BLADE** green, narrowly ovate to lance-ovate, 2-pinnate-pinnatifid to 3-pinnate; with stalked glands, especially on rachis and costae. **PINNAE** tending to be widest near middle or near base. **PINNULES:** Basal basiscopic pinnules of basal pinnae shorter than adjacent basiscopic pinnules; margins with pointed or spine-tipped teeth. **SORI** attached on veins away from margins. **INDUSIA** roundish with a narrow sinus, 0.5–1 mm across, minutely glandular. **PHENOLOGY:** Leaves survive a summer and a winter. New leaves emerge in May as leaves from the previous year senesce; spores are released from August through winter.

IDENTIFICATION: In Minnesota, *D. intermedia* is most likely to be confused with the more common *D. carthusiana.* Many people think the leaves of *D. intermedia* are more finely divided than those of *D. carthusiana,* but that is somewhat subjective. Objectively, the small size of the basal basiscopic pinnule on the basal pinnae (dichotomy 6) is the best field character to identify *D. intermedia.* To confirm identification, check for tiny, stalked glands on the rachis. Be aware the glands are very small and can be hard to see even with a hand lens, and they might not be seen on overwintered leaves.

NATURAL HISTORY: *Dryopteris intermedia* occurs in cool temperate and subboreal forests in the northeastern United States and adjacent parts of Canada. In Minnesota, it is locally common in parts of the northeast, and rare or infrequent elsewhere. Its habitat is invariably within mesic forests, either deciduous or coniferous. The largest populations are found in steep, forested ravines and on rocky slopes. But single plants have been found in a variety of rather ordinary-looking woods. It seems that most of our *Dryopteris* species are evergreen, to some extent, but *D. intermedia* more consistently than most. Although delicate looking, the leaves seem to survive even the worst Minnesota winter unscathed beneath the snow. The leaves resume photosynthesis in the spring before they are replaced by new leaves.

Finely divided leaves have a lacy look.

Sori on undersides of pinnules.

Tiny stalked glands on the rachis.

In a typical forest setting.

Basal basiscopic pinnules are short.

Dryopteris marginalis (L.) Gray
Marginal Wood Fern

RHIZOMES horizontal, to about 10 cm long, occasionally branched. **LEAVES** monomorphic, remaining green through winter, 30–90 cm long, 12–35 cm wide. **PETIOLE** scaly, especially toward the base; scales orange to yellowish brown; lacking glands. **BLADE** bluish green, somewhat leathery, narrowly elliptic to ovate-lanceolate, 2-pinnate, nonglandular. **PINNAE:** Basal pinnae not significantly reduced in size; margins of pinnules with blunt or rounded teeth, or nearly entire. **SORI** attached near margins of ultimate segments, usually at a notch or sinus.

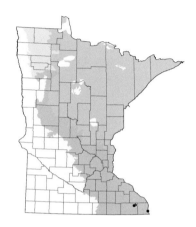

INDUSIA roundish, 0.5–1 mm across, lacking glands. **PHENOLOGY:** Poorly known for Minnesota. Apparently both sterile and fertile leaves remain green through much of the winter.

IDENTIFICATION: The leaves of *D. marginalis* often have a dark blue-green color, especially the lower surfaces. They are somewhat leathery in texture and are consistently 2-pinnate. The leaves might look like those of other *Dryopteris*, especially *D. filix-mas*. But in the case of *D. marginalis*, nearly all the leaves will be fertile (in season), producing large, round sori along the margins of the pinnules, hence the name *marginalis*. Look for them at a notch or a sinus. This is the only *Dryopteris* in Minnesota with sori located in that position, and they are relatively easy to see on the undersides of the leaves. It is the feature botanists look for in the field.

NATURAL HISTORY: *Dryopteris marginalis* is endemic to eastern and central parts of the United States and adjacent parts of Canada. It is very rare in Minnesota, having gone undetected until 1981. It has been found, to date, only in deciduous woodlands in bluff country in the southeastern corner of the state. It is most likely to be found in moist or well-drained sandy or stony soils, and in partial shade. It will not likely be restricted to the interior of unfragmented forests. It seems well adapted to edges, and woodlands with a patchy canopy. Based on its range-wide distribution, it could possibly be found in northeastern Minnesota, probably on forested slopes. Nothing in its habitat requirements reveals why it should be so rare in Minnesota. Apparently, it simply reaches the northwestward limit of its geographical range in eastern Minnesota, most likely a result of climate, but specifics are unknown.

On a forested slope in Fillmore County.

Leaves stay green through winter.

Petioles have orangish scales near the base.

Sori are found at notches along the margins of pinnules.

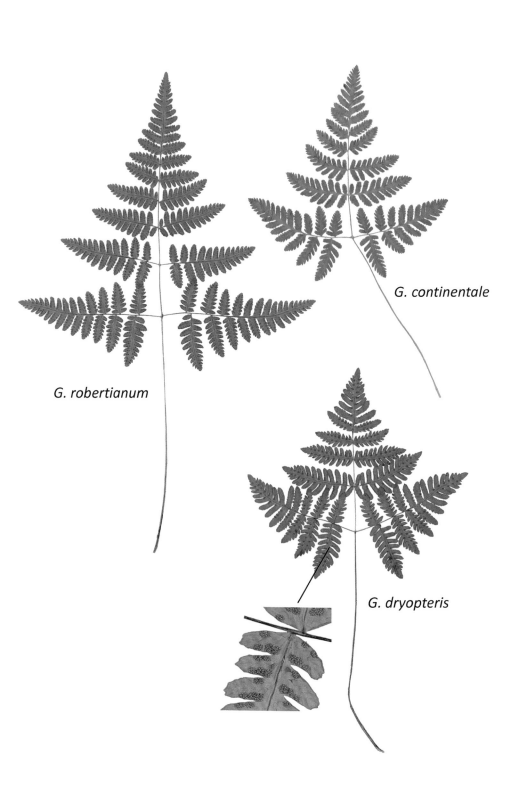

G. robertianum

G. continentale

G. dryopteris

GYMNOCARPIUM (OAK FERNS)

The genus *Gymnocarpium* is currently placed in the family Cystopteridaceae, which has 3 genera and a total of about 37 species. There are at least 8 species of *Gymnocarpium* in the world. They are found in north temperate regions of North America and Eurasia. There are 6 species in North America and 3 in Minnesota. There are also 2 named (sterile) hybrids that have been found in the northeastern part of the state.

KEY TO NONHYBRID *GYMNOCARPIUM*

1. Rachis and leaf surfaces glabrous; the lowest pair of pinnae greatly enlarged to the point of each being about 75–90 percent as large as the portion of the blade above the lowest pinnae, therefore the blade appearing ternate (made up of 3 nearly equal parts) . . . . *G. dryopteris*
1. Rachis and at least the lower surface of the leaf moderately or densely covered with tiny, clear or white, stalked glands (about 0.05 mm long and may require magnification to see); the lowest pair of pinnae each about 50–75 percent as large as the portion of the blade above the lowest pinnae, therefore the blade not as convincingly ternate.
    2. The second pair of pinnae from the base sessile or on a stalk ≤ 0.5 mm long; the basal pinnules on these pinnae half to fully as large as the adjacent pinnules; leaf glabrous on upper surface. . . . . *G. continentale*
    2. The second pair of pinnae from the base usually with a stalk 8–15 mm long, or if sessile then the basal pinnules on these pinnae about half the size of the adjacent pinnules; leaf sparsely glandular on upper surface . . . . *G. robertianum*

HYBRIDS

G. ×intermedium Sarvela is the sterile hybrid between *G. dryopteris* and *G. continentale*. A close examination of Minnesota specimens reveals that this hybrid is not uncommon in northeastern Minnesota, where the ranges of the two parent species overlap. All known occurrences are from cliff habitats, like those of *G. continentale*.

G. ×brittonianum (Sarvela) K. M. Pryor & Haufler is the sterile hybrid between *G. dryopteris* and *G. disjunctum*. Three Minnesota specimens of this hybrid have been confirmed by a specialist. All were found in moist forest habitats in the northeastern counties. Paradoxically, the nearest known population of *G. disjunctum* is in western Montana, which raises the question of how an ostensibly sterile hybrid involving this species could be found in Minnesota. No conclusive answer is forthcoming.

Gymnocarpium continentale (Petrov) Pojark
Nahanni Oak Fern

[*G. jessoense* subsp. *parvulum* Sarvela]

RHIZOMES horizontal, to 25+ cm long, slender, branching often. **LEAVES** monomorphic, dying back in winter. **PETIOLE** pale greenish to straw-colored, 8–30 cm long; glabrous or with minute stalked glands distally, and with broad brown scales basally. **BLADE** triangular, oblique to the petiole, 2-pinnate-pinnatifid, 6–15 cm long, 5–20 cm wide; upper surface glabrous; lower surface moderately glandular. **RACHIS** and costae with minute stalked glands. **PINNAE:** The lowest pair significantly enlarged and stalked; the remaining pinnae progressively smaller and sessile or the second lowest pair on an

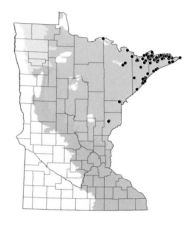

apparent stalk ≤ 0.5 mm long; margins of ultimate segments entire or scalloped. **INDUSIA** absent. **PHENOLOGY:** Leaves emerge in May and die back in autumn. Sporangia are seen from midsummer through autumn.

IDENTIFICATION: Comparing the 3 species of oak fern, look first for tiny, stalked glands. They are easiest to see on the rachis and costae, but they are tiny and will require a hand lens. They are white or clear and very small, about 0.05 mm long. *Gymnocarpium continentale* and *G. robertianum* both have stalked glands; *G. dryopteris* has none. To separate *G. continentale* from *G. robertianum*, find where the second-lowest pinnae pair attach to the rachis. If it is *G. continentale*, the pinnae will be attached without a stalk. If it is *G. robertianum*, the corresponding pinnae will usually have an obvious stalk, which settles the matter. In cases where the pinnae of *G. robertianum* lack a stalk, the basal pinnules of the pinnae will be only about half size and skew outward. It is also fair to consider the different habitats and geographic distributions of the two species.

NATURAL HISTORY: *Gymnocarpium continentale* is found across boreal and subboreal regions of North America and Eurasia. In Minnesota, it typically occurs in small crevices on north- or east-facing cliffs, and associated talus that accumulates at the base of cliffs. These are cool, mossy retreats shaded or partially shaded by trees or by the position of the cliff. *Gymnocarpium continentale* is common and predictable in these situations, at least in the northeastern corner of the state, where there are concentrations of large cliffs composed of noncalcareous rock. It is almost certain to be the only species of *Gymnocarpium* found in such habitats.

In a crevice of a sandstone cliff, Pine County—July 26.

Brown scales at base of petiole.

Stalked glands on rachis.

Late-season plants viewed from above.

Gymnocarpium dryopteris (L.) Newman
Western Oak Fern

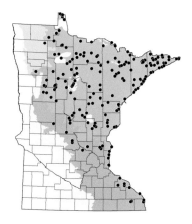

RHIZOMES horizontal, to 30+ cm long,
slender, branching often. **LEAVES**
monomorphic, dying back in winter.
PETIOLE pale greenish to straw-colored,
8–30 cm long; with broad brown or yellow-
brown scales near base, otherwise
glabrous. **BLADE** broadly triangular to
ternate, oblique to the petiole, 2-pinnate-
pinnatifid, 5–15 cm long, 7–20 cm wide,
glabrous or rarely with a few stalked glands
on the lower surface. **RACHIS** glabrous or
rarely with a few stalked glands. **PINNAE:**
The lowest pair greatly enlarged and
stalked, the remaining sessile and
becoming progressively smaller; margins of ultimate segments entire or
crenulate. **BASAL PINNULES** of the second lowest pair of pinnae about equal in size
or slightly smaller than adjacent pinnules. **INDUSIA** absent. **PHENOLOGY:** Leaves
emerge in May and die back in autumn. Sporangia are seen from midsummer
through autumn.

IDENTIFICATION: The first thing to know when identifying *G. dryopteris* is that the
surface of the leaves has no glands. Glands are outgrowths of the epidermis and
are very small, standing about 0.05 mm high (about half the thickness of a sheet
of paper). If present, they will appear as small white dots at 10× magnification.
Look for them along the rachis, especially where the pinnae join the rachis. If no
glands are seen, then the plant in question is *G. dryopteris*. Experts will consider
geography (widespread) and habitat (forests), but they will always check for
glands.

NATURAL HISTORY: *Gymnocarpium dryopteris* occurs across northern parts of
North America and Eurasia. It is common in the northern half of Minnesota,
becoming uncommon southward. Habitats in northern Minnesota are about
evenly divided between upland forests composed of various common tree species
and swamp forests dominated mostly by lowland tree species. In swamps, it will
usually be growing in well-aerated hummocks or slightly elevated microhabitats
around the bases of trees. In nearly all cases, it will be shallowly rooted in loose
material such as coarse peat, fine woody humus, or leaf duff. Habitats in southern
Minnesota are mostly in noncalcareous loamy soils in upland forests of oak or
maple. In all habitats, it tends to form small colonies with interlayered leaves
about ankle high.

Looking down from above; rocky woods in Pine County—May 28.

Leaves are smooth, lack stalked glands.

G. dryopteris in foreground, Pine County—May 23.

Gymnocarpium robertianum (Hoffm.) Newman
Scented Oak Fern

RHIZOMES horizontal, to 20+ cm long,
slender, branching often. LEAVES
monomorphic, dying back in winter.
PETIOLE pale greenish to straw-colored,
12–28 cm long; with tiny, stalked glands
distally, and broad brown scales proximally.
BLADE triangular, oblique to the petiole,
2-pinnate-pinnatifid to partially 3-pinnate,
10–20 cm long, 12–25 cm wide; upper
surface sparsely glandular; lower surface
moderately glandular. RACHIS and costae
glandular. PINNAE: The lowest pair
noticeably enlarged and stalked; the second
pair stalked, or if sessile then the basal

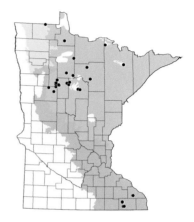

pinnules about half the size of the adjacent pinnules and skewed outward;
margins entire or scalloped. INDUSIA absent. PHENOLOGY: Leaves emerge in May
and die back in autumn. Sporangia are seen from midsummer through autumn.

IDENTIFICATION: *Gymnocarpium robertianum* is a medium-size fern—on
average somewhat larger than the other two Minnesota oak ferns. The leaves
invariably have stalked glands on the rachis and costae. They are tiny, but their
great numbers usually make them visible at 10× magnification and conspicuous
at 20×. The presence of glands will tell you it is not *G. dryopteris*. To rule out
G. continentale, look at the second pair of pinnae from the base and see how they
are attached to the rachis. Those of *G. robertianum* are usually on a stalk 8–15 mm
long. In some cases they won't be stalked, in which case there will be a
disproportionately small pair of pinnules right at the base of the pinnae, and they
will be skewed outward.

NATURAL HISTORY: *Gymnocarpium robertianum* is found in north temperate and
subboreal habitats in northeastern North America and Eurasia. In northern
Minnesota, it is found in mineral-rich conifer swamps, usually in wet, mossy
habitats dominated by northern white cedar, often with black spruce and
sometimes tamarack or balsam fir. However, *G. robertianum* is rare in Minnesota.
It is not found in every northern habitat that might seem suitable. In southern
Minnesota, *G. robertianum* is found exclusively near cold-air vents on algific talus
slopes. This is a unique habitat consisting of limestone talus covered by mosses
and shaded by trees. Algific slopes harbor a number of northern species
seemingly out of place in southern Minnesota. These are presumed to be relics of
the Pleistocene vegetation.

In a typical habitat: conifer swamp, Beltrami County.

Sori lack indusia.

The tiny white flecks are stalked glands.

The leaf is nearly an equilateral triangle.

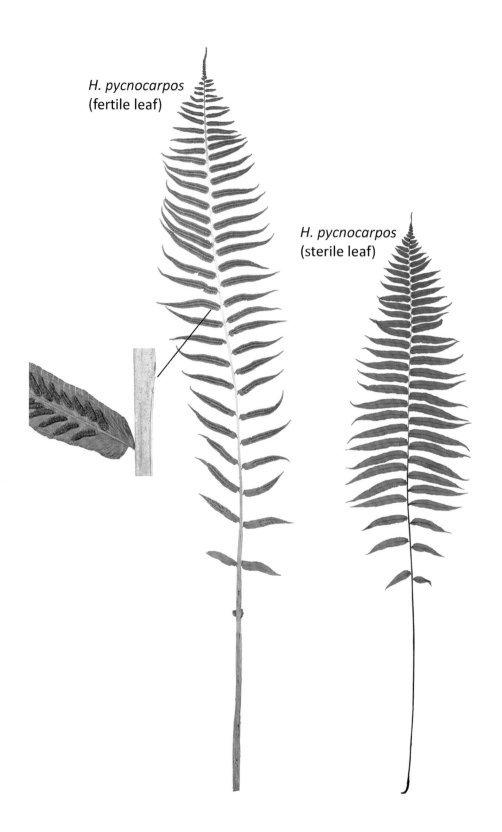

H. pycnocarpos
(fertile leaf)

H. pycnocarpos
(sterile leaf)

HOMALOSORUS (GLADE FERN)

The species presented here as *Homalosorus pycnocarpos* (narrow-leaved glade fern) had been placed in the genus *Athyrium* by some and in the genus *Diplazium* by others. It now sits alone in the monotypic genus *Homalosorus*, which was created for this species in 1977. The genus resides in the small and rather obscure family Diplaziopsidaceae (2 genera and 4 species), which was created in 2011. The difficulty biologists have had finding a place for this species on the tree of life does not mean it is difficult to identify. To the contrary. Among Minnesota ferns, it is distinctive in many ways, primarily in being 1-pinnate. This means the leaf is divided into a single series of long, slender segments (pinnae). Each pinna is on a short but distinct stalk. Other than *Homalosorus*, this architecture is seen only in *Polystichum* (p. 277) and *Asplenium* (p. 181), which are contrasted in dichotomy 4 (p. 171).

Homalosorus pycnocarpos (Sprengel) Pichi-Sermolli
Narrow-Leaved Glade Fern

[*Diplazium pycnocarpon* (Sprengel) Broun; *Athyrium pycnocarpon* (Sprengel) Tidestrom]

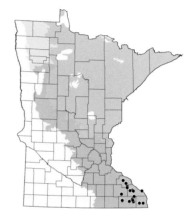

RHIZOMES horizontal, to about 15 cm long, branching occasionally. **LEAVES** 1-pinnate, 50–110 cm long, 10–22 cm wide, somewhat dimorphic; fertile leaves generally longer than sterile leaves, with narrower and stiffer pinnae, and appearing later in the season; all leaves dying back by winter. **PETIOLE** ± glabrous, predominately greenish or straw-colored. **BLADE** narrowly oblong to narrowly elliptic or lanceolate; apex abruptly acuminate; base slightly tapered; rachis with scattered hairs or essentially glabrous. **PINNAE** lanceolate to oblong-lanceolate (sterile) or narrowly linear-lanceolate (fertile); margins entire or shallowly scalloped; apex acuminate; base attached by a short stalk. **SORI** oblong, straight or slightly curved. **INDUSIA** laterally attached, vaulted, persistent. **PHENOLOGY:** The first leaves emerge in early May and are sterile. Fertile leaves appear in July and are best seen in August. All leaves die back by winter.

IDENTIFICATION: *Homalosorus pycnocarpos* is a tall, slender-leaved fern of moist, shady forests in the southeastern corner of the state. Significantly, the leaf is 1-pinnate, meaning it has only one series of divisions, composed of long, slender, narrow-pointed pinnae. Each pinna is attached to the rachis by a short stalk. The margins of each pinna are smooth, not serrated or toothed. In structure, *H. pycnocarpos* most resembles *Asplenium platyneuron* (ebony spleenwort, p. 182) and *Polystichum acrostichoides* (Christmas fern, p. 278), but the pinnae of those species have serrated margins.

NATURAL HISTORY: *Homalosorus pycnocarpos* is endemic to temperate regions of eastern North America. In Minnesota, it is found in the rugged southeastern counties, where it grows in forested ravines and deep stream valleys, usually on north-facing slopes, where it is protected from the warming and drying effects of sunlight. It generally roots in deep, well-drained loamy or clayey soil. Soils are never wet but always moist, even in periods of little rainfall. The rhizomes grow slowly and branch occasionally. Eventually one rhizome can form a rather dense colony a meter or more across. The first leaves to emerge in the spring are sterile; they do not produce sporangia. They serve only to photosynthesize. In midsummer, the fertile leaves emerge. They are taller, stiffer, have narrower pinnae, and are loaded with sporangia.

In a typical forest setting, Winona County—June 16.

Sori on underside of fertile leaf—August 16.

Sterile leaf—June 16.

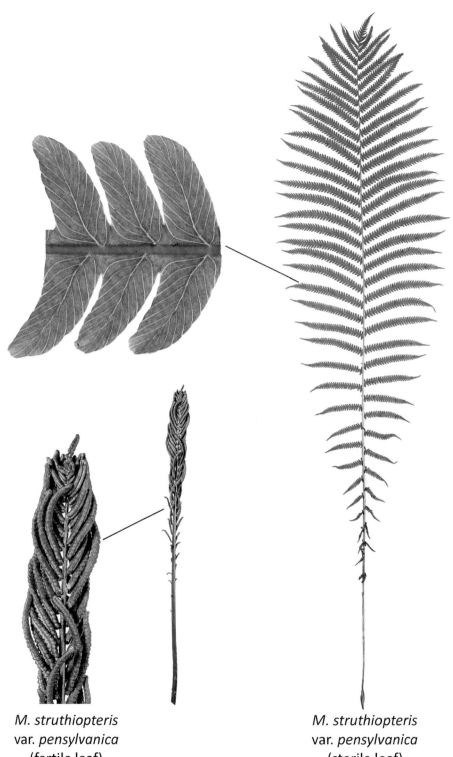

M. struthiopteris
var. *pensylvanica*
(fertile leaf)

M. struthiopteris
var. *pensylvanica*
(sterile leaf)

MATTEUCCIA (OSTRICH FERN)

The genus *Matteuccia* includes only one species, *M. struthiopteris* (ostrich fern), which occurs in cold temperate and boreal regions of North America, Europe, and Asia. The species has been separated into two distinct varieties. The Eurasian plants are var. *struthiopteris,* while the North American plants are var. *pensylvanica.* There is evidence the two varieties could be considered distinct species.

The genus *Matteuccia* has been placed in a small family named Onocleaceae, which contains only 4 genera and a total of 5 species. The only other member of the family that occurs in Minnesota is *Onoclea sensibilis* (sensitive fern, p. 258).

Matteuccia struthiopteris var. *pensylvanica* (Willd.) C. V. Morton
Ostrich Fern

RHIZOMES of 2 types: The leaf-producing structure is vertical, cylindrical, to about 10 cm across and 20 cm high; the invasive propagating structure is horizontal, slender, to 50+ cm long (reportedly to 3 m). **LEAVES** strongly dimorphic. **STERILE LEAVES** green, high-arching in vaselike clusters, 50–200 cm long, 12–38 cm wide, dying back by winter; petiole 5–40 cm long; blade oblanceolate, 1-pinnate-pinnatifid; pinnae linear, sessile, glabrous or glabrate; segment margins entire; veins pinnate; lateral veins unforked. **FERTILE LEAVES** erect; initially green, becoming brownish

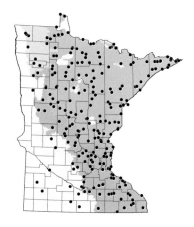

and woody; persisting through winter, 25–60 cm long, 3–8 cm wide, 1-pinnate. **SORI** ± round, covered by inrolled pinna segments. **INDUSIA** vestigial.

PHENOLOGY: Sterile leaves emerge in late April or early May, reach full size by July, die back by winter; fertile leaves appear in June, mature in the fall, survive winter, and release spores the following spring.

IDENTIFICATION: The sterile leaves of *M. struthiopteris* var. *pensylvanica* are arranged in a tight, vaselike cluster. They are large, sometimes reaching shoulder height, and have a peculiar paddle shape when laid flat. The fertile leaves will seem a puzzle. They come from the center of the "vase" and stand about knee high. They fail to expand and quickly turn brown—looking like a failed experiment. They serve just one purpose: to produce spores and release them to the wind. They can be seen standing upright all winter, much like those of sensitive fern (*Onoclea sensibilis*, p. 258).

NATURAL HISTORY: *Matteuccia struthiopteris* var. *pensylvanica* is widespread in boreal and cool temperate regions across much of northern North America. It is common in Minnesota, particularly in moist, seasonally wet forests, especially along streams. It is sometimes found in forest clearings along utility corridors and ditch banks. It does best in partial shade on fertile, weakly acidic soils with a high moisture content. The new leaves grow from a tight cluster of buds in the center of a vertical, cylinder-shaped rhizome. From near the base of the vertical rhizome will come 2–5 slender, horizontal rhizomes that grow beneath the ground for 50 cm or more. Each will start a new vertical, leaf-producing rhizome at its tip. This can result in exponential growth with numerous densely packed plants.

Fiddleheads—May 7.

Fertile leaves still green, Rice County—June 23.

Fertile leaf in winter—February 19.

A mesic, deciduous forest in Hennepin County—-May 21.

M. gracilis
(ventral surface)

M. gracilis
(dorsal surface)

MYRIOPTERIS (LIP FERNS)

The genus *Myriopteris* was segregated from the much larger genus *Cheilanthes* in 2013. It is now a genus of 47 species found primarily in arid regions of North and Central America. Only one species is known to occur in Minnesota: *M. gracilis.* Members of the genus *Myriopteris* are closely related to species in the genus *Pellaea* (cliffbrake ferns, p. 261), although they look quite different. Members of both genera are small rock plants of dry, open habitats.

In the University of Wisconsin herbarium, there is a solitary specimen of *M. lanosa* labeled as having been collected along the St. Croix River in Wisconsin in 1866. If information on the label is correct, it would be hundreds of miles outside its normal range in the southeastern states. Because the St. Croix River divides Minnesota from Wisconsin, *M. lanosa* is sometimes credited with occurring in Minnesota, which seems highly unlikely. *Myriopteris lanosa* looks similar to *M. gracilis,* but the smallest leaf segments are somewhat elongate rather than round, and are in the range of 3–5 mm long rather than 1–3 mm.

Myriopteris gracilis Fée
Slender Lip Fern

[*Cheilanthes feei* T. Moore]

RHIZOMES compact, short-branched, with persistent brown scales. LEAVES monomorphic, remaining nominally green through winter, 4–20 cm long, 1–4 cm wide. PETIOLE persistent, wirelike, round in cross-section, dark brown to black. BLADE linear-oblong to lanceolate, 2-pinnate-pinnatifid to 4-pinnate; rachis similar to petiole. PINNAE green; upper surface strigose; lower surface and margins with a dense covering of long, tangled hairs. ULTIMATE SEGMENTS round to slightly oblong, bead-like, the largest 1–3 mm long. VEINS obscure. SORI ±

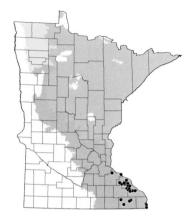

continuous around segment margins. INDUSIA false (poorly differentiated), formed by the partially incurving margins of the ultimate segments. PHENOLOGY: Leaves remain viable, if not green, over winter and during drought; the replacement interval is unknown. Spores shed with pinnae throughout the year.

IDENTIFICATION: *Myriopteris gracilis* is a small, compact cliff fern with an overall gray-green color when seen from above. In dry periods, especially in late summer, the leaves turn completely gray and curl up; the whole plant may appear dead. The smallest segments of the leaf are often called bead-like and are no more than 3 mm across. They are cup-shaped (the cup facing downward). The cavity of the "cup" has a row of sori along the margin and is filled with a tangled mass of long hairs.

NATURAL HISTORY: *Myriopteris gracilis* is a xerophyte that occurs primarily in semiarid regions of the western United States, with outposts in the Ozarks and the Driftless Area of the central states. In Minnesota, it seems to grow exclusively on dry, sunny cliffs of dolomite or limestone. These are extreme habitats where few other species can survive. It does not establish quickly on cliffs that are created by roadcuts or quarrying, and it has not been found on stone structures such as bridge foundations. To prevent desiccation in time of drought, the pinnae curl up to expose the hair-covered undersides to the desiccating wind. When this happens, they may look dead but revive when conditions improve. Suitable habitat for *M. gracilis* is quite uncommon in Minnesota and is found primarily in the southeastern counties. Where favorable conditions do exist, this species can be expected to occur. In that sense, it is rather predictable.

Wedged tightly into a rock crevice—
September 29.

On a limestone cliff, Winona County.

Upper surface of leaf tip.

Lower surface covered with brown hairs.

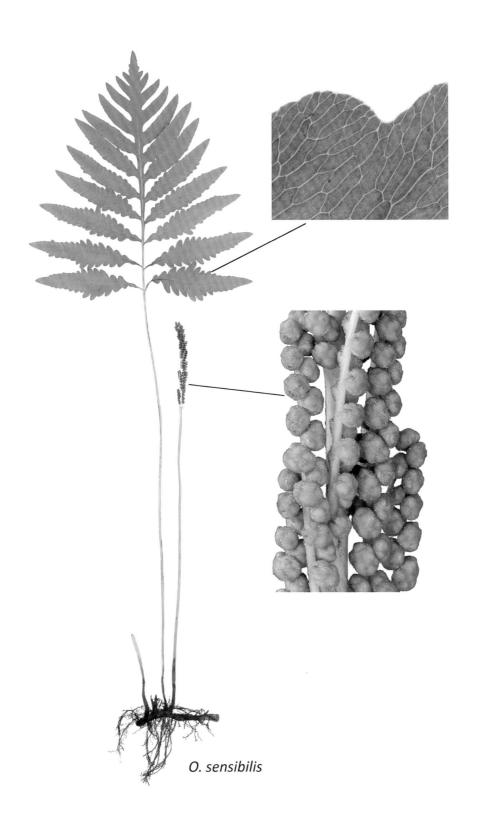

O. sensibilis

ONOCLEA (SENSITIVE FERN)

The genus *Onoclea* has only one species, *O. sensibilis* (sensitive fern). It occurs in the eastern half of North America and parts of eastern Asia. It is closely related to *Matteuccia struthiopteris* (ostrich fern, p. 250), although the two species are rarely confused.

The current classification scheme has the genera *Onoclea* and *Matteuccia* placed together in the small family Onocleaceae. The family contains 4 genera and a total of perhaps 5 species. All show extreme dimorphism of the leaves, meaning the leaves come in 2 distinct forms. The form that produces the sporangia, called the fertile leaf (sporophyll), is highly modified. It is comparatively short, slender, greenish and leathery, eventually becoming blackish and almost woody. It stands erect all winter. The photosynthetic form, called the sterile leaf (trophophyll), is a broad, green leaf. It has no sporangia and dies back in autumn. Both forms grow together from the same rhizome.

Onoclea sensibilis L.
Sensitive Fern

RHIZOMES horizontal, slender, branching
often, to 35+ cm long. LEAVES strongly
dimorphic. STERILE LEAVES green to
yellow-green, 30–120 cm long, 15–40 cm
wide, dying back in autumn; petiole 15–50
cm long; blade ovate to deltate,
predominately 1- or rarely 2-pinnatifid,
although often pinnate at base; rachis
winged; primary segments 5–15 per side,
narrowly elliptic to linear; margins entire,
sinuate, or lobed. VENATION: Segments
with a distinct midvein and reticulate
lateral veins. FERTILE LEAVES initially green
and leathery, becoming blackish and
marcescent, 2-pinnate, 25–65 cm long, 1–5 cm wide, persisting through winter.
SORI covered by strongly revolute margins of pinnules. INDUSIA absent or
vestigial. PHENOLOGY: Sterile leaves appear in early to mid-May, develop over the
summer, and die back with the first frost in autumn. Fertile leaves appear in June,
mature by autumn, and survive the winter to release their spores in late winter
and early spring.

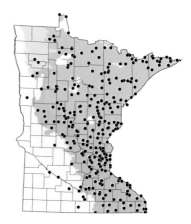

NATURAL HISTORY: *Onoclea sensibilis* is notable for a number of things, including
the extreme dimorphism of its leaves. The fertile leaf bears no resemblance to the
sterile leaf. It is slender, blackish (in winter), somewhat woody, and stands only
about knee high. It is common to see these standing in snow-covered marshes.
They are similar to the fertile leaves of *Matteuccia struthiopteris* var. *pensylvanica*
(ostrich fern, p. 250). The sterile leaves of *O. sensibilis* look more like a typical fern
leaf but are pinnatifid, meaning that all the divisions of the leaf are connected to
each other rather than separate and distinct.

NATURAL HISTORY: *Onoclea sensibilis* is widely distributed in eastern and central
North America and in Asia. In Minnesota, it is typically found in soggy or mucky
soil at the edge of a woodland marsh, swale, or wet meadow, sometimes deep in
swamps. Soils may be perpetually saturated or only moist. Full sunlight might be
preferred, but shade is tolerated. On occasion, individuals are found in an upland
forest far from a wetland. Such rogues, although not uncommon, are probably not
part of a self-sustaining population. Rhizomes are slender and shallow; they grow
quickly and branch often. This can result in dense colonies several meters across,
especially where competing vegetation has been suppressed. The common name
"sensitive fern" refers to the susceptibility of the leaves to frost.

Sterile leaves thrive all summer, die with first frost—July 9.

Fertile leaf—
August 11.

Sterile leaf and fertile leaf—July 29.

At a wetland edge, Isanti County—June 11.

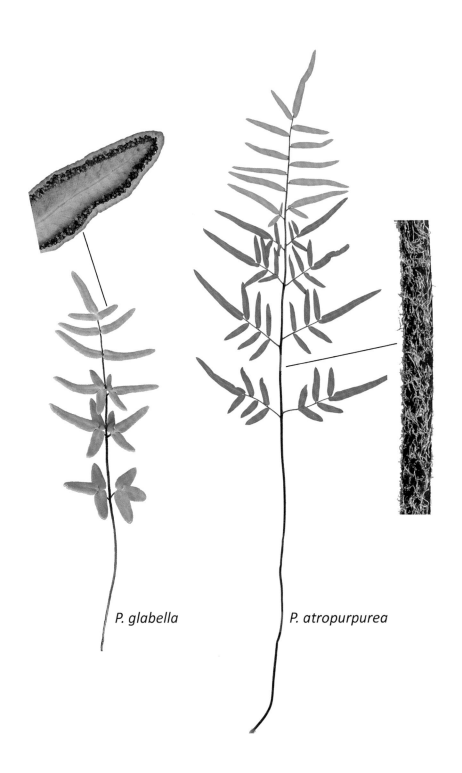

P. glabella

P. atropurpurea

PELLAEA (CLIFF-BRAKE FERNS)

The genus *Pellaea* has about 40 species scattered over much of the world. There are thought to be 15 in the United States and 2 in Minnesota. The genus is in the subfamily Cheilathoideae of the family Pteridaceae. There are 22 other genera and an estimated 426 species in the subfamily. These are the famed "cheilanthoid ferns," which are adapted to hot, dry, sunny habitats and are found in arid regions of the world. The only other member of this subfamily to occur in Minnesota is *Myriopteris gracilis* (slender lip fern, p. 254).

KEY TO *PELLAEA*

1. Rachis and costae covered with a dense tangle of hairs; the larger leaf segments
   2–4 cm long . . . . *P. atropurpurea*
1. Rachis and costae lacking hairs, or with only a few scattered hairs; the larger leaf
   segments 1–2.5 cm long . . . . *P. glabella*

Pellaea atropurpurea (L.) Link
Purple Cliff-Brake

RHIZOMES compact, short-branched.
LEAVES 10–35 cm long (usually 15–25),
3–10 cm wide; somewhat dimorphic with
fertile pinnules somewhat narrower than
sterile pinnules, and often twisted out of
plane with the leaf. **PETIOLE** persistent,
2–15 cm long, reddish black, shiny, hairy.
BLADE 1-pinnate distally, 2-pinnate
proximally, linear-lanceolate; rachis and
costae reddish black, densely hairy. **PINNAE**
distally simple, proximally with 1–5 pairs
of pinnules. **PINNULES AND SIMPLE**
PINNAE linear-oblong, stiff and leathery;
stalked, or sessile with a narrow base; the

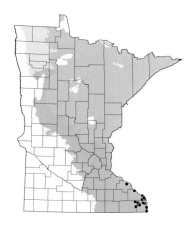

larger ones 2–4 cm long; lower surface with hairs along midrib; upper surface
glabrous; apex obtuse to barely acute; base truncate, occasionally auriculate or
hastate; margins entire, inrolled; veins obscure. **INDUSIA** false, formed by inrolled
leaf margins. **PHENOLOGY:** Leaves remain minimally green through winter and
restore in early spring when new growth begins. Spores are shed predominately
in summer.

IDENTIFICATION: To most people, *P. atropurpurea* and the closely related *P. glabella*
will stand out as oddities among Minnesota ferns. More than anything, it is the
thick, leathery, widely spaced leaf segments, not to mention their habit of
growing on bare rocks. To tell the two species apart, check the rachis. In the case
of *P. atropurpurea*, it will be covered in tangled hairs. There will be few if any hairs
on *P. glabella*. The purple color of the petiole, as implied by the name, does not
help separate it from *P. glabella*. And although *P. atropurpurea* is usually larger and
has more pinnae than *P. glabella*, there is considerable overlap.

NATURAL HISTORY: *Pellaea atropurpurea* occurs at scattered locations across much
of subboreal North America, extending southward to Central America. In
Minnesota, it is associated with bedrock outcrops on south-facing bluff prairies in
the southeastern border counties. It is usually rooted in crevices of sandstone or
dolomite, or sometimes in the sand that has eroded from the parent rock and
accumulated at the base of the outcrop. Plants are usually exposed to full sunlight
or may be partially shaded by an overhanging ledge. Habitats of the two species of
Pellaea are essentially the same, and where their ranges overlap, the two often
occur together, although *P. atropurpurea* is the rarer of the two by a considerable
margin.

On a sandstone outcrop, Houston County—July 1.

On a steep, rocky, bluff prairie.

Upper surface of a lower pinna.

Lower surface covered with sori.

Pellaea glabella subsp. *glabella* Mett. ex Kuhn
Smooth Cliff-Brake

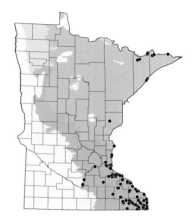

RHIZOMES compact, short-branched.
LEAVES essentially monomorphic, 5–30 cm
long (usually 10–15), 1–5 cm wide. **PETIOLE**
persistent, 2–15 cm long, reddish brown,
shiny, glabrous or with scattered hairs.
BLADE 1-pinnate, or 2-pinnate proximally;
roughly oblong; rachis similar to petiole.
PINNAE stiff and leathery; those on distal
portion simple; those on proximal portion
likely consisting of 3 pinnules. **PINNULES
AND SIMPLE PINNAE** oblong to lanceolate,
short-stalked or sessile, the larger ones
1–2.5 cm long, glabrous except for
occasional hairs on the underside near the
midrib; apex obtuse; base truncate or broadly tapered; margins entire, inrolled.
VEINS obscure. **INDUSIA** false, formed by inrolled leaf margins. **PHENOLOGY:**
Pinnae and pinnules shrivel and turn brown in winter, and restore in early spring
when new growth begins. Spores are shed in summer and fall.

IDENTIFICATION: Among ferns, the genus *Pellaea* is generally distinctive. But
telling the two Minnesota species apart requires a quick check for hairs on the
rachis. Most people can see the hairs on *P. atropurpurea* without magnification;
P. glabella subsp. *glabella* will appear smooth. Differences in size and number of
pinnae mentioned in the key work best with "maximally" developed specimens.

NATURAL HISTORY: There may be as many as 4 subspecies of *P. glabella*, all
endemic to North America but geographically isolated from one another. The only
subspecies known to occur in Minnesota is subspecies *glabella*, which is limited to
eastern and central parts of the country. It is an apogamous tetraploid, meaning it
is a nonsexual species that originated by a doubling of the chromosomes of a
closely related subspecies. It still produces fertile spores that develop into
gametophytes, but in this case the gametophytes cannot interbreed and are
called nonsexual. In southeastern Minnesota, it is easy to find *P. glabella* subsp.
glabella on vertical exposures of sedimentary bedrock. It occurs on sandstone,
limestone, and dolomite with about equal frequency. It is usually in the open
where it gets direct sunlight, or sometimes in shaded situations. Where suitable
conditions occur, *P. glabella* subsp. *glabella* is common, although never abundant.
In northeastern Minnesota, it occurs on igneous rock, such as basalt, and is
quite rare.

Bedrock exposure on a bluff prairie overlooking Rushford, Fillmore County—July 28.

Underside of a fertile leaf—
September 29.

Nestled tightly in a sandstone crevice—May 30.

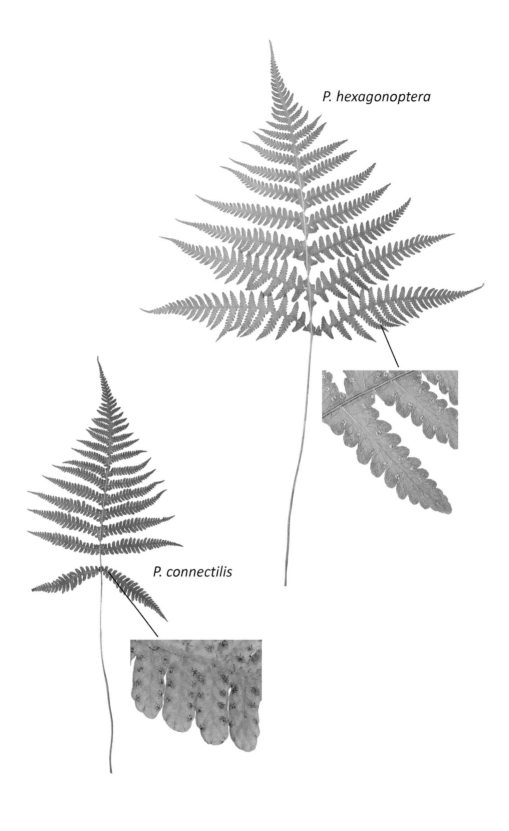

P. hexagonoptera

P. connectilis

PHEGOPTERIS (BEECH FERNS)

Worldwide, there are 6 species in the genus *Phegopteris*. The genus has been placed in the family Thelypteridaceae, a huge family with 37 genera and an estimated 1,190 species. Three species of *Phegopteris* occur in forests of North America, 2 of which are found in Minnesota.

The leaf blade of a typical *Phegopteris* has a triangular shape; broad or narrow, depending on the species. The primary divisions of the leaf may seem separate, but a closer look will reveal they are connected to each other (completely or in part) by a thin band of leaf tissue that runs along the rachis. When such is the case, the leaf is said to be pinnatifid. When the primary divisions are also pinnatifid, the whole leaf is considered 2-pinnatifid. This is easy to overlook but an important detail when trying to navigate the key to genera (p. 171). In this one feature, our species of *Phegopteris* are like *Onoclea sensibilis* (sensitive fern, p. 258) but unlike nearly every other fern in Minnesota.

KEY TO *PHEGOPTERIS*

1. The larger leaves 15–35 cm wide (usually > 20 cm); the lowest pair of pinnae usually connected to the pair directly above by a narrow band of tissue along the rachis; the lowest pinnae 3–7 cm wide; the larger segments of the lowest pinnae 2–5 mm long, with distinctly lobed margins . . . . *P. hexagonoptera*

1. The larger leaves 10–25 cm wide (usually < 20 cm); the lowest pair of pinnae usually not connected along the rachis to the pinnae pair directly above; the lowest pinnae 1.5–3 cm wide; the larger segments of the lowest pinnae 0.7–2 cm long, with unlobed margins
. . . . *P. connectilis*

Phegopteris connectilis (Michx.) Watt
Narrow Beech Fern

[*Thelypteris phegopteris* (L.) Slosson]

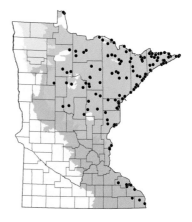

RHIZOMES horizontal, slender, frequently branching, to 30+ cm long. **LEAVES** monomorphic, dying back in winter, 15–55 cm long, 6–25 cm wide (usually 12–18 cm). **PETIOLE** 8–40 cm long; with pale hairs dense distally and sparse proximally, and often with scattered brown scales. **BLADE** triangular to narrowly triangular, usually somewhat longer than wide, predominately 2-pinnatifid, although 1-pinnate-pinnatifid at base. **PINNAE**: The lowest pair 1.5–3 cm wide, reflexed and twisted out of plane, separate from those above; more distal pairs connected along the rachis. **ULTIMATE SEGMENTS**: Margins ciliate, entire or scalloped; the larger segments 0.7–2 cm long; surfaces with appressed hairs, especially along veins. **SORI** round, attached on veins near margins. **INDUSIA** lacking. **PHENOLOGY**: Leaves emerge in spring and die back in autumn. Sporangia are visible from midsummer to autumn.

IDENTIFICATION: The most noticeable feature of *P. connectilis* is the lowest pair of pinnae, which jut downward and forward, seeming to break the symmetry of the leaf. The closely related *P. hexagonoptera* does the same thing. To separate the two species in the field, botanists tend to rely on a seemingly insignificant feature: In the case of *P. hexagonoptera,* all the pinnae are connected or nearly connected to the pair directly above by a thin band of leaf tissue running along the rachis. The situation with *P. connectilis* is similar except the lowest pair are clearly separate. Surprisingly, it seems to work nearly every time. For confirmation, check the segments of the lowest pinnae; those of *P. connectilis* are smaller than those of *P. hexagonoptera,* and they are unlobed.

NATURAL HISTORY: *Phegopteris connectilis* is widespread in boreal and cool temperate regions of North America and Eurasia. It is one of the more common and characteristic ferns of forests in northern Minnesota, occurring under a canopy of either needle-leaved or broad-leaved trees. It is usually found in moist acidic soils, often on slopes with thin, rocky soil. It also occurs in low, swampy forests, although not in the wettest parts of a swamp, and certainly not in standing water. In good habitat, it may form large patches of evenly spaced leaves corresponding to an intricate network of underground rhizomes.

Can form large patches in good habitat.

Note the jutting angle of the lowest pinnae.

Sori are round, lack indusia.

Lowest pinnae separate from the rest.

Phegopteris hexagonoptera (Michx.) Fée
Broad Beech Fern

[*Thelypteris hexagonoptera* (Michx.) Nieuland]

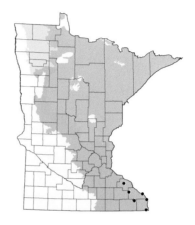

RHIZOMES horizontal, frequently branching, slender, to 30+ cm long. **LEAVES** monomorphic, dying back in winter, 25–75 cm long, 15–35 cm wide (usually 20–30 cm). **PETIOLE** 10–50 cm long, ± glabrous or with sparse pale hairs distally. **BLADE** broadly triangular, usually somewhat wider than long, 2-pinnatifid. **PINNAE:** The lowest pair 3–7 cm wide, somewhat reflexed and twisted out of plane, connected to the pinnae above by a narrow band of tissue along the rachis. **ULTIMATE SEGMENTS** ciliate, entire or the largest ones lobed or pinnatifid; 2–5 cm long; surfaces with stiff appressed hairs, especially along the veins. **SORI** round, attached on veins toward margins. **INDUSIA** lacking. **PHENOLOGY:** Leaves are seasonal, emerging in spring and dying back in autumn. Sporangia are visible from midsummer to autumn.

IDENTIFICATION: The common names "broad beech fern" versus "narrow beech fern" (*P. hexagonoptera* versus *P. connectilis*) refer to the proportions of the leaf blade. But that character alone is not enough to separate difficult specimens. Most of the meaningful differences have to do with size rather than proportions. Broad beech fern is simply a larger plant, especially the lowest pair of pinnae. They will be wider, and the individual segments of the pinnae will be longer and distinctly lobed, sometimes even pinnatifid. Also check to see if the lowest pair of pinnae are connected to the pair immediately above by a narrow band of leaf tissue that runs along the side of the rachis (such a rachis is said to be "winged"). If connected, or nearly connected, that will strongly indicate *P. hexagonoptera*.

NATURAL HISTORY: *Phegopteris hexagonoptera* is found in the eastern half of the United States and adjacent parts of southern Canada, reaching the western edge of its range rather abruptly in the southeastern corner of Minnesota. Favorable habitats are mesic forests, typically on north-facing slopes in shaded stream valleys. Such habitats support many fern species, but in Minnesota, *P. hexagonoptera* is one of the rarest. It typically occurs in rhizomatous colonies, meaning that individual leaves arise singly from a discrete place along a network of slender rhizomes rather than clustered in a tight, vaselike configuration.

Cloning, not clumping, Winona County—
July 10.

Leaf broadly triangular, 2-pinnatifid.

Where the rachilla joins the rachis (botanist's
jargon).

Pinnae connected along rachis by a
"wing."

P. virginianum

POLYPODIUM (POLYPODY FERNS)

The fern genus *Polypodium* resides in the family Polypodiaceae, which consists of perhaps 65 genera and an estimated 1,652 species. There are about 40 species in the genus *Polypodium*. Most occur in the tropics, where many are epiphytic in rainforests. There are 11 species in North America, primarily in rocky areas of the west. North American *Polypodium* has been described in *Flora of North America* as a "complex assemblage of interactive species" (Haufler et al. 1993, 315). As daunting as that might sound, only one species, *P. virginianum,* occurs in Minnesota, and it is seldom misidentified.

Polypodium virginianum L.
Rock Polypody

[*Polypodium vulgare* var. *virginianum* (L.) D. C. Eaton]

RHIZOMES horizontal, shallow, to 20+ cm long, with frequent branches. **LEAVES** monomorphic, remaining green in winter, to 40 cm long and 2–7 cm wide, stiff and somewhat leathery. **PETIOLE** jointed at base, greenish to straw-colored, with narrow wings (decurrent tissue) distally, glabrous. **BLADE** narrowly oblong to lanceolate, 1-pinnatifid, usually widest near or below the middle, evenly tapered to an acute apex, only slightly if at all narrowed at base; rachis usually glabrous. **SEGMENTS** oblong, 3–9 mm wide; margins entire to shallowly toothed or scalloped; apex rounded to blunt; veins obscurely pinnate, midvein black, lateral veins ending in hydathodes before reaching the margins.

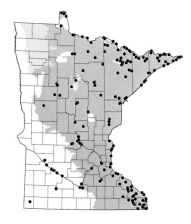

SORI nearly circular. **INDUSIA** absent. **PHENOLOGY:** Fertile leaves are produced through the summer and into the fall, with spores being released during the winter and the following spring. All leaves stay green through winter.

IDENTIFICATION: The leaves of *P. virginianum* are thick and somewhat leathery. They typically stand stiffly erect or nearly so, but they do not stand very tall. The structure of the leaf is consistently pinnatifid, meaning all the leaf segments are connected at their base, making identification relatively simple.

NATURAL HISTORY: *Polypodium virginianum* is found primarily in boreal and temperate regions of the eastern and central United States and Canada. Most of the records from Minnesota are associated with somewhat dry, shady, rocky habitats, such as cliffs, talus, outcrops, and sometimes mossy boulders. But a substantial number of occurrences have been found growing in soil, particularly sandy soil on steep, forested slopes and in ravines. It seems that loose, coarse-textured, acidic soils are preferred but circumneutral soils are sometimes tolerated. It really does not need much in the way of soil; the rhizomes are shallowly rooted and very tough. Occasionally a few pioneering individuals are found in unpromising habitat such as hummocks in a swamp or a road embankment. This may be another example of a population testing the suitability of new habitat. The leaves of *P. virginianum* are notably tolerant of desiccation. Perhaps more than once during a summer dry spell, the plants will lose most of their unbound water but will recover quickly when it rains, like a desert plant, with no ill effects.

Underside of leaf.

In a rock crevice, Pine County—October 3.

Leaves stand stiffly erect—
September 6.

On a steep, sandy hillside, Washington
County—August 29.

sterile leaf   fertile leaf

P. braunii   *P. acrostichoides*

POLYSTICHUM (HOLLY FERNS)

Polystichum is a large genus occurring worldwide. There are about 500 known species, with about 15 occurring in the United States and 2 in Minnesota. The genus is currently placed in the family Dryopteridaceae along with perhaps 25 other genera and more than 2,000 species.

In addition to the 2 species of *Polystichum* that are known to occur in Minnesota, there is a third species that bears mention. It is *P. lonchitis* (northern holly fern), a western species with isolated populations in the western Great Lakes region. It is sometimes reported to occur in Minnesota, but substantial evidence to support that claim is lacking. If it does occur in Minnesota, it would likely be in rocky habitats near the northeastern tip of the state. It has long, slender, 1-pinnate leaves like *P. acrostichoides,* but it does not have the peculiar aspect of half-size pinnae at the top of the fertile leaf. Also, the pinnae of *P. lonchitis* continue to the very base of the leaf, leaving little if any petiole.

KEY TO *POLYSTICHUM*

1. Leaves 1-pinnate, 6–12 cm wide . . . . *P. acrostichoides*
1. Leaves 2-pinnate, 10–25 cm wide . . . . *P. braunii*

Polystichum acrostichoides (Michx.) Schott
Christmas Fern

RHIZOMES compact, occasionally to 10 cm
in length, branching occasionally. LEAVES
remaining green in winter, 30–80 cm long,
6–12 cm wide, partially dimorphic; fertile
leaves about ¼ longer than sterile leaves.
PETIOLE 8–18 cm long, with both broad
and slender yellow-brown scales. BLADE
1-pinnate, narrowly elliptic to linear-
lanceolate, tapered gradually to an acute
apex, narrowed little if at all to the base;
rachis scaly in the manner of the petiole.
PINNAE irregularly oblong; base truncate to
broadly tapered, with an acroscopic auricle;
apex acute or blunt; margins with spine-

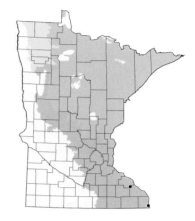

tipped teeth; lower surface with hairs along the midrib; upper surface glabrous or
nearly so; fertile pinnae (found distally) about half the size of corresponding
sterile pinnae. SORI round, often confluent. INDUSIA entire, peltate. PHENOLOGY:
Poorly known for Minnesota. All leaves likely remain green over winter.

IDENTIFICATION: On average, the fertile leaves of *P. acrostichoides* are longer and
more erect than the sterile leaves. Otherwise, they resemble the sterile leaves,
except for one unusual feature. The pinnae in the upper portion of the leaf bear
all the sporangia, and they are disproportionately small. They are no more than
half the size as would be expected if the whole leaf were sterile. In the absence of
fertile leaves, *P. acrostichoides* might look most like *Homalosorus pycnocarpos*
(narrow-leaved glade fern, p. 246) or a greatly oversized *Asplenium platyneuron*
(ebony spleenwort, p. 182). All three species have somewhat erect, 1-pinnate
leaves, and occur in similar habitats in the southeastern corner of the state. But
among these look-alikes, only *P. acrostichoides* has spine-tipped teeth along the
margins of the pinnae. Also, the rachis and petiole of *P. acrostichoides* are covered
with orangish, papery scales.

NATURAL HISTORY: *Polystichum acrostichoides* is found in the eastern half of
temperate North America, barely reaching Minnesota at the northwestern edge of
its range. Little is known about *P. acrostichoides* in the state, other than it is very
rare. There are no recent records from the state, but it will likely be found again,
and probably in the stream-dissected terrain in the southeastern corner of the
state, most likely in a deep, wooded ravine or a densely forested stream valley.

In a typical forest setting—July 8.

Fertile leaf—July 30.

Acroscopic auricles.

Fertile pinnae—July 30.

Ventral view—July 8.

Polystichum braunii (Spenner) Fée
Braun's Holly Fern

RHIZOMES compact, occasionally to 10 cm
in length, branching infrequently. LEAVES
monomorphic, remaining green in winter,
30–75 cm long, 8–25 cm wide. PETIOLE
2–8 cm long, densely covered with both
broad and slender yellow-brown scales.
BLADE dark green above, pale gray-green
beneath, 2-pinnate, narrowly elliptic,
tapered evenly at both ends; rachis scaly in
the manner of the petiole. PINNAE sessile,
widest at the base, tapering to an acute
apex. PINNULES lined with spine-tipped
teeth; base truncate to broadly tapered,
attached at one corner with a broad, short
stalk; acroscopic auricle poorly developed; upper surface with long hairs or
occasionally glabrous; lower surface with narrow hair-tipped scales. SORI round,
in rows between midrib and margin. INDUSIA laciniate, peltate. PHENOLOGY: The
leaves release most of their spores in August and September and remain green
through winter.

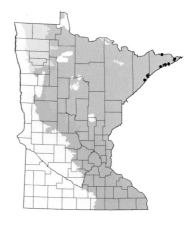

IDENTIFICATION: *Polystichum braunii* is not an overly large or conspicuous fern. It
will likely not attract the attention of a casual hiker, but a number of interesting
details set it apart from more common ferns. The pinnae extend nearly to the
bottom of the leaf, getting progressively smaller. The result is a very short petiole,
and a leaf with almost perfect transverse symmetry. The rachis and petiole are
conspicuously covered with large, orangish, papery scales. The margins of the leaf
segments are lined with low, broad-based teeth, each tipped with a slender spine.
If these details are noticed, then identification is confirmed.

NATURAL HISTORY: In North America, *P. braunii* occupies small, isolated ranges in
the Great Lakes region eastward to the Canadian maritime provinces, and in the
Pacific Northwest. It is also found in parts of Eurasia. In Minnesota, it has been
found in deep, shaded ravines, river gorges, and narrow canyons in the
northeastern corner of the state. It also occurs along small, intermittent, low-
gradient streams and heavily forested slopes. It is usually rooted in moist soil with
high organic content and shaded by white cedar, yellow birch, or sugar maple.
These are all habitats with many ferns, yet *P. braunii* is among the rarest, and is
very hard to find without prior knowledge. Among local botanists, it has the
reputation of being hidden in remote, inaccessible forests.

Leaves arise in a vaselike cluster.

Very short petiole.

Papery scales on rachis.

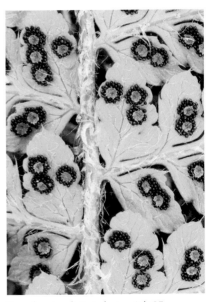

Round sori; peltate indusia—July 17.

P. aquilinum
subsp. *latiusculum*

PTERIDIUM (BRACKEN FERNS)

The genus *Pteridium* is one of 10 genera in the family Dennstaedtiaceae. It occurs essentially worldwide and contains perhaps 4 species. The only species of *Pteridium* that occurs in Minnesota is *P. aquilinum* (common bracken fern or just bracken). It is widespread in the Northern Hemisphere and is thought to contain as many as 11 subspecies. At least 3 subspecies are known to occur in the United States, but only subspecies *latiusculum* (eastern bracken) is believed to occur in Minnesota.

Pteridium aquilinum subsp. *latiusculum* (L.) Kuhn
Eastern Bracken

RHIZOMES horizontal, long, slender, smooth, frequently branched. LEAVES monomorphic, dying back in winter, 35–180 cm long, 25–85 cm wide. PETIOLE 15–100 cm long; greenish or straw-colored, with a dark base; glabrous or with patches of short hairs, attached at a distinct swelling on a short, vertical branch of the rhizome. BLADE stiff and leathery, broadly triangular or ovate, oblique to the petiole; 3-pinnate, or 3-pinnate-pinnatifid proximally, 20–80 cm long; surfaces and costae glabrous or sparsely hairy. PINNAE margins minutely hairy, inrolled; basal

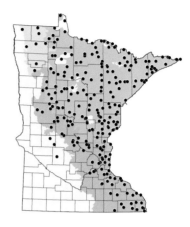

pinnae remote, greatly enlarged; terminal segment of each pinna elongated. SORI ± continuous, covered by outer false indusium and inner true indusium.

PHENOLOGY: Leaves typically emerge aboveground in early May and reach full size in June. Sporangia generally mature from late July through August or September and release most of their spores before winter.

IDENTIFICATION: *Pteridium aquilinum* subsp. *latiusculum* is one of the largest ferns in Minnesota, typically reaching waist or even chest high. It keys out next to the oak ferns (*Gymnocarpium*) because of the 3-parted triangular leaf blade (p. 172). But the oak ferns are small, delicate, ankle-high ferns, which will not be mistaken for eastern bracken when seen in the field.

NATURAL HISTORY: *Pteridium aquilinum* subsp. *latiusculum* occurs in Eurasia and much of eastern North America, including Mexico. It is ubiquitous throughout the forested region of Minnesota; its pervasiveness cannot be overstated. It is normally mild-mannered, although omnipresent, occupying its own small niche in the forest. But when the forest is cleared or otherwise compromised, it seems to slip the bonds of whatever might have restrained it before. Its seemingly eternal rhizome system gives it supreme dominance belowground. Aboveground, its chemical defenses protect it from insect pests, grazing herbivores, and pathogens. This is a superplant. Although locally aggressive, it does not seem to have expanded its original range in Minnesota. It grows in a wide range of soil types but appears to do best in moderately acidic, well-drained loam and sandy loam, and where soils are thin and rocky. It does not occur in permanent wetlands and evidently does not compete well in prairie soils or in agricultural soils. It thrives in full sun as well as shade.

Note 3-parted (ternate) leaf—June 24.

A solid carpet of bracken—May 21.

Newly emerging leaf—May 25.

LYNDEN B. GERDES

Leaf margins lined with hairs; lateral veins forked.

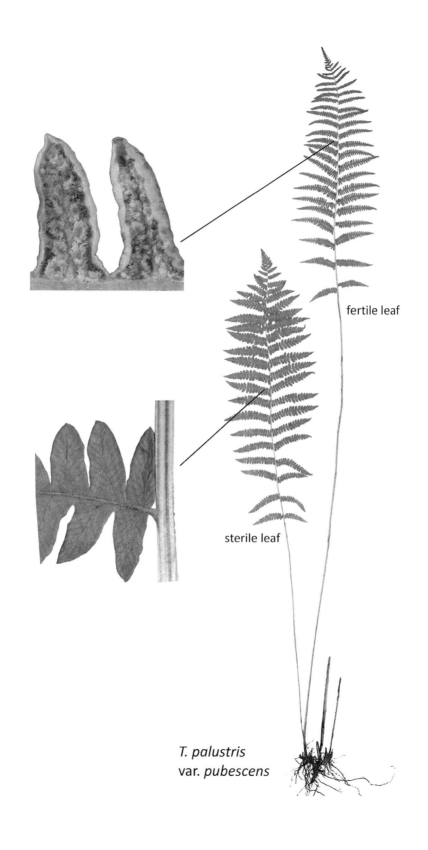

fertile leaf

sterile leaf

T. palustris
var. *pubescens*

THELYPTERIS (MARSH FERNS)

The genus *Thelypteris* is in the family Thelypteridaceae, one of the largest of fern families with about 1,200 species occurring worldwide, mostly in tropical and subtropical regions. As many as 37 genera are sometimes recognized in the family, 2 of which occur in Minnesota, *Phegopteris* and *Thelypteris*. The genus *Thelypteris* has only 2 species, 1 of which occurs in Minnesota, *T. palustris* var. *pubescens* (eastern marsh fern).

Thelypteris palustris var. pubescens (Lawson) Fernald
Eastern Marsh Fern

RHIZOMES horizontal, slender, to 35+ cm
long, smooth, occasionally branched.
LEAVES dying back in winter, (20)30–100
cm long, 6–18 cm wide, somewhat
dimorphic; fertile leaves longer, narrower,
more erect, with inrolled margins. **PETIOLE**
slender, straw-colored with a darkened
base, 9–45 cm long, with long, slender
hairs distally and sometimes sparse scales
proximally. **BLADE** lanceolate to narrowly
ovate, 1-pinnate-pinnatifid, tapering to an
acute apex, narrowed only slightly to a
truncate base; rachis hairy. **PINNAE** sessile
or nearly so; segments oblong, entire, base

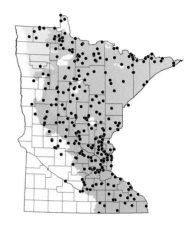

broadly attached, apex blunt or broadly pointed, hairy on costae and sometimes
midrib; venation pinnate, lateral veins forked. **SORI** round, ± confluent.
INDUSIA round, often glandular. **PHENOLOGY:** Sterile leaves emerge in early May
and reach full size in June or July; fertile leaves appear in July and mature in
August. All leaves die back with the first frost. Spores are released in autumn and
during the winter.

IDENTIFICATION: In the field, *T. palustris* var. *pubescens* can look like a small,
slender *Athyrium filix-femina* var. *angustum* (northern lady fern, p. 190). But the
leaves of *A. filix-femina* var. *angustum* are 2-pinnate, meaning the smallest leaf
segments are separate from each other, and they are lined with pointed teeth.
The smallest segments of eastern marsh fern are all connected along their
bases (1-pinnate-pinnatifid), and the margins are not toothed. Sterile leaves of
T. palustris var. *pubescens* far outnumber the fertile leaves, and although the two
leaf forms do look somewhat different, both will come out at the same place in
the key.

NATURAL HISTORY: The typical variety of *T. palustris* (*T. palustris* var. *palustris*) is
found in Eurasia. *Thelypteris palustris* var. *pubescens* occurs in the eastern half of
the United States and adjacent parts of Canada. It is common in wetlands
throughout the forested region of Minnesota. Habitats include swamps, fens,
sedge meadows, marshes, and floating mats. Although it might appear delicate, it
is highly competitive in dense vegetation and commonly grows unsheltered from
the elements. Soils are usually saturated peat or muck, sometimes sodden loam.
The rhizomes do well when continually saturated but also survive when the
substrate is only moist. It tolerates a certain amount of shade but needs direct
sunlight for a portion of the day to thrive.

With tufted loosestrife, Sherburne County—
June 11.

Sterile leaf—June 24.

Underside of pinnae showing sori—September 17.

Fertile leaf—August 5.

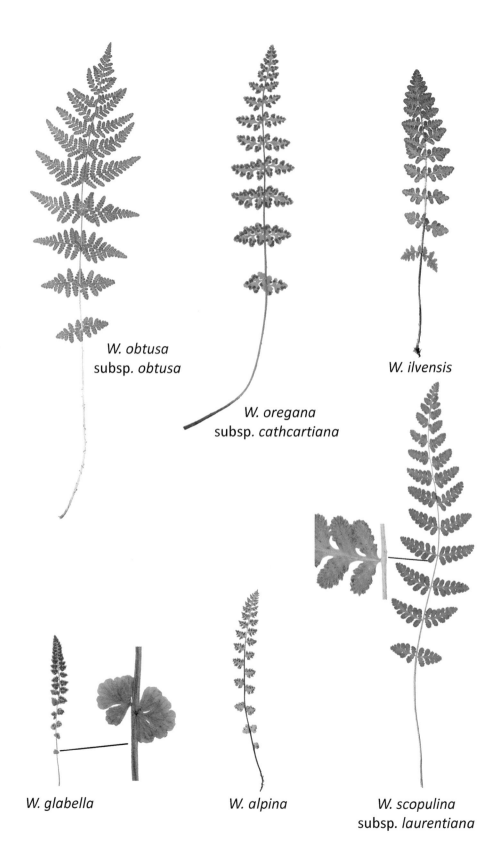

W. obtusa
subsp. *obtusa*

W. oregana
subsp. *cathcartiana*

W. ilvensis

W. glabella

W. alpina

W. scopulina
subsp. *laurentiana*

WOODSIA (CLIFF FERNS)

The genus *Woodsia* is the sole member of the family Woodsiaceae. There are about 40 species of *Woodsia* in the world, occurring primarily in boreal and temperate habitats of the Northern Hemisphere, with some species in Central and South America and southern Africa. There are 10 species of *Woodsia* in North America and 6 in Minnesota.

Confusion with species of *Cystopteris* (bladder ferns, p. 199) is common. The only single character that will separate all *Woodsia* from all *Cystopteris* is the indusium. The indusia of *Cystopteris* are said to be bladder-shaped; that is, the sporangia will appear to be partially contained in a sack- or cup-shaped structure lying on its side. The indusia of *Woodsia* seem to encircle the sporangia from below, with either spidery arms or scalelike segments. Features of the indusium are difficult to see and somewhat ephemeral. Alternatively, look for 3 characters: hydathodes, stalked glands, and jointed petioles. The presence on any 2 will confirm *Woodsia* in a comparison with *Cystopteris*.

Hydathodes are associated with the veins of the leaves and are just visible to the unaided eye. A vein will end in a hydathode, if a hydathode is present, just before reaching the margin of the leaf. It will look like a continuation of the vein, but it will be thicker than the vein and have a contrasting color or texture. If a hydathode is not present, the vein will continue unchanged to the margin.

Stalked glands are very small but can be critically important. There will likely be a variety of hairs, scales, or chaff growing from the epidermis of any fern, but the "tiny, stalked glands" mentioned in the key are the smallest and most specific. The stalk will be rather stout, and it will have a roundish structure at the top, like a golf ball sitting on a tee. They will be clear, white, or yellow.

Jointed petioles are a feature highlighted in the key. The joint is visible as a slightly discolored or swollen node a few centimeters above the base of the petiole. It is small but distinct. After separation (abscission), the lower portion of each petiole is retained on the rhizome, creating a somewhat even stubble that persists and accumulates for years. Rather than looking for the petiole stubble, which can sometimes be found on ferns without jointed petioles, it is recommended that an intact petiole be inspected for the joint.

1. Petioles disarticulating at a joint a few cm above the base; leaves lacking tiny, stalked glands; indusia composed of many long, tangled, hairlike segments; margins of ultimate leaf segments entire or scalloped.

    2. Leaves (especially the rachis) moderately to densely covered with long, pale hairs and narrow scales; basal pinnae somewhat elongate, typically about twice as long as broad, and with 2–5 pair of distinct segments . . . . *W. ilvensis*

    2. Leaves with only a few scattered hairs or scales, or none at all (disregarding the hairs that form the indusia); basal pinnae ovate or hemispherical, less than twice as long as broad, and with only 1–2 pairs of distinct segments.

        3. Petioles dark reddish brown or purplish; rachis usually with a few scattered hairs or narrow scales; basal pinnae somewhat longer than broad. . . . . *W. alpina*

        3. Petioles straw-colored or greenish; rachis lacking hair or scales; basal pinnae broader than long . . . . *W. glabella*

1. Petioles not disarticulating at a joint; leaves (especially lower surface and rachis) with tiny, stalked glands; indusia composed of scalelike segments, only the tips sometimes hairlike (easiest to see early in development); margins of ultimate leaf segments with ± pointed, triangular teeth.

    4. Leaves with long, clear, multicelled (segmented) hairs; stalked glands yellow . . . . *W. scopulina* subsp. *laurentiana*

    4. Leaves without such hairs, although hairlike scales (broader and flatter than hairs) sometimes seen on rachis; stalked glands clear.

        5. Petioles entirely pale green or straw-colored; indusia consisting of a few broad segments with short tips; the larger pinnae 3–6 cm long, with 4–10 distinct segments along each margin . . . . *W. obtusa* subsp. *obtusa*

        5. Petioles brown to dark brown or dark purple on proximal half; indusia consisting of a few to several segments with long, narrow tips; the larger pinnae rarely as much as 3 cm long, and rarely with more than 5 distinct segments along each margin . . . . *W. oregana* subsp. *cathcartiana*

STERILE *WOODSIA* HYBRIDS KNOWN TO OCCUR IN MINNESOTA

Species of *Woodsia* seem to hybridize freely, but the offspring are sterile, meaning the spores of a hybrid are deformed and do not germinate. Hybrids exist as scattered individuals among co-occurring and reproducing populations of their parent species. Although hybrids can be recognized by having abortive spores and morphological features intermediate between the two parents, the determination of a hybrid *Woodsia* specimen is very difficult and perhaps best left to specialists. The following hybrids have been confirmed to occur in Minnesota.

Woodsia ×*abbeae* Butters (*W. ilvensis* × *W. oregana*)

Woodsia ×*gracilis* (G. Lawson) Butters (*W. ilvensis* × *W. alpina*)

Woodsia ×*maxonii* R. M. Tryon (*W. oregana* × *W. scopulina*)

Woodsia alpina (Bolton) S. F. Gray
Alpine Cliff Fern

RHIZOMES compact, short-branched.
LEAVES monomorphic, dying back in
winter, 3–20 cm long, 1–2.5 cm wide.
PETIOLE reddish brown to dark purple;
sparsely scaly, at least near base, otherwise
glabrous; jointed at a swollen node a few
cm above the base, the proximal portion
persisting. **BLADES** ± linear, 1-pinnate-
pinnatifid to questionably 2-pinnate,
lacking glands; lower surface with few
narrow scales and hairs; upper surface
glabrous; rachis with a few widely scattered
hairs and slender scales. **PINNAE** ovate-
lanceolate, longer than wide, tapered to a

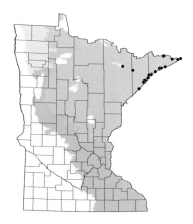

rounded or broadly pointed apex; largest pinnae with 2–4 pairs of lateral lobes
(segments); margins entire or broadly crenulate; veins imperfectly pinnate,
ending in hydathodes. **INDUSIA** consisting of hairlike segments. **PHENOLOGY:**
Poorly known; spores apparently shed mid-July through September.

IDENTIFICATION: The first dichotomy of the key separates *W. alpina*, *W. glabella*,
and *W. ilvensis* from the others. They all have jointed petioles, lack stalked
glands, and have no "teeth" along the margins of the leaf segments. Among these
3 species, *W. ilvensis* usually stands out as being larger in general appearance and
"scaley." The remaining *W. alpina* and *W. glabella* are very similar and easily
confused. Most of the petioles of *W. alpina* are dark brown or purplish black at
maturity, while those of *W. glabella* are greenish or straw-colored. Also, the pinnae
on the lower half of the leaf blade of *W. alpina* are somewhat longer than they are
broad, while those of *W. glabella* are broader than long.

NATURAL HISTORY: It has been determined that *W. alpina* originated in the distant
past as a fertile hybrid between *W. ilvensis* and *W. glabella*. It has been evolving on
its own for a long time and is now a distinct species, able to exploit a unique
ecological niche. It now occurs at widely scattered locations in arctic, alpine, and
boreal habitats in North America and Eurasia. In Minnesota, it is quite rare, found
only in sheltered crevices on north-facing cliffs along Lake Superior and in the
Border Lakes region between Minnesota and Ontario. The cliffs are often situated
in narrow river gorges or overlooking deep, oligotrophic lakes. The microhabitat is
typically cool, moist, and well shaded.

On a north-facing cliff, Cook County—July 31.

Leaf from above.

Rachis and petiole are reddish brown.

Woodsia glabella R. Br. ex Richardson
Smooth Cliff Fern

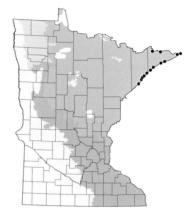

RHIZOMES compact, short-branched.
LEAVES monomorphic, dying back in
winter, 3–13 cm long, 0.8–1.8 cm wide.
PETIOLE greenish or straw-colored, scaly
near base, otherwise glabrous; jointed at a
swollen node a few cm above the base,
proximal portion persisting. **BLADES** ±
linear, 1-pinnate-pinnatifid, evenly tapered
to an acute apex, narrowed somewhat to
the base, glabrous; rachis glabrous.
UPPER PINNAE triangular in outline;
somewhat longer than wide; apices angled;
bases broadly tapered; margins entire,
with 2–3 pairs of distinct lateral lobes.
LOWER PINNAE hemispherical; somewhat wider than long; apices broadly
rounded; bases truncate; margins crenulate, with 1 pair of distinct lateral lobes.
VEINS imperfectly pinnate, ending in hydathodes. **INDUSIA** consisting of hairlike
segments. **PHENOLOGY:** Imperfectly known in Minnesota; spores apparently shed
mid-July through September.

IDENTIFICATION: *Woodsia glabella* is, on average, the smallest cliff fern in
Minnesota. The leaves are usually about the length and width of a finger, and
there may not be many of them. From any distance, it will look very much like
W. alpina, but there are a few small differences. Most importantly, the petioles of
W. glabella are straw-colored or pale green. Also, the basal pinnae are smaller,
proportionally broader and rounder, and have fewer lobes. Curiously, these
differences apply only to the lower pinnae; the upper pinnae of the two species are
essentially identical.

NATURAL HISTORY: *Woodsia glabella* occurs in far northern regions of North
America and Eurasia. It is a small, compact fern well adapted for life in the arctic.
It occurs in Minnesota at the extreme southern edge of its range and is quite rare.
It is found exclusively in sheltered cliff habitats along the shore of Lake Superior,
and north-facing cliffs associated with the larger lakes along the Minnesota/
Ontario border. These are shady, cool, moss-filled cracks and seams on vertical
cliff faces where small amounts of wind-borne soil and eroded rock material
accumulate. The chemical nature of rocks in these habitats is generally considered
circumneutral or alkaline, but the small microhabitats that support this species
may not represent the textbook version of geology of the region. And the degree to
which the plant interacts with the rock is not known.

In a rocky crevice, Lake County—September 6.

The length and width of a finger.

Petiole and rachis are greenish, smooth.

Woodsia ilvensis (L.) R. Br.
Rusty Cliff Fern

RHIZOMES compact, short-branched.
LEAVES monomorphic, dying back in
winter, 6–27 cm long, 1–4 cm wide.
PETIOLE jointed at a swollen node a few cm
above the base, proximal portion
persisting; green to brown, or dark purple
in late season; hairy and scaly, lacking
glands. **BLADES** narrowly lanceolate to
narrowly oblong-elliptic, 1-pinnate-
pinnatifid to 2-pinnate, lacking glands;
lower surface with hairs and narrow scales;
upper surface with sparse hairs or nearly
hairless; rachis with abundant hairs and
scales. **PINNAE** ovate-lanceolate to narrowly

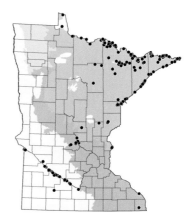

triangular, longer than wide, gradually tapered to a rounded or broadly angled
apex; largest pinnae with 3–6 pairs of distinct lateral segments; margins entire
or broadly scalloped; veins imperfectly pinnate, ending in hydathodes.
INDUSIA consisting of long, hairlike segments. **PHENOLOGY:** Growth begins in
early May; sporangia develop in June and early July; spores are released in late
July through August.

IDENTIFICATION: *Woodsia ilvensis* is the most common and predictable *Woodsia* in
Minnesota. In fact, finding any *Woodsia* in Minnesota other than *W. ilvensis* is
noteworthy. The rusty color that gives *W. ilvensis* its common name is seen on the
undersides of the leaves and is caused by the densely packed sporangia, the
hairlike indusia, and the scales. The stiff stubble left behind when the leaves are
shed each fall accumulates for a number of years and becomes conspicuous on
older robust plants. This feature is important to note but is not exclusive to this
species.

NATURAL HISTORY: *Woodsia ilvensis* is widespread in northern parts of North
America and Eurasia. In Minnesota, it seems to be common wherever there are
extensive exposures of igneous or metamorphic bedrock, excepting quarries and
roadcuts. Such exposures are usually the result of glacial scouring or subsequent
erosion. In other words, *W. ilvensis* is not limited by climate as much as geological
history. In general, look for it on cliffs, talus, modest outcrops, and boulder fields,
especially where exposed to the sun for some portion of the day. It is the hardiest
of the Minnesota *Woodsia,* although in the harshest environment it can be very
small and compact, almost mosslike. The leaves will turn brown and shrivel
during dry summers, although that will not kill the plant.

On bedrock with *Cladonia arbuscula*, Lake County.

In a cliffside crevice, Cook County.

Indusia consist of long, hairlike segments.

Rachis and petiole are hairy and scaly.

Woodsia obtusa subsp. *obtusa* (Spreng.) Torr.
Blunt-Lobed Cliff Fern

RHIZOMES compact, short-branched.
LEAVES monomorphic, 15–45 cm long,
4–12 cm wide; fertile leaves dying back in
winter; sterile leaves remaining green.
PETIOLES not disarticulating at a joint, not
persisting, pale green to straw-colored,
with minute stalked glands and scales.
BLADE 2-pinnate or 2-pinnate-pinnatifid;
with small, clear, stalked glands; rachis
similarly glandular and sparsely scaly.
PINNAE narrowly lanceolate to narrowly
triangular, 2–4 times as long as wide,
gradually tapered to a blunt tip, each with
4–10 pairs of deeply lobed segments

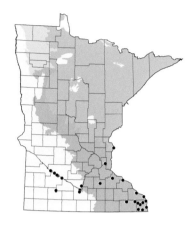

(sometimes identifiable as pinnules); margins irregularly dentate with short, blunt
teeth; veins pinnate, ending in hydathodes. **INDUSIA** glandular, consisting of
broad segments. **PHENOLOGY:** Leaves begin growth in May, sporangia mature in
July and August, and spores shed in autumn and winter.

IDENTIFICATION: This is, on average, the largest Minnesota *Woodsia*. Leaves are
commonly 20–30 cm long by midsummer. Where you find *W. obtusa* subsp.
obtusa, it is possible the much rarer *W. oregana* subsp. *cathcartiana* will be
nearby. They may look similar, but *W. obtusa* subsp. *obtusa* has pale-colored
petioles, and it has larger leaves, although there is some overlap. It is also possible
that *W. obtusa* subsp. *obtusa* will be mistaken for a *Cystopteris,* but the rachis of
W. obtusa subsp. *obtusa* is covered with tiny, stalked glands, which can usually be
seen with the unaided eye.

NATURAL HISTORY: *Woodsia obtusa* is endemic to temperate forests of the eastern
half of the country and is divided into two subspecies corresponding to cytotypes.
Subspecies *obtusa* is a tetraploid found throughout the range of the species,
including Minnesota. Subspecies *occidentalis* is a diploid that occurs only in the
south-central states and does not occur in Minnesota. In Minnesota, *W. obtusa*
subsp. *obtusa* is found occasionally to infrequently on the vertical faces of bedrock
outcrops in southern Minnesota, including sedimentary, igneous, and
metamorphic rock. Rocks tend to be circumneutral to alkaline, although local
conditions seem to prevail over the chemical nature of the rock. The rocks are
typically in a forest setting, usually cool, moist, and shaded. It may also occur in
exposed, sunny spots where it is able to survive desiccation during dry spells.

Tiny flecks are
stalked glands.

Mossy cliff habitat, Rice County—June 23.

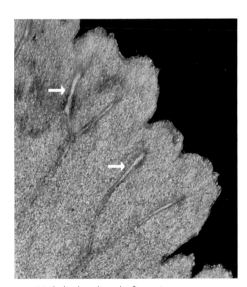

Hydathodes along leaf margin.

Leaves are 2-pinnate-pinnatifid.

Woodsia oregana subsp. *cathcartiana* (B. L. Robins.) Windham
Oregon Cliff Fern

RHIZOMES compact, short-branched.
LEAVES monomorphic, dying back in
winter, 10–30 cm long, 2–5 cm wide.
PETIOLE reddish brown to dark purple on
proximal half, with minute stalked glands
and few if any scales, not disarticulating at
a joint yet proximal portion persisting.
BLADE linear to linear-elliptic, 1-pinnate-
pinnatifid to 2-pinnate; rachis with clear,
stalked glands and occasionally sparse
scales. **PINNAE** narrowly triangular to
somewhat oblong, mostly 1.5–3 times as
long as wide, gradually tapered to blunt
apex, with 2–5(6) pair of distinct segments;

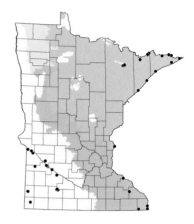

margins and costae with or without clear, stalked glands; margins irregularly
dentate with short, blunt teeth; veins imperfectly pinnate, ending in hydathodes.
INDUSIA consisting of narrow, usually filamentous, segments. **PHENOLOGY:**
Leaves begin growth in May, sporangia develop over the summer, and spores are
released in late summer and autumn.

IDENTIFICATION: Nothing about the appearance of *W. oregana* subsp. *cathcartiana*
will immediately separate it from the other *Woodsia* found in Minnesota.
Identification will be arrived at by a process of elimination. Somewhere on the
leaf, usually the rachis, there will be tiny, stalked glands. They will be clear, not
yellow. Petioles are usually dark-colored on the lower half and pale-colored on the
upper half. The lower portions of the petiole do persist on the rhizome after the
rest of the leaf has been shed, but they do not disarticulate at a joint. Also, note
the irregular teeth on the margins of the leaf segments.

NATURAL HISTORY: There are 2 subspecies of *Woodsia oregana*, each
corresponding to a different chromosome number and geographic range.
Subspecies *oregana* is a diploid confined to the Pacific Northwest of North
America. Subspecies *cathcartiana* is a tetraploid ranging from the southwestern
United States to eastern Canada. Its range includes Minnesota, where it is
widespread but comparatively rare. Habitat is primarily cracks or crevices in
vertical exposures of bedrock, such as cliffs or lesser promontories. Rock types
vary and include sedimentary, igneous, and metamorphic. The microhabitat is
usually moist and shaded, typically in a forest setting, but it tolerates dry, sunny
habitats, including south-facing exposures in the prairie region, where it seems
able to survive desiccation in dry summers.

Granite outcrop habitat, Yellow Medicine County.

Sheltered in a protective rock crevice—June 27.

Segments lined with jagged "teeth."

Flourishing in a harsh environment.

Woodsia scopulina subsp. *laurentiana* Windham
Laurentian Cliff Fern

RHIZOMES compact, short-branched.
LEAVES monomorphic, dying back in
winter, 10–32 cm long, 2–6 cm wide.
PETIOLE reddish brown, sometimes with
sparse stalked glands and nonglandular
hairs, not disarticulating at a joint yet
proximal portion persisting. **BLADE**
narrowly lanceolate to narrowly ovate-
lanceolate, 1-pinnate-pinnatifid to
2-pinnate; surfaces with long, clear,
multicellular hairs; lower surface and
rachis with tiny, yellow, stalked glands.
PINNAE 2–3 times as long as wide, tapered
evenly to a blunt apex; the larger pinnae

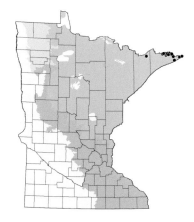

with 4–9 pairs of distinct segments; margins irregularly dentate with short, blunt
teeth; veins pinnate, ending in hydathodes. **INDUSIA** segments narrow or the tips
hairlike. **PHENOLOGY:** Leaves begin growth in May, sporangia develop during June
and July, and spores are released from late July through September.

IDENTIFICATION: *Woodsia scopulina* subsp. *laurentiana* is a substantial rock fern,
perhaps more likely to be mistaken for a *Cystopteris* than another *Woodsia*. It is the
only Minnesota *Woodsia* with bright, golden-yellow glands. But the glands are very
small. It will require magnification to see them, but they will appear obvious
when seen. At the end of each growing season, the leaf blade breaks off, leaving a
portion of the petiole attached to the rhizome, which can persist for 5 or 6 years.
But these petioles do not break off smoothly at a joint like those of *W. ilvensis*,
W. alpina, or *W. glabella*. They break unevenly and are irregular in length, with
torn, jagged edges.

NATURAL HISTORY: *Woodsia scopulina* is endemic to the United States and Canada.
It is divided into 3 subspecies largely based on chromosome number. Subspecies
scopulina and subspecies *appalachiana* are diploids and do not occur in Minnesota.
Subspecies *laurentiana* is a tetraploid and occurs primarily in the northwestern
United States and the Upper Great Lakes region, including Minnesota. It is
decidedly rare in Minnesota, found on cliffs in the Rove Formation along the
Border Lakes in the northeastern corner of the state. The cliffs are diabase and
slate in a Precambrian terrain. The plants frequently occur on lower portions of
the cliff face in vertical and horizontal cracks, small ledges, and chutes just above
the adjoining talus. These are characteristically cool, moist, and shaded situations,
most often facing northward.

A mossy ledge on a cliff in the Rove Formation, Cook County—June 4.

Wedged into a tight crevice.

The yellow dots are tiny glands.

GLOSSARY

aerial Relating to something in the air as opposed to underground or underwater; e.g., aerial stems of a fern or lycophyte are stems that are aboveground.

acroscopic Facing or pointed toward the apex or distal end of the axis on which the structure is attached. This usually relates to an "upward" pointing portion of a leaf.

acuminate Forming an angle less than 30 degrees with the sides somewhat concave.

allopolyploid A polyploid whose chromosomes were contributed by two or more species.

annual A plant that completes its life cycle in one year, living for just one year. Sometimes applied to a portion of a plant, such as a leaf, that survives just one year.

apiculate Abruptly terminating in a small, triangular apex.

apogamy Development of an embryo without fertilization; especially the development in some ferns of a sporophyte from an unfertilized gametophyte.

appressed Tightly pressed against a surface.

ascending Growing obliquely upward.

auriculate Having a rounded, ear-shaped lobe or appendage, usually at the base of a leaf or segment of a leaf.

axil The acroscopic angle formed between any two attached organs such as a pinna and rachis.

basal A somewhat general term referring to the base of something. In practice not necessarily the actual base, but something near the base or with some relationship to the base; i.e., basal pinnae will be the pinnae closest to the base of the plant.

basiscopic Facing or pointed toward the base or proximal end of the axis on which the structure is attached. This usually relates to a "downward" pointing portion of a leaf.

blade The broad portion of a leaf, as distinct from the petiole.

bulblet A small asexual propagule produced by a nonsexual portion of a plant, which is capable of developing into a free-living individual (ramet) upon becoming detached from the parent plant. A form of clonal reproduction seen in *Cytsopteris bulbifera*.

circumboreal Inhabiting boreal regions of North America and Eurasia.

clone A plant or group of plants produced asexually from one ancestor, to which they are genetically identical.

cone A compact reproductive structure with a central axis bearing closely spaced, spirally arranged sporangia. As used here, it is synonymous with strobilus.

costa (*pl.* costae) The major axis of a pinna.

crenate Scalloped, as in the margins of a leaf segment, with low, rounded teeth.

crenulate Finely crenate.

deciduous Falling off or shed seasonally, or at some specific stage of development in the life cycle.

decumbent A stem or branch of a stem lying along the ground with the growing tip curving upward.

decurrent A structure, such as a pinna or pinnule, extending down the stem below the point of attachment rather than attaching narrowly or abruptly.

determinate Genetically limited in growth; often applied to a plant or a structure of a plant that grows for a biologically predetermined period of time, or to a specific reproductive stage, then ceases growth or dies.

dimorphic A plant having two distinct shapes or sizes; often applied to fertile vs. nonfertile forms of a leaf.

distal Toward or near the apex; away from the center.

dichotomous branching A pattern of branching in which the divisions are equal in size, shape, and position; also referring to an identification key in which two parallel but exclusive choices are offered.

elliptic Possessing the form of an ellipse; a closed plane geometric form resembling an elongated circle, widest at the middle and narrower at the two equally curved ends.

endemic Used in an exclusionary way to describe the geographic occurrence of a species; e.g., a plant said to be endemic to North America occurs only in North America.

entire Having a smooth margin, as in the margin of a leaf or leaf segment that is not toothed, scalloped, or otherwise divided.

evergreen A plant that retains green leaves through summer and winter, a condition sometimes known as wintergreen.

family The taxonomic rank between order and genus, composed of genera that are more closely related to one another than to any genera of other families.

fern A taxonomic class identified as the Polypodiopsida, within the division Pteridophyta, including the Equisetales but excluding the Lycopodiales, Isoetales, and Selaginellales (among Minnesota plants), which are usually considered lycophytes rather than ferns.

fertile Bearing or capable of bearing offspring through a sexual process; in the case of ferns and lycophytes, producing gametes. This is effected by spores produced in sporangia. A leaf or portion of a leaf is said to be fertile if it produces spores (as in a sporophore or sporophyll); otherwise it might be called sterile (as in a trophophore or trophophyll).

gametophyte In the life cycle of plants with alternating generations such as ferns and lycophytes, it is the haploid phase that bears the sex organs, producing the zygote from which the sporophyte arises. It exists as an independent but inconspicuous plant body on or beneath the soil surface.

gemma (pl. gemmae) An asexual propagule; a modified bud of tissue that detaches from the parent and develops into a new individual.

genus (*pl.* genera) The taxonomic rank between family and species, composed of species that are more closely related to one another than to any species of other genera.

glabrate Becoming glabrous.

glabrous Smooth; without hairs, glands, or scales.

gland An epidermal outgrowth containing or secreting resinous or waxlike substances; single-celled or several cells stacked to create a linearly segmented structure.

hair An epidermal outgrowth, single-celled or an elongate row of cells stacked single-file, to one degree or another resembling a mammalian hair.

hastate Having the shape of an arrowhead with laterally pointing basal lobes; triangular with two spreading lobes at the base.

heterosporous Producing spores of two types (sizes), one male and one female. The smaller of these, the microspore, is male and the larger megaspore is female. A condition seen (among Minnesota ferns and lycophytes) in Isoetales, Selaginellales, and Salviniales.

homosporous Producing spores of a single type (size) that are not differentiated by sex. A condition seen (among Minnesota ferns and lycophytes) in Lycopodiales, Equisetales, Ophioglossales, Osmundales, and Polypodiales.

hybrid The offspring resulting from the cross between parents of different species or subspecies.

hydathode A specialized pore on the leaves of certain plants that functions in the exudation of water. Often appears as a swollen or darkened linear area on the upper surface of the leaf at the ends of the veins.

indeterminate Genetically unlimited in growth. Often applied to a plant or a portion of a plant, typically the main stem, that continues to grow indefinitely without being limited by a terminal cone.

indusium (*pl.* indusia) A usually thin, membranous or scalelike epidermal structure that partially or fully covers the young sporangia of a fern.

internode The portion of a stem between any two nodes.

lanceolate Shaped like the head of a lance, with a long-tapering apex and a short-tapering base; widest some distance above the base but well below the middle.

linear Long and narrow, with parallel sides resulting in a uniform or nearly uniform width.

lobe A roundish or flattish projection or division of something, such as might occur along the margin of a leaf, separated from others by sinuses or fissures.

lycophyte (*syn.* lycopod) Any member of a distinct class of plants called the Lycopodiopsida, which include (among Minnesota plants) species in the orders Lycopodiales, Isoetales, and Selaginellales; generally considered pteridophytes but not ferns.

marcescent The retention of dead plant organs that normally are shed, such as leaves that die at the end of the growing season but remain attached to the plant.

megasporangium (*pl.* megasporangia) In heterosporous pteridophytes, a sporangium bearing megaspores.

megaspore A large spore of a heterosporous pteridophyte that produces a female gametophyte.

megasporocarp A structure (sporocarp) that bears megasporangia.

microphyll The leaf of a lycophyte, small in size, possessing a single unbranched vein and lacking a petiole.

microsporangium (*pl.* microsporangia) In heterosporous pteridophytes, a sporangium that bears microspores.

microspore A small spore of a heterosporous pteridophyte that produces a male gametophyte.

microsporocarp A structure (sporocarp) that bears microsporangia.

monomorphic An organism that exhibits only one shape, commonly applied to species for which the fertile vs. sterile sporophyte of a fern do not differ significantly in form.

morphology The study of the size, shape, and structure of animals and plants. The term usually refers to the general aspects and outward appearance of form, in contrast to anatomy, which typically pertains to internal structures and finer details of structure.

mycorrhizal fungi Specific soil fungi that engage in symbiotic relationships with plants. The fungi colonize the underground portions of a host plant, providing increased water and nutrient absorption capabilities while the plant provides the fungus with carbohydrates derived by photosynthesis. Occasionally, as in the case of a fern gametophyte, a nonphotosynthetic plant acts more as a parasite than a symbiont.

oblong A symmetrical plane (2-dimensional) shape best described as a rectangle with rounded corners. The length is longer than the width, with approximately parallel sides.

oligotrophic In reference to a lake, characterized by low amounts of mineral nutrients, resulting in a sparse growth of plants, especially algae. Often referred to as soft-water lakes.

order Part of the taxonomic hierarchy used in biology; fitting between class and family and indicated by the suffix -iales. Composed of related families, which in turn are composed of related genera and species. All members of an order are presumed to have been derived from a common ancestor.

ovate The classic shape of a chicken egg in outline with the broader end at the bottom.

perennial Plants that persist for at least 3 growing seasons. Generally the top portion of the plant dies back each winter and regrows the following spring from rhizomes or other underground structures.

petiole (*syn.* stipe) When applied to ferns, the structure of a leaf that connects the base of the blade to the rhizome.

phenology The study of periodic events in biological life cycles and how these events are influenced by seasonal variations in climate and day length.

pinna (*pl.* pinnae) A primary, stand-alone (separate and distinct) division of a fern leaf.

pinnate (of a fern leaf) Having pinnae (primary divisions) arranged on each side of a common stalk, the rachis. The simplest structure of a compound fern leaf.

pinnatifid A leaf structure in which the margins are incised more than halfway but not all the way to the axis.

pinnule A division of a pinna that is attached by a stalk or is at least narrowed at the base.

pinnulet A division of a pinnule that is attached by a stalk or is at least narrowed at the base.

proximal Toward or near the base.

pseudowhorl A false whorl.

rachis The central axis of a compound leaf, often appearing as a continuation of the petiole into the blade of a leaf.

reflexed Bent backward or downward.

reticulate Resembling a closed mesh-like or netlike network.

rhizome An underground stem that produces the leaves and roots; typically a perennial structure, sometimes annual. The same structure, if it grows over the surface of the ground, is called a stolon. Some authors of fern books use the term *rhizome* exclusively without regard to its position or appearance.

scale A thin, flat, multicellular, epidermal outgrowth found on the leaves and sometimes rhizomes of certain ferns. Resembling the scale of a fish or a reptile.

segment Used in this book to describe the smallest discrete division of a leaf without concern for the shape or location of the division being described. Encompasses terms such as *pinnule, pinnulet,* or *lobe* when such fine distinctions are not necessary or cannot be reliably discerned.

serrate Having a row of sharp, forward-pointing teeth along the margin.

serrulate Minutely serrate.

sessile Lacking a petiole or stalk, thereby attaching directly by the base.

sheath A tubular structure enveloping the nodes on a stem of *Equisetum,* composed of highly modified leaves.

sorus (pl. sori) A discrete cluster of sporangia, exclusive of the indusium.

spatulate Having the shape of a spatula; narrow at the base and gradually becoming wider distally to a rounded apex. Nearly or quite spoon-shaped.

spinulose Indicating the presence of spines; bearing elongated conical processes.

sporangium (pl. sporangia) A spore-producing structure.

spore A unicellular reproductive structure produced within the sporangium that germinates to produce a gametophyte.

sporophyll In ferns, a leaf that bears sporangia. In lycophytes, a leaf (microphyll) subtending a sporangium.

sporophore In the Ophioglossales, the separate fertile (sporangia-bearing) branch of the leaf.

sporophyte In ferns and lycophytes, the conspicuous green plant that produces the asexual spores; the asexual stage in plants exhibiting an alternation of generations.

spreading Diverging progressively in different directions, such that the distance between leaf tips widens at an increasing rate.

stem In most terrestrial ferns and certain lycophytes, a horizontal underground (rhizome) or surficial (stolon) structure that produces the roots, leaves, and in some species branches that may become vertical and bear sporangia.

sterile A structure such as a leaf that lacks sexual reproductive structures; a leaf that has no sporangia associated with it.

stolon A long, horizontal stem that grows over the surface of the ground and produces roots, leaves, and branches at points along its length.

stomate (*pl.* stomata or stomates) A small, single-cell pore on the surface of a leaf that is used for gas exchange.

ternate Having three equal or nearly equal parts attached at a single point.

trophophore In the Ophioglossales, the separate sterile (lacking sporangia) branch of the leaf.

trophophyll A leaf of a fern or lycophyte that lacks sexual reproductive structures (sporangia).

velum In *Isoëtes,* the membranous covering of the sporangium-containing cavity in the base of the leaves.

whorl Having 3 or more similar structures inserted at a single point along an axis, as leaves on a stem.

BIBLIOGRAPHY

This is a partial list of useful scientific publications that have relevance to the study of ferns and lycophytes in Minnesota. They may be too technical for some readers but are valuable for anyone seeking a deeper understanding of the subjects covered in this book. A few are cited in the text, but most are not.

Anderson, D. S., R. W. Haug, and W. R. Smith. 2021. Noteworthy collections—Westward range extension of *Dendrolycopodium obscurum* (L.) A. Haines (Lycopodiaceae), including new state records for Minnesota, U.S.A. *Great Lakes Botanist* 60(1–2): 72–78.

Barker, M. S., and W. D. Hauk. 2003. An evaluation of *Sceptridium dissectum* (Ophioglossaceae) with ISSR markers: Implications for *Sceptridium* systematics. *American Fern Journal* 93(1): 1–19.

Beitel, J. M., and J. T. Mickel. 1992. The Appalachian firmoss, a new species in the *Huperzia selago* (Lycopodiaceae) complex in eastern North America, with a new combination for the western firmoss. *American Fern Journal* 82(2): 41–46.

Brunton, D. F., and H. J. Bickerton. 2018. New records for eastern mosquito fern (*Azolla cristata*, Salviniaceae) in Canada. *Canadian Field-Naturalist* 132(4): 350–359.

Christenhusz, M. J. M., et al. 2019. Phylogenetics, classification and typification of extant horsetails (*Equisetum*, Equisetaceae). *Botanical Journal of the Linnean Society* 189: 311–352.

Dauphin, B., et al. 2017. A worldwide molecular phylogeny provides new insight on cryptic diversity within the moonworts (*Botrychium* s. s., Ophioglossaceae). *Systematic Botany* 42(4): 620–639.

Davis, C. C., W. R. Anderson, and K. J. Wurdack. 2005. Gene transfer from a parasitic flowering plant to a fern. *Proceedings of the Royal Society B* 272: 2237–2242.

Farrar, D. R., and A. V. Gilman. 2017. Relationships in the *Botrychium campestre* (Ophioglossaceae) complex. *Brittonia* 69(3): 265–275.

Farrar, D. R., and C. L. Johnson-Groh. 1990. Subterranean sporophytic gemmae in moonwort ferns *Botrychium* subgenus *Botrychium*. *American Journal of Botany* 77(9): 1168–1175.

Farrar, D. R., and C. L. Johnson-Groh. 1991. A new prairie moonwort (*Botrychium* subgenus *Botrychium*) from northwestern Minnesota. *American Fern Journal* 81(1): 1–6.

Gacca, E., and E. Ballesteros. 1993. Population and individual variability of *Isoetes lacustris* L. with depth in a Pyrenean lake. *Aquatic Botany* 46(1): 45–47.

Gastony, G. J. 1988. The *Pellaea glabella* complex: Electrophoretic evidence for the derivations of the agamosporous taxa and a revised taxonomy. *American Fern Journal* 78(2): 44–67.

Gerdes, L. B. 2001. A contribution to the flora of the Rove Slate Bedrock Complex land-type association, Northern Cook County, Minnesota, USA. Master's thesis, School of Forestry, Michigan Technological University.

Gildner, B. S., and D. W. Larson. 1992. Seasonal changes in photosynthesis in the desiccation-tolerant fern *Polypodium virginianum*. Oecologia 89: 383–389.

Gilman, A. V., and D. R. Farrar. 2015. *Botrychium michiganense* sp. nov. (Ophioglossaceae), a new North American moonwort. *Journal of the Botanical Research Institute of Texas* 9(2): 295–309.

Gilman, A. V., and W. L. Testo. 2015. Use of gemma characteristics to identify North American *Huperzia* (Lycopodiaceae). *American Fern Journal* 105(3): 145–161.

Grusz, A. L., and M. D. Windham. 2013. Toward a monophyletic *Cheilanthes*: The resurrection and recircumscription of *Myriopteris* (Pteridaceae). *PhytoKeys* 32: 49–64.

Haines, A. 2003. *The Families Huperziaceae and Lycopodiaceae of New England: A Taxonomic and Ecological Reference.* Bar Harbor, Maine: V. F. Thomas.

Haufler, C. H., M. D. Windham, and T. A. Ranker. 1990. Biosystematic analysis of the *Cystopteris tennesseensis* (Dryopteridaceae) complex. *Annals of the Missouri Botanical Garden* 77: 314–329.

Haufler, C. H., et al. 1993. *Polypodium*. In *Flora of North America North of Mexico,* vol. 2, ed. Flora of North America Editorial Committee, 315–323. New York: Oxford University Press.

Hauke, R. L. 1963. *A Taxonomic Monograph of the Genus* Equisetum *Subgenus* Hippochaete. Weinheim: J. Cramer.

Hauke, R. L. 1978. A taxonomic monograph of *Equisetum* subgenus Equisetum. *Nova Hedwigia* 30: 385–455.

Johnson, D. M. 1986. Systematics of the New World species of *Marsilea* (Marsileaceae). *Systematic Botany Monographs* 11: 1–87.

Johnson-Groh, C., and J. M. Lee. 2002. Phenology and demography of two species of *Botrychium* (Ophioglossaceae). *American Journal of Botany* 89(10): 1624–1633.

Kelloff, C. L., et al. 2002. Differentiation of eastern North American *Athyrium filix-femina* taxa: Evidence from allozymes and spores. *American Fern Journal* 92(3): 185–213.

Khrapko, O. V., and N. A. Tsarenko. 2015. Adaptive strategies of two species from the family Onocleaceae. *Contemporary Problems of Ecology* 8(2): 148–154.

Landi, M., and C. Angiolini. 2011. Population structure of *Osmunda regalis* in relation to environment and vegetation: An example in the Mediterranean area. *Folia Geobot* 46: 49–68.

Lellinger, D. B. 2002. *A Modern Multilingual Glossary for Taxonomic Pteridology.* Washington, D.C.: American Fern Society.

Li, J., and C. H. Haufler. 1994. Phylogeny, biogeography, and population biology of Osmunda species: Insights from isozymes. *American Fern Journal* 84(4): 105–114.

Lu, J., et al. 2011. Biogeographic disjunction between eastern Asia and North America in the *Adiantum pedatum* complex (Pteridaceae). *American Journal of Botany* 98(10): 1680–1693.

MacFarlane, M., and R. MacFarlane. 2021. Distribution of species of *Botrychium* (Ophioglossaceae) in north-northwestern Minnesota. *Great Lakes Botanist* 60(3–4): 82–96.

Marrs, R. H., and A. S. Watt. 2006. Biological flora of the British Isles: *Pteridium aquilinum* (L.) Kuhn. *Journal of Ecology* 94: 1272–1321.

Marschner, F. J. 1974. *The Original Vegetation of Minnesota (Map Scale 1:5000,000)*. St. Paul, Minn.: USDA Forest Service, North Central Forest Experiment Station.

McMaster, R. T. 1996. Vegetative reproduction observed in *Ophioglossum pusillum* Raf. *American Fern Journal* 86(2): 58–60.

Metzgar, J. S., H. Schneider, and K. M. Pryer. 2007. Phylogeny and divergence time estimates for the fern genus *Azolla* (Salviniaceae). *International Journal of Plant Science* 168(7): 1045–1053.

Metzgar, J. S., et al. 2008. The paraphyly of *Osmunda* is confirmed by phylogenetic analysis of seven plastid loci. *Systematic Botany* 33(1): 31–36.

Moore, J. W., and R. M. Tryon Jr. 1946. A new record for Isöetes melanopoda. *American Fern Journal* 36(3): 89–91.

Moran, R. C. 1982. The *Asplenium trichomanes* complex in the United States and adjacent Canada. *American Fern Journal* 72(1): 5–11.

Moran, R. C. 1983. *Cystopteris tenuis* (Michx.) Desv.: A poorly understood species. *Castanea* 48: 218–223.

Peck, J. H. 1980. *Equisetum ×litorale* in Illinois, Iowa, Minnesota and Wisconsin. *American Fern Journal* 70(2): 33–38.

PPG1. 2016. A community-derived classification for extant lycophytes and ferns. *Journal of Systematics and Evolution* 54(6): 563–603.

Prange, R. K., and P. V. Aderkas. 1985. The biological flora of Canada. 6. *Matteuccia struthiopteris* (L.) Todaro, Ostrich Fern. *Canadian Field-Naturalist* 99(4): 517–532.

Primack, R. B. 1973. Growth patterns of five species of *Lycopodium*. *American Fern Journal* 63(1): 3–7.

Pryor, K. M., and C. H. Haufler. 1993. Isozymic and chromosomal evidence for the allotetraploid origin of *Gymnocarpoum dryopteris* (Dryopteridaceae). *Systematic Botany* 18(1): 150–172.

Reid, J. D., G. M. Plunkett, and G. A. Peters. Phylogenetic relationships in the heterosporous fern genus *Azolla* (Azollaceae) based on DNA sequence data from three noncoding regions. *International Journal of Plant Science* 167(3): 529–538.

Rutz, L. M., and D. R. Farrar. 1984. The habitat characteristics and abundance of *Equisetum ×ferrissii* and its parent species, *Equisetum hyemale* and *Equisetum laevigatum,* in Iowa. *American Fern Journal* 74(3): 65–76.

Stensvold, M. C., and D. R. Farrar. 2017. Genetic diversity in the worldwide *Botrychium lunaria* (Ophioglossaceae) complex, with new species and new combinations. *Brittonia* 69(2): 148–175.

Swartz, L. M. 2002. The morphological and genetic distinctness of *Botrychium minganense* and *B. crenulatum* as assessed by morphometric analysis and RAPD markers. *American Fern Journal* 92(4): 249–269.

Taylor, W. C., and N. T. Luebke. 1988. *Isöetes ×hickeyi:* A naturally occurring hybrid between *I. echinospora* and *I. macrospora*. *American Fern Journal* 78(1): 6–13.

Tryon, A. 1957. A revision of the fern genus *Pellaea* section *Pellaea*. *Annals of the Missouri Botanical Garden* 44: 125–193.

Tryon, A., R. Tryon, and F. Badre. 1980. Classification, spores, and nomenclature of the marsh fern. *Rhodora* 82: 461–474.

Tryon, R. M. 1948. Some Woodsias from the North Shore of Lake Superior. *American Fern Journal* 38(4): 159–170.

Tryon, R. 1980. *Ferns of Minnesota,* second edition, revised. Minneapolis: University of Minnesota Press.

Wagner, G. M. 1997. *Azolla*: A review of its biology and utilization. *The Botanical Review* 63(1): 1–26.

Wagner, W. H. 1960. Periodicity and pigmentation in *Botrychium* subg. *Sceptridium* in the northeastern United States. *Bulletin of the Torrey Botanical Club* 87(5): 303–325.

Wagner, W. H. 1961a. On the relative development of the fertile segments in *Botrychium dissectum* and *B. oneidense*. *American Fern Journal* 51(2): 75–81.

Wagner, W. H. 1961b. Roots and the taxonomic differences between *Botrychium oneidense* and *B. dissectum*. *Rhodora* 63(750): 164–175.

Wagner, W. H. 1986. Three new species of moonworts (*Botrychium* subg. *Botrychium*) endemic in western North America. *American Fern Journal* 76(2): 33–47.

Wagner, W. H. 1989. *Lycopodium hickeyi*: A new species of North American clubmoss. *American Fern Journal* 79(3): 119–121.

Wagner, W. H., and D. M. Johnson. 1981. Natural history of the ebony spleenwort, *Asplenium platyneuron* (Aspleniaceae), in the Great Lakes area. *Canadian Field-Naturalist* 95(2): 156–166.

Wagner, W. H., and L. P. Lord. 1956. The morphological and cytological distinctness of *Botrychium minganense* and *B. lunaria* in Michigan. *Bulletin of the Torrey Botanical Club* 83(4): 261–280.

Wagner, W. H., and F. S. Wagner. 1981. New species of moonworts, *Botrychium* subg. *Botrychium* (Ophioglossaceae), from North America. *American Fern Journal* 71(1): 20–30.

Wagner, W. H., and F. S. Wagner. 1982. *Botrychium rugulosum* (Ophioglossaceae), a newly recognized species of evergreen grapefern in the Great Lakes area of North America. *Contributions from the University of Michigan Herbarium* 15: 315–324.

Wagner, W. H., and F. S. Wagner. 1990. Notes on the fan-leaflet group of moonworts in North America with descriptions of two new members. *American Fern Journal* 80(3): 73–81.

Wagner, W. H., and F. S. Wagner. 1994. Another widely disjunct, rare and local North American moonwort (Ophioglossaceae: *Botrychium* subg. *Botrychium*). *American Fern Journal* 84(1): 5–10.

Waterway, M. J. 1986. A reevaluation of *Lycopodium porophilum* and its relationship to *L. lucidulum* (Lycopodiaceae). *Systematic Botany* 11(2): 263–276.

Watt, A. S. 1940. Contributions to the ecology of bracken (*Pteridium aquilinum*) 1. The rhizome. *New Phytologist* 39: 401–422.

Wittig, R., R. Jungmann, and H. Ballach. 2007. The extent of clonality in large stands of *Lycopodium annotinum* L. *Flora* 202: 98–105.

INDEX

WELBY R. SMITH is the state botanist with the Minnesota Department of Natural Resources in St. Paul. His previous books include *Trees and Shrubs of Minnesota* (2008), *Native Orchids of Minnesota* (2012), and *Sedges and Rushes of Minnesota* (2018), all published by the University of Minnesota Press.

RICHARD W. HAUG has been a native plant enthusiast and photographer for forty years. His photographs have been featured in many publications, including *Northland Wildflowers*, *Native Orchids of Minnesota*, and *Sedges and Rushes of Minnesota*.